T0163349

Gibson's
Last Stand

Sports and American Culture Series
Roger Launius, Editor

University of Missouri Press
Columbia and London

Gibson's Last Stand

The Rise, Fall, and Near Misses
of the St. Louis Cardinals, 1969–1975

Doug Feldmann

Copyright © 2011 by
The Curators of the University of Missouri
University of Missouri Press, Columbia, Missouri 65201
Printed and bound in the United States of America
First paperback printing, 2013
All rights reserved
5 4 3 2 1   17 16 15 14 13

Cataloging-in-Publication data available from the Library of Congress
ISBN 978-0-8262-2012-7

∞™ This paper meets the requirements of the
American National Standard for Permanence of Paper
for Printed Library Materials, Z39.48, 1984.

Cover design: Susan Ferber
Design and composition: Jennifer Cropp
Typefaces: Rockwell and Minion

To Gus Kuczka, my uncle and a Cardinal fan forever

Contents

Preface

With little knowledge of what it would launch in the subsequent years of my life, I attended my first St. Louis Cardinals baseball game on June 19, 1974, at the age of four. After scurrying my legs as quickly as possible to stay with my family up the long, winding ramps to the top of old Busch Stadium—which at that time was still the *new* Busch Stadium—I imagine my next experience was the same as most first-timers. Standing with mouth agape upon emerging from the narrow tunnels into the seating area, I was stunned at the massive expanse of the lower deck and field that sank far below, as if I were gazing into the Grand Canyon with an equal magnificence of beauty. We had been up in the Arch just a couple hours earlier, and both heavenly views seemed all the same to me. Suddenly anointed as the master of the universe, I was now in command of all my favorite players down on the field, pretending to maneuver them as I did with my baseball cards on our living room floor.

As my mother handed me a game program she had purchased, I noticed that the presumed starting lineups for the evening were already printed on the card—something particular to the stadium operations in St. Louis, but not in most other big league parks, which leave the spaces blank. At the bottom of the Cardinals' batting order, I saw a name with the number *45* next to it. Before today, I had heard of their starting pitcher for the game, Bob Gibson, but had never seen him in action on television. Someone sitting near us informed me that this hurler was the team's longtime ace. Being more critical of players than the average four-year-old, I was not too impressed with this pitcher once the game began, and by the time we left the ballpark later that night, this Gibson guy had permitted the San Francisco Giants a total of fourteen hits and had lost the game, dropping the individual season record of this so-and-so to 3–8, making him quickly forgotten in my mind. I had been, instead, more interested in a new guy for the Cardinals named "Bake" who had stolen a base in the game. Not giving number 45 any more thought beyond quick relapses of anger for his blowing the contest, I next looked forward to the obligatory postgame pizza we always enjoyed at the Knotty Pine in Breese, Illinois, on the way back to my uncle's house. Getting out of the car in the parking lot, the first thing I always did was look at the temperature on the bank clock down the street. In summertime in the St. Louis area, it always seemed to be in the nineties—even now in the blackness of midnight, with the only illumination in Breese being the colorful electric Knotty Pine sign and the streetlights, which hung like small frosted moons along U.S. 50 until vanishing from my eyes' reach.

Little did I know at the time was that the Bob Gibson I had witnessed was a shadow of his former self. By this June night in 1974, he was now a man fighting pain in his pitching arm as well as in both legs, struggling in the twilight of a career that was once dominant and straining to summon the power he had, in past seasons, unleashed on batters with unparalleled fury.

Glancing over the scorecard that my family helped me to fill, I noticed that this pitcher Gibson—even though he was besieged by the Giants' bats all night long—was permitted to complete the entire contest by his manager of ten years, Albert "Red" Schoendienst. Schoendienst had grown up playing ball with my father in Clinton County, Illinois—appropriately from the village of Germantown, just four miles due south from the Knotty Pine—and had always been loyal to Gibson, never short on confidence to give his best pitcher the chance to finish what he started. No one took the ball from the pitcher in Gibson's greatest season of all, the turbulent summer of 1968, when he started thirty-four games and pitched every inning in twenty-eight of them, while shutting out the opponent in almost half of those complete games. "I doubt we'll ever see that happen again," Gibson said in the 1990s in mourning that closing salvo of the golden era of baseball. The ensuing changes in the game would be partially blamed on him, as his pitching success caused team owners in later years to believe that cash-paying customers instead wanted base hits and home runs. But as far as Gibson was concerned, pitchers after 1968 never stood a chance as the strike zone was shrunk, the mound was lowered, and the age-old "rancor" between the pitcher and hitter, as he liked to put it, was ultimately softened into a more politically correct version of the sport. "It's really sad that everybody blames the pitchers for not completing ballgames. It really has nothing to do with the pitchers. It has to do with the way the game is played today."

The right-hander would make only thirty-three more starts in a Cardinals uniform after the one I witnessed, hanging up his spikes for good after the 1975 season.

As our car rolled westward on U.S. 50 through Trenton and Aviston before pulling into the Knotty Pine, we caught a few more sounds of the mighty KMOX radio station in St. Louis, by then the longtime home of the Cardinals (and now so once again). Now in his fifth season as the Cards' lead announcer after many more patiently waiting in a secondary role, Jack Buck had concluded his postgame show with one of his usual closing lines: "If you're driving home from the game, watch out for the other guy—he's dangerous." Buck's voice, as well as his message, always reassured me; throughout all the changes of Gibson's final years with the Cardinals, Buck's presence—along with that of his partner, Mike Shannon—was the one constant with the ball club as the team on the field endured numerous changes in personnel, attempting to recapture the glory days of the 1960s.

If only I could, just one more time, be riding on some isolated patch of road, somewhere in southern Illinois on another steamy June night, and hear Buck once again.

"Turn the radio on," he would implore his listeners at his induction speech to the Radio Hall of Fame in 1995. "You will hear a friend. You will enjoy, you will learn, you will imagine, you will improve. Turn the radio on—in your car, in your home, in prison, on the beach, in the nursing home. You will not be alone—you will not be lonely."

Acknowledgments

The author wishes to thank all the talented newspaper writers who have covered the Cardinals over the years, especially those whose resources contributed the most to this book—Neal Russo, Ed Wilks, Mike Eisenbath, and of course Bob Broeg, who in turn learned his craft from the great J. Roy Stockton. And to Annette Wenda, my copy editor, whose fine attention to detail and creative suggestions improved this book greatly.

Gibson's Last Stand

1   Like Family

The Cardinal players were uncommonly proud to be part of those [1960s] teams. . . . [T]hey won through intelligence, playing hard and aggressively, and because they had a sense of purpose that cut across racial lines in a way that was still extremely unusual in the world of sports.

—David Halberstam, *October 1964*

"Northrup hit a fastball away, and that's where we try to pitch him—to make him hit the ball to center field," Bob Gibson said of the sudden blow that struck downtown St. Louis, Missouri, like a lightning bolt, late into the afternoon sky of October 10, 1968. "Things were never the same again."

In the latter part of his comment, Gibson was referring not only to the outcome of baseball's world championship that year, but also to what he felt was a larger and undesirable tilt of the sport into an era of selfishness and unnecessary meddling by outside forces.

The final minutes of the baseball era Gibson cherished were contained in the 1968 World Series, which had been an even draw up until the point he was describing. His St. Louis Cardinals, rulers of the National League for the past two seasons, were tied with the American League titleholder Detroit Tigers at three games apiece to require a decisive seventh contest, which was scoreless when Jim Northrup strutted to the plate with one out in the seventh inning. At that very moment, the final curtain was coming down on one of the greatest individual pitching performances in any baseball season. Personally posting 13 of the record 339 shutouts issued in the Major Leagues that year, Gibson had dismantled opposing bats during the summer with a 1.12 earned run average—the lowest in more than fifty years by a starting pitcher and the third lowest in the twentieth century. And for an encore, Gibson had already struck out a World Series–record seventeen batters in Game 1 of the fall classic. As the sun was setting in St. Louis over one of the final afternoon games in World Series history, Gibson had used 91 fastballs among his 144 pitches as the St. Louis schoolkids were rushing home to catch hometown broadcaster Harry Caray describe the remaining action. Being the workhorse of the Cardinals' pitching staff, Gibson understandably had admitted to being tired in the final few weeks of the season, but surged onward as his team sought to become the first National League club since 1922 to repeat as World Series champions. In a short time, an announcement would come that Gibson outdistanced batting champion Pete Rose of the Cincinnati Reds for the Most Valuable Player award in the National League by a 242–205 vote.

A few days after his Game 1 masterpiece, Gibson had easily beaten the Tigers and their own ace pitcher, Denny McLain, once again in Game 4 in Detroit by a 10–1 margin. A final knockout punch by the big right-hander now appeared inevitable. But here in the seventh of the final battle, the Redbird hurler found himself in trouble for the first time in the series. He was fighting to keep the Tigers at bay to give the Cardinals a chance, hoping to keep it a scoreless tie as baseball's world championship had turned into a three-inning duel as Gibson went to work on Northrup. He had been able to retire Mickey Stanley and Al Kaline, the first two Detroit batters of the inning, but afterward had permitted Norm Cash and Willie Horton to occupy first and second bases on singles.

Standing at attention far behind Gibson in center field was Curt Flood, the Cardinals' Gold Glove–winning outfielder and his most trusted defender. When the voting was finally revealed, Flood would finish fourth in the MVP tally himself, trailing only Gibson, Rose, and San Francisco's slugging first baseman, Willie McCovey. Gibson's ironclad defensive platoon—including Flood, sure-handed shortstop Dal Maxvill, and others—had, for years, permitted him to challenge hitters whimsically, and almost recklessly. Gibson, in fact, once suggested to a reporter that he thought he would never throw a no-hit game, as over the course of a typical contest he made far too many mistakes.

His first offering to Northrup caught a good deal of the plate, and the hitter let loose on a long drive that caused the surprised Gibson to snap his head suddenly to his right, watching the white sphere sail far through the autumn midwestern clouds. "When I saw Flood looking for the ball," Gibson continued in reflecting on the moment, "I knew I was in trouble."

Flood—considered the preeminent center fielder of his day—initially broke inward toward home plate on the ball, but soon realized the error of his judgment. As he struggled to reverse his momentum in a 180-degree turn, the drive soared over Flood's head, rolling to a rest at the base of the center-field wall as

Horton and Cash scored the first runs of the game with Northrup easily galloping into third with a triple. "The hardest ball to judge is one right at you," said Gibson's teammate and fellow pitcher Nelson Briles, who had started Games 2 and 5 of the series and was now watching from the dugout steps. "And when he [Flood] didn't recognize it and tried to recover, he slipped and just wasn't able to quite get back to it. Had he not slipped, he would have caught the ball. . . . [W]e had the series in our hands, and just didn't close the deal. Pure and simple."

Truly dejected for one of the first times all year, Gibson made another mistake to the next batter in Detroit catcher Bill Freehan, who laced a sharp double to the gap between Flood and Lou Brock in left field, giving the Tigers a 3–0 advantage. Playing out the last few innings of his career and running over from right field was the great Roger Maris, helpless to assist on the play. It was an emotional turn of events from which the Cardinals could not recover. Detroit left-hander Mickey Lolich took advantage, the surprise hero off the mound for the Tigers in the postseason who had risen to the occasion in lieu of McLain. Lolich finished off his third win of the series by closing out a 4–1 final score, giving the upstart Detroit men the victory over the stunned Cardinals. It was revenge for the Motor City from thirty-four years earlier, when in 1934 another great Cardinals' pitcher, Dizzy Dean, dominated the Tigers in Game 7 in Detroit for the world title.

The St. Louis players—some of the best paid in the game, compliments of owner August A. Busch Jr. and his megasuccessful beer brewery—were quickly accused of being caught in a complacent attitude as the local press and a large number of fans were crestfallen. Many were looking to particularly pin the downfall on Flood and his gaffe, supposedly emblematic of the general lackadaisical approach of a team more concerned with sporting Nehru jackets and expansive (and expensive) hairstyles rather than focusing on their jobs. Money had caught hold of the team and held them hostage. Gibson, however, always gave balanced assessments of his teammates and insisted that the will to win was still preeminent in the majority of them. He was never too critical or too flattering of the men who wore his uniform, and was as such with Flood in this glaring instance as well. Thus, he quickly added the following sentence for the disappointed local writers covering the morbid St. Louis locker room: "He has saved many a ballgame for me."

Nonetheless, his defense of his coworker would not seem to alter public opinion, at least among the ranks of Cardinal fans. A week later, Gibson was walking in the St. Louis airport when a woman approached him. Expecting the typical request for an autograph—which Gibson despised under most circumstances away from the ballpark, while he was trying to mind his own business—Gibson was dumbfounded by the woman's question of him.

"Do you still speak to Curt Flood?" she wanted to know.

He responded, "Lady, how can you ask me that?"

It was just one of many moments of interaction with the public that left Gibson shaking his head, wondering if the average person would ever understand the day-to-day pressures, the up-and-down relationships, and often-deep turmoil that invariably beset a Major League Baseball team, as with any other profession. Despite the growing money issue in baseball, Gibson and the Cardinals still regarded each other like family, but executives in the front office, all the way up to Busch and his general manager, Vaughan "Bing" Devine, felt it was time to reinvent the roster after nearly a decade of stability. The team had maintained its core of key players throughout the 1960s, much resembling the Atlanta Braves of the 1990s with the interchange of only an occasional minor part over the course of several successful seasons. The first of these important "spare parts" for the Cardinals would be Maris, a man originally from the Midwest who encountered personal horrors in New York with the Yankees for the apparently horrific crime of pursuing a home run record. Maris was most pleased for the chance to come to St. Louis in 1967, a refreshing escape from the perpetual scrutiny he suffered. Maris would be, however, only the first of many hired hands to switch to a St. Louis uniform over the coming seasons. What was once a stable roster became a litany of new faces brought in by Devine each off-season, hoping to find the right formula to keep the Cardinals among the National League's elite. But as he sought approval from Busch—known around St. Louis simply as "Gussie"—Devine found the right combination of personalities ever harder to find as the business side of the game hurled itself into its most turbulent decade. Busch was sensing an evolution of the modern baseball player. It was a change in which players, now armed with an attorney on one side and a tax consultant on the other, were no longer typical brewery employees. And his first such run-in with a player was ironically Maris, and ironically, the topic was the brewery itself.

When Maris came aboard in 1967, he arrived with more political capital than the typical player had acquired in a trade to date. He proceeded to engage in separate business negotiations with Busch, with the player seeking ultimate control of an Anheuser-Busch distributorship in Florida upon his retirement from baseball. At the conclusion of the 1967 schedule, Gussie promised the distributorship to Maris if he would play one more season in 1968, to which Maris agreed; when Gussie tried to make the same promise if Roger would play just one more year in 1969, Maris held firm, reminding the colonel that a promise had already been made. Gussie relented, and soon Roger was off to oversee the operations at the company's Gainesville, Florida, plant. While Busch had gotten productive time that he wanted out of the player (including two National

League pennants), he was finding—perhaps for the first time—that he could not control people in his baseball business as minutely as he could in his beer operations.

Therefore, when Maris would not budge, Devine felt compelled to go after another qualified veteran outfielder to take his place for 1969. Available was Cincinnati's Vada Pinson, who had nailed at least sixteen homers a year for the past nine seasons. So he phoned Reds general manager Bob Howsam—the very man who had taken over for Devine in St. Louis in 1964, after Devine's first stint at the job with the Cardinals—and brokered a deal to make Pinson the next "hired gun" to come to the Cardinals, in turn sending to Cincinnati rising young Cardinal prospects in outfielder Bob Tolan and pitcher Wayne Granger. For the first time since his rookie year of 1958, Pinson had been unable to play in an entire season in 1968 due to injuries; Devine, however, was confident he would be healthy for the Cards in '69. "Virtually everybody approved the trade," recalled Bob Broeg, the veteran beat writer who covered the Cardinals for the *St. Louis Post-Dispatch*. Broeg, however, was not sure that Pinson would be the same player he had been in Cincinnati. "I certainly agreed that Pinson would add some experience, but I didn't have the same feeling I'd had about him earlier." In addition, Broeg felt that the Cardinals should be cautious in making deals with Howsam. "I believe Stan Musial [the Cardinal great who would later serve in 1967 as the Cardinals' general manager himself] had something when he said, 'I won't deal with Howsam because he took too many of our guys with him, and they know the Cardinals' personnel better than we know his.'"

Trying to maintain a steady course with the recent World Series loss and the departure of Maris was Cardinals manager Albert "Red" Schoendienst, who received news of the Pinson deal just as the team was getting on a plane to tour Japan. Schoendienst's surname translated to "good service" in German, appropriate to his twenty-one-year contribution to the Cardinal organization by 1969 (and a Cardinal career that would stretch decades longer afterward as well). He had made an additional trip to Japan several years earlier with the team, when Musial gained recognition as the most prominent American to spend time in that country since Douglas MacArthur. "We had a lot of formal dinners," Schoendienst would later recall of the late 1968 voyage, as the team was still worn out from the long season and the grueling World Series that fell short. "And most of them were served in the traditional Japanese style, meaning all the guests took off their shoes and sat on the floor and ate on a very low table. That was okay for a while, but then it started getting old." They were the toasts of baseball—not only in St. Louis, the Midwest, or even just the United States, but beyond the borders as well, to any shore where the game was revered. Outside of New York, they were the most handsomely paid club; the men knew that theirs was a special assembly, a team with the potential to go down in history as one of the best ever. It was composed of a diverse cast of individuals with a common goal, and despite the retirement of Maris and the departure of promising youngsters in Tolan and Granger, it was imagined that Pinson would add greatly to their continued success as well. "The Cardinal players were uncommonly proud to be part of those [1960s] teams, for they won not by dint of pure talent or pure power—San Francisco was far richer in terms of pure talent," writer David Halberstam believed. "Rather, they won through intelligence, playing hard and aggressively, and because they had a sense of purpose that cut across racial lines in a way that was still extremely unusual in the world of sports."

When the Cardinals returned home from the Far East, they discovered that Major League Baseball had changed things to favor the hitter for 1969, which came to be known in some circles as the "Gibson Rules" after the dominating performance by the Cardinal pitcher the previous season. "I respectfully decline the honor, thank you," Gibson would assert decades later about the title. Instead of being honored by his direct connection to the greatest season ever for pitchers, he was conversely disturbed in witnessing a larger destruction that was taking place of the traditional inner battles of the sport. "I will accept no responsibility for what baseball did to itself," he added about the rule changes that were imminent. Most specifically, the pitcher's mound was lowered to 67 percent of its typical height for 1969 (from fifteen inches high down to ten), the first adjustment to the actual geometric outlay of the game in nearly fifty years—and something that Gibson (in addition to his philosophical disagreements with the move) also claimed would contribute to arm problems he would develop a few years later, exacerbated by yet another change. "My slider wasn't bothered much," Gibson determined. "My control, on the other hand, was bothered plenty, but not by the height of the mound. They shrank the damn strike zone." A greater crime in his estimation, Gibson was referring to how umpires were ordered to shave down all four edges of the zone after 1968, in particular the high strike that used to be called at the batter's armpits. Now, the upper reaches of the strike zone were lowered to the jersey letters of the hitter. "But," Gibson summarized about the effects of the changes in 1969 and beyond, "the umpires seldom called a strike at the letters. After a while, they never did."

Still, for Gibson, even worse than the lowering of the mound and the shrinking of the strike zone was a third dagger that came from the baseball Brutuses, the additional command given to umpires to warn pitchers who threw too far inside on the batter—something "Gibby" thought was essential to his success. It was an issue that the pitcher and the batter had resolved by themselves for decades in the game, and now such situations were to be placed in the hands of a third party—the umpire, who in the past had largely abstained from such confrontations. "The commissioner's office was reaching straight into my pocket," Gibson further mourned about his predestined, self-fulfilling drop in effectiveness—and, presumably, a coinciding drop in salary. He knew that things would never be the same, for the almighty dollar had finally applied its death grip on the game. It was becoming obvious, at least to Gibson, that the powers-that-be believed that offensive excitement—in lieu of appreciation for a well-pitched, well-defended game—would send more people through the turnstiles. There was a windfall to be made, and Gibson (perhaps ironically) was simultaneously enjoying it as one of the highest-paid players in the game. "The rancor between the pitcher and the hitter, which characterized the game in my time and [Babe] Ruth's and [Ty] Cobb's and Musial's, has been legislated out in favor of a kinder, gentler game in which there is more cheap offense for the paying customer," Gibson concluded about the contemporary version of baseball.

But by the early months of 1969, Gibson was also forming the opinion that the St. Louis Cardinals outfit in its entirety was doing things to *harm itself from within* as well, from the laborers on the field all the way up through the management in the brewery. A common thread throughout the 1960s for the Cardinals was the sense of camaraderie that pervaded the organization; the Cardinals were indeed among the most racially integrated teams in Major League Baseball, had performed as a cohesive unit on the field as well as any team in recent memory, and were well paid and well loved by their owner—who had already made his fortune in another business and thus paid close attention to his club simply because he was its biggest fan.

But for Gussie Busch *and* Bob Gibson, the Cardinals—which to them had been "like family"—were starting to grow further apart with each passing season. The pitcher had arrived at the organization in 1957 whereas the owner had taken over in 1953, as they dedicated their professional baseball careers to St. Louis. For Gibson, the game—meant to be his savage, individual battle between pitcher and hitter—had become less recognizable from the form in which he had learned it. But for Busch, his personal albatross was a gulf of mistrust that was slowly beginning to grow between him and his baseball employees, beginning with one man in his radio broadcasting booth.

2 Becoming a Business

Bob Gibson is a picnic to catch because he works rapidly and is always around the plate with his pitches.

> —Ted Simmons, quoted in Bob Broeg,
> "Ted Simmons: Losing Drives Me Crazy!"

A few weeks after the Cardinals' World Series loss, a cold, rainy evening blanketed the St. Louis area on November 3, 1968. Harry Caray, owner of the team's beloved radio voice since World War II, was taking a nighttime stroll along Kingshighway near Forest Park. Caray had been a St. Louis man all his life, growing up on the near north side of the city and breaking into the big leagues as a broadcaster the same season Schoendienst made his debut as a player. He had been born Enrico Carabina, reputedly taking his later, more recognized name from the stage moniker of a 1940s performer.

In the blur of the inclement evening, an automobile appeared suddenly from around a corner and struck Caray near the Chase Park Plaza Hotel. He instantly suffered two broken legs, a broken nose, and a dislocated shoulder from the incident. While his body would heal, the ramifications of the event—and what had possibly caused it—would reverberate around St. Louis and Caray's career for years to come.

Gussie Busch was frantically worried about Caray from the time the owner received a phone call about the accident. Busch had long loved him and personally saw to it that the broadcaster received round-the-clock care. After spending a month in a hospital bed, Caray in December would be flown by Busch in Gussie's private plane to his winter home at Pass-a-Grille on St. Pete Beach in Florida—near the Cardinals' spring training home since 1947—for further mending.

Harry was no different from Gussie's troops on the field, for Busch saw each man in the Cardinal family as one of "his boys," and after taking over as owner in 1953, he rewarded his baseball employees with salaries that no team outside of New York or Boston had ever seen. Back in the 1870s, when noted educator William Torrey Harris arrived as the superintendent of St. Louis Public Schools, he recruited an "all-star" lineup of teachers by paying them handsomely; in a like manner, Busch attracted top talent to his Anheuser-Busch brewery with high-scale pay rates and had figured he could simply do the same in his pursuit of baseball talent. After gaining ownership of the team, one of his first such targets was the acquisition of a rising young infielder with the Chicago Cubs named Ernie Banks. The owner of the Cubs was Philip K. Wrigley, a man who like Busch had procured a fortune in another field and held on to his team as an endeared novelty. Accustomed to being able to purchase the people he wanted, Gussie was incensed when Wrigley turned down his offer of five hundred thousand dollars for Banks. Turning to one of his many advisers, the scorned brewmaster listened wryly as the assistant mumbled, "Uh, Mr. Busch . . . Mr. Wrigley needs half a million dollars about as much as you do." Wrigley, with his chewing gum empire, always wished to be on the cutting edge of his business as well; as an example, in a few years he would be proud to announce that his gum was the first product sold using a Universal Product Code, or UPC, scanned at a checkout line the morning of June 26, 1974, at a grocery store in Troy, Ohio.

Over time, Busch would settle into understanding the differences in business acumen between baseball and his original field. He came to take great individual "ownership" in his players, looking after them with interest on a personal level and demanding almost daily updates from Devine and his other general managers over the years about the players' health, recent performances, and even private difficulties they may have been facing with which he might be able to help. One of his great joys was interacting with the players' families at the annual company picnic each August, from which nearly everyone left feeling a little closer to the boss at the end of the day. Often, the picnics would be a showcase for the latest portrait of the Busch family painted by Flood, a gifted artist in addition to being a skilled ballplayer. While no one—including Flood, Devine, Musial, or Schoendienst—ever dared calling him anything other than "Mr. Busch," the owner was generally viewed as a man who wished to be as common as anyone. He loved to play gin rummy on the Cardinals' team train with whoever wished to be dealt in, with the only requirement being that each participant, when thirsty, call for a "Bud" and not a "beer" from the porter.

Being the team's biggest fan, he was naturally as soured from the Cards' 1968 World Series collapse as anyone. Ten years after purchasing the club (as well as the team's ballpark from the previous landlords, the St. Louis Browns, who had moved on to Baltimore), Gussie could be heard hollering encouragement to the team from behind the dugout in the 1964 championship games, cheering as loudly for them against the Yankees like a St. Louis–born sailor home on leave from the war. He deeply relished the strong roster of players built by Devine throughout the 1960s—though often even claiming a majority of the credit for these brushstrokes on the masterpiece instead of Devine and the other general managers. He believed he had assembled a collection of players who were as loyal to him as he was to them. But as spring training of 1969 was approaching, the impact of the youth counterculture that had enveloped the country over the past decade had now seemingly found its way to the starched image of the St. Louis Cardinals personnel.

Busch had been able to starch the image by carefully handpicking his management team. During his time as the general manager in St. Louis in the mid-1960s, Bob Howsam—much in the spirit of his mentor, Branch Rickey—did his best to instill a true "uniform" appearance in the players, such as high-rolled pants, clean shaves, closely cropped hair, and other signs of conformity, team-oriented policies that by 1969 he was now working to establish in Cincinnati as the general manager with the Reds. In beginning his own second term as general manager after Howsam, however, Devine now seemed to be inheriting a club that had lost a portion of its focus and drive. And as a handful of players were beginning to check into their winter quarters at the Sheraton Inn in St. Petersburg, Florida, to begin preparing for the 1969 schedule, they glanced around to notice fewer of their 1968 teammates present. Something had struck the Cardinals' family that had never before been seen en masse—a large collection of contractual holdouts, news that enraged Gussie Busch.

The first blow to the morale of the owner had been when Gibson appeared as a guest of Johnny Carson on *The Tonight Show* on February 4 and revealed—in carefully chosen language—that the Major League Baseball Players' Association (MLBPA) had suggested that the union members consider the possibility of striking in advance of the 1969 regular season. In addition to augmented contributions on the owners' part to the players' pension and insurance funds (a move to which the owners had been clearly opposed in making their own views public), Gibson also asserted that the players wanted maintenance of the same and an ongoing percentage of the television revenues, moneys that were rapidly multiplying in the modern game.

When news of the interview got back to Gussie Busch, a new wall had suddenly been erected between him and his players, and what had previously been a friendly, wholesome all-American sport to the beer baron now, nearly overnight, became just another cutthroat aspect of his business with which he had to deal, whereby disunity must be crushed with an iron fist. And thus, the owner would take matters into his own hands in a few weeks, confronting the Cardinal wing of his brewery in a manner and location he had not utilized previously— by raging at them in their own locker room.

It was becoming increasingly apparent to writers covering the team that despite the loss in the World Series the past autumn, an inflated sense of self-importance had suddenly struck the well-paid players. The first of the combatants against the brewery in contract negotiations had been second baseman Julian Javier, a likable, steady player whom Schoendienst—a fine Keystoner himself—called the best ever at the position in pursuing pop flies in the outfield. In addition, Javier was considered by Schoendienst to be one of the finest hitters against left-handed pitching he had ever seen, comparing him in this regard to former St. Louis greats Danny Litwhiler and Whitey Kurowski. Although never a National League Gold Glove winner at second base in the midst of the Bill Mazeroski era in Pittsburgh, Javier was among the steadiest at the position as had been seen in baseball in the 1960s. After a career-high .281 batting average in 1967 that landed him ninth in the MVP voting, his batting mark (as with most other hitters the following season) fell to .260 in 1968. Even so, Javier imagined himself a large-enough part in the Redbird machine to request another raise in salary (Javier stood his ground despite the fact that, only twelve months earlier, Devine's assistant Jim Toomey had spent a good deal of March 1968 jet-setting back and forth between St. Petersburg and the Dominican Republic, attempting to get Javier signed and in camp at that time as well). Javier once again appeared in no hurry to arrive in Florida, instead passing the time by tending to his small cocoa bean farm in the Dominican Republic and lounging with his five daughters, who ranged in ages from nine to one.

In addition to the growing concern over Javier whereabouts, Flood and fellow star outfielder Lou Brock were each seeking increases to $100,000 a year in their pay rates. And Gibson—while nonetheless having decried the departure of the "old-fashioned game"—was not above seeking a modern pay rate for himself, looking for $125,000, with some reports in the St. Louis media claiming he was calling for as much as $140,000 per year. With training camp already under way for a week by March 1—the same day that Yankee legend Mickey Mantle announced that he was leaving the game—a total of nine unsigned players from the previous year's big league roster were missing from Cardinal practices. ("My right knee is what they call '100% disability'—there's nothing left to fix," Mantle told the press. "If I kept playing, I would only keep lowering my average. I have known for two years that I couldn't hit anymore, but I kept trying.") Musial, having stepped aside for Devine's return one year earlier but still serving as an adviser to him and Busch, scolded those who were holding out. "They're out of line," he said bluntly. "We've always been very fair with them, but individually few of them had the kind of season last year that would merit large increases. And I know, on the strength of what they've done, Bob Gibson is the only $100,000 ballplayer." Busch agreed, for in an isolated case, he was happy to pay Gibson the hefty raised he had wanted, as it was obvious that the pitcher had more to do with the 1968 pennant than any other player. The others, however, Busch found not only to be undeserving of what they wanted but also ungrateful for what they already had. Broeg noticed that Busch was "aghast to find pay increases [for 1969] spurned by players who had not contributed in proportion to the team's [1968] success." Ironically, Musial himself was the first $100,000 player eleven years prior, further evidence of how Busch often led the way in generosity to his players in the pre–free agency days of baseball, money typically seen only by the likes of New York stars such as the departing Mantle.

Also among the absentees from the St. Louis training camp were key pitchers Briles, Steve Carlton, and Ray Washburn as well as position players Shannon and Maxvill, leaving Orlando Cepeda, catcher Tim McCarver, and the newly acquired Pinson as the only regulars with finalized deals by the first of March. "It's unfortunate that we don't have the time for leisurely negotiations," added Devine to Musial's sentiment on Bing's fifty-second birthday. He then uttered next what symbolized the simplistic negotiating atmosphere of the era, with figures that would be considered laughable in modern times: "Whenever we're $4,000 to $5,000 apart I know we can get together. From $6,000 to $8,000 I feel we'll have no real trouble, either, but when the differential is $10,000 or more, I know we've got a difficult situation."

It was Flood who was looking for the biggest jump in pay, whose proposal of $100,000 was a substantial leap from his 1968 rate of $72,500 (in spite of his batting average having dropped from .335 to .301). The AWOL Javier, meanwhile, was desiring nearly a 300 percent raise, even after his own twenty-one-point hitting plunge. And the promising young Carlton, who had a dismal second half off the mound in 1968, was thought to have the least bargaining power among the holdouts. Even so, he was as adamant about his own salary demands as anyone, a pouting stance that would be seen by the left-hander more than once in the future as well. Almost overnight, the organization had found itself saddled with a throng of players who only wanted, wanted, and wanted some more. "Maybe someday," Devine dreamed idyllically, "a ballplayer will say, 'Look, it's been nice getting those World Series checks and more chances at endorsements. We've got a good shot at least another $7,500 or $10,000 or more, so I'll take a reasonable raise and sign."

The attitude of the modern player was certainly shocking to those on the administrative side of the game—including the field managers, such as Schoendienst and his foe in the World Series in Tigers manager Mayo Smith. In another angle on the issue, Smith was bemoaning the number of players who were suddenly trying to hit home runs in a backdoor attempt to grab a piece of the new money coming into the game. "Did you know that there were more than 20,000 strikeouts in the major leagues last season?" Smith pointed out in the spring of 1969. "Now, that's an awful lot of air blowing around. And it's the same old story. Too many guys are still swinging for home runs. And you can't make them realize that they don't have to hit a lot of homers to drive Cadillacs. Dal Maxvill's driving a Cadillac, isn't he? And how many homers has he hit?" In terms of the individual contract discussions between Cardinal players and Devine's management team, Busch did not directly involve himself in the negotiations at the time; he insisted, however, that Devine, Toomey, and Musial keep him apprised of the dealings, often cornering Bing with the question, "Did you get so-and-so signed yet???" To discourage the duration of holdouts from lengthening, Devine even showed an inclination to waive the standard $250-a-day fine for players who were late to camp—a good deal in relation to salaries of the day—if they showed a good-faith effort to get there.

Despite being absent from camp himself for the first few days, McCarver admitted that he needed at least six weeks of spring training and was miffed that some of the important pitchers were not yet in camp with only five weeks to go before the start of the regular season. But with fewer teammates with whom to work for the time being, he now had an extra opportunity to tutor the team's nineteen-year-old prized rookie catcher, Ted Simmons, who had been taking classes at the University of Michigan and had recently reported to Florida. The son of a horse trainer from suburban Detroit, the athletically gifted Simmons had been a productive switch-hitter since the age of thirteen and was also a force on the high school football field as a fullback. He had received a college football scholarship offer to stay in Ann Arbor, but also held gridiron invitations from Michigan State, Ohio State, and Purdue. Baseball remained his true love, and he thus chose to sign with the Cardinals and scout Mo Mozalli for a bonus of $50,000. Simmons then wasted no time in sailing through the team's Minor League system, having been named the Most Valuable Player in the California League in 1968 in leading all in batting average (.331) and runs batted in (117) while adding 28 home runs. The twenty-seven-year-old McCarver, meanwhile, weighed in at 210 pounds as spring workouts began, which was more than 20 pounds heavier than when he entered pro ball ten years earlier— which was after McCarver's own stellar high school football career landed him scholarship offers from coast to coast as well.

Lou Brock had been yet another normally sound hitter who saw his batting average drop in 1968. While being one of the holdouts, in short time, he would come to terms with Devine and Toomey (as did Washburn), agreeing to a raise near the $85,000 range. Washburn's salary went up to $35,000, as Carlton also finally inked for $27,000. While not requesting a particularly high figure, Washburn's situation particularly irritated Devine because of the pitcher's past history of needing time to get ready, as McCarver had implied. "Ray should come in [to finalize his contract] because he's a slow starter who has had a case history of arm trouble," the general manager had grumbled a few days earlier. When previously asked about how he would conduct spring exercises with several key individuals still out of the fold, a concerned Schoendienst just shrugged his shoulders. "I play the hand I'm dealt," he said. But by March 4, however, all of his players would be under contract—including Gibson, who received what he had been seeking in hauling in a Cardinal-record $125,000, as well as Flood, who reaped a healthy raise himself, up to $90,000. In whipping out a pen at his desk and doing some quick final numbers, Devine estimated that the twenty-five-man roster would nearly crack the $1 million figure overall.

In addition to the new salary demands, adding to Busch's growing dismay was the fact that many of the players were showing off their new collections of flashy clothing, jewelry, and hairstyles, making the scene nearly unrecognizable from a typical Major League locker room. And compounding the increasingly circuslike atmosphere was the recent addition of pitcher Bo Belinsky during the off-season, a hurler with mediocre statistics over his six-year big league career but with a reputation for late-night carousing with every notable woman who traversed Sunset Boulevard in Hollywood (Belinsky would be sold to the California Angels before the start of the 1969 season, not pitching in the Major Leagues again until August, when he was dealt to the Pittsburgh Pirates).

With several of the veterans late in getting to camp, other rookies besides Simmons were taking advantage of the opportunity to show off their skills to the coaching staff. In addition to the new catcher, the one all were curious to see was nineteen-year-old left-handed pitcher Jerry Reuss, the local St. Louis prep phenomenon from Ritenour High School. The arrival of Reuss had been so anxiously anticipated by the organization that he ate up one of the fifteen "protected" roster spots the team needed to submit to the National League offices in advance of the special 1969 expansion draft, a directive that would help stock the new franchises coming in San Diego and Montreal. Protecting Reuss from the expansion draft was a decision that came with the risk of leaving several veteran pitchers unprotected, but many were of the opinion that Reuss, a 1967 graduate of Ritenour, might be able to help the big league club almost immediately. "He's not far away," Schoendienst projected on the young pitcher's ETA to the majors. "He can really hum that ball, and he's got the poise and physique, too." Added Red's pitching coach Billy Muffett about the pitcher's advanced poise and makeup, "He's old for his years."

Reuss had recalled how, while dominating the high school ranks, nearly every Major League team was scouting him at Ritenour—with the glaring exception of his hometown Cardinals, and he naturally wondered why. The reasoning was later revealed: the Cards did not want to initially display a heightened interest in Reuss, in an effort to lower the other clubs' rating of him and to hopefully leave the pitcher available to St. Louis (based on the notion that other teams would relent if the hometown club, who presumably had scouted the player the most often and with the most scrutiny, was not interested). The hoax paid off, as Reuss was bypassed by both leagues in the first round of the 1967 draft, with St. Louis claiming him with its second-round choice (after taking Simmons in the first).

As a teenager, Reuss had never been convinced that his future would be as a hurler, for in his first high school practice as a freshman, two of Jerry's coaches at Ritenour (Lee Engert and Pete Hensel) had invited the players to run out to whichever positions they preferred to pursue. Seeing a high number of youngsters scramble toward his first choice of first base, Jerry spontaneously changed directions in midstride and headed for the pitcher's mound. It was a decision that altered history for the midtown high school in Overland, as Ritenour would claim back-to-back Missouri State Championships in baseball in 1966 and 1967.

In his first season of Minor League ball, Reuss had posted a 1.86 ERA in fifty-six innings at Cedar Rapids before being promoted to the Cardinals' higher-level farm team in the Texas League at Little Rock. Throughout his Minor League progress, Reuss came across several players who, like himself, had been high school stars; some had relied too heavily on their natural skills and would end up failing, but Reuss adapted quickly to advanced levels of competition and continued to improve. He issued strong numbers at Little Rock as well, with a 2.17 ERA along with 86 strikeouts in 112 innings. Looking for a well-rounded life, Jerry had also been finding time to squeeze in college credits at Southern Illinois University and Central Missouri State University when he was able to do so (while at CMSU, he even broadcasted high school basketball games on a Warrensburg station).

However, high school bonus babies were not the only young prospects making their marks in the initial absence of the veterans in the Cardinals' 1969 training camp. One such fellow was Charles "Boots" Day, a twenty-one-year-old outfielder from upstate New York signed in 1966 out of a tryout camp. To the impression of the Cardinal coaches, Day was executing the same type of magnificent catches in center to which people were accustomed to seeing Flood make. And with Javier holding out, the team was compelled to give youngster Steve Huntz a chance to fill in at second base and had also toyed with the idea of having Maxvill move over from short to second. Huntz, at the age of twenty-one, had attained his first few big league at-bats with the Cards in 1967, having been acquired from the Baltimore Orioles organization in 1964 after batting .249 in the minors at Appleton for that summer. The Cleveland native had just been married over the winter and was looking to secure a big league job on a regular basis. He had taught himself to be a switch-hitter long ago at the age of ten, when he and his friends had to minimize the distance they could hit the ball in the confines of their small Cleveland sandlot—thus, all the boys agreed to bat left-handed. Huntz had been a three-sport star at the city's storied St. Ignatius High School, and like Simmons and McCarver had scholarship offers for football to several Big Ten schools. After graduation, he was about to pack his bags for Villanova University in Philadelphia when the Orioles arrived with a signing-bonus offer of fifteen thousand dollars plus four years of college tuition when he was ultimately finished with baseball. "That was quite an inducement," Huntz recalled. "With three younger kids, my folks couldn't afford to send me to college." While toiling through the Minor Leagues, Huntz returned home to the Cleveland area to pursue a degree in English at nearby Kent State University, with a desire to one day be a high school teacher. He credited Joe Medwick, the former Cardinals star slugger and last Triple Crown winner in the National League in 1937, in helping him grow as a hitter through the minors as Medwick coached the young batters.

Like Huntz, McCarver, Simmons, and several others, the Cardinals' roster in the late 1960s was dotted with tremendous all-around athletes who had enjoyed stellar high school careers on the gridiron and the basketball floor as well, and another such prep standout arrived in a December 1968 trade from the San Diego Padres, pitcher Dave Giusti. Born in Seneca Falls, New York, Giusti grew up in Syracuse and played college baseball and basketball at Syracuse University, pitching for SU head coach and former Major League hurler Ted Kleinhans, who showed him a new way to throw a change-up. Giusti had also received football offers to SU and Florida State University, but turned them down because of a fear of recurring concussions he had suffered from his high school days on the football field. A scholar as well, Giusti had already earned bachelor's and master's degrees in physical education from SU by 1967, by which time he had already been a veteran of six Major League seasons with the Houston Colt .45s and, later, the Houston Astros. "I don't think my wife would appreciate this," Giusti revealed upon the family's late move to St. Louis in March 1969, despite the trade occurring in December, "but one of the main reasons we stayed in Houston this past winter was so that I could play golf three or four times a week."

Giusti, one of the many new faces in spring camp in 1969, had been acquired from Houston for popular catcher Johnny Edwards (who, as a veteran like McCarver, was dealt in light of the imminent development of Simmons as the heir to the position). Given a chance to bolster the Cardinals' bull pen, he was hit hard in his spring training debut for the Cards on March 14, allowing nine hits and seven runs while retiring only one batter's worth of work. Giusti threw thirty-eight pitches in the rough inning before Muffett went out to retrieve him, but both the pitching coach and Schoendienst were convinced that Giusti would be an effective member of the staff in the future.

While Giusti was pitching, Gussie Busch was sitting next to Bing Devine in the box seats at Al Lang Field in St. Petersburg, as Busch was making his first public appearance of the spring. Stating that "this is the latest I've ever reported to camp," Busch was anxious to assess the early status of his club and was certain that the pieces were in place for a drive to a third-straight pennant. As he and Devine sat together, quiet discussion began to emerge between the men of a potentially earthshaking trade—one that would manifest itself just three days later.

Slugging, fun-loving first baseman Orlando Cepeda's time with the Cardinals began, literally, with the birth of the "new" Busch Stadium in downtown St. Louis in May 1966. On the eighth of that month, Cepeda took one of the final at-bats by a visiting player in what has become known as "Busch Stadium I" —also known then as Sportsman's Park—moments before the San Francisco Giants sealed a 10–5 win in the final game at the old yard. In the locker room afterward, Cepeda and Cardinals pitcher Ray Sadecki learned they were changing sides, and Cepeda immediately prepared to join the Cards on a brief road trip to Chicago while the finishing touches were being placed on the new St. Louis stadium by the riverfront, with a grand opening of the new ballpark slated for May 12.

Since that momentous time in mid-May 1966, Cepeda had been viewed as the heart and soul of the club, often seen climbing on top of the "money trunk" (where players kept their valuables locked up during games) in the clubhouse to lead the team in cheers, shouting out in broken Spanish, "Viva El Birdos!" He secured the 1967 National League Most Valuable Player award with a .325 average and league-best 125 RBIs but had batted only .103 in the 1967 World Series. His fall in the playoff had preceded his worst regular-season statistics ever in 1968 in seeing his average drop to .248 at the age of thirty (despite leading the Cardinals in game-winning hits with 12). To make matters worse for Cepeda, it had also been revealed that he had been running up large amounts of personal debt over the course of many months heading into 1968. And in the midst of trying to resolve his myriad financial issues, he had even been seen running back into the Cardinals' locker room in between innings of games at Busch Stadium to use the telephone—and, on one occasion it was reported, to even meet with one of his "creditors" in the stadium tunnel to discuss an under-the-table repayment plan.

While Busch publicly expressed optimism about the 1969 season, privately he was becoming very disturbed with the attitude he was starting to notice in the players—and Cepeda had become a prominent example of what he considered to be a growing trend of laziness and irresponsibility among the modern big leaguers. As a result, Cepeda's trade to the Atlanta Braves for Joe Torre on March 17, 1969, would signal the first of many moves he commanded Devine to make over the next few years, hoping to reestablish the hallmark Cardinal loyalty and competitiveness from years past with the right formula of new "employees." The move of Cepeda stunned many of the remaining Cardinals, who felt that in spite of the World Series loss to Detroit, the roster should be left alone; it was obvious, such players claimed, that the team had immense talent, and thus any problems would be temporary and resolved naturally. Gibson was among the first and most vocal in this regard. "Management was messing in a major way with a club that had run away with two straight pennants," the ace pitcher believed. "Trading Cepeda signaled to us, loud and clear, that things would no longer be the same around the Cardinal clubhouse."

Despite Gibson's feelings for Cepeda, Torre would become one of Gibson's best friends over the next couple of years on the team (in addition, he would also become one of the few Cardinal players willing to challenge Gibson on the field when the pitcher was not at his best). The slugger, meanwhile, had similarly been involved in his own difficulties with his bosses in Atlanta. And while Gibson and other Cardinals were concerned about the team's giving up one of the few true home run power sources in their lineup in Cepeda, people such as former St. Louis general manager Frank Lane—Devine's first predecessor from the 1950s—thought the payoff with Torre would be greater. "Cepeda will hit a lot of home runs in that smaller Atlanta ballpark, Gussie," he told Busch in forecasting the players' 1969 output. "But I'll tell you this: every time Torre goes to bat for you, he'll see [Braves general manager] Paul Richards' face on the ball." Torre was quite happy to be leaving Atlanta, having had several angry brushes with Richards regarding his contract. Not believing that Torre had performed up to par the past two seasons, Richards was not concerned when the New York native Torre—who sold municipal bonds for a company on Wall Street in the off-season—announced that, once again in early 1969, he planned to hold out for a better contract.

"I can't compare Torre with Cepeda defensively at first base," Devine acknowledged after the deal was consummated, "but we believe he's good enough with the glove. And we believe he'll give us a good bat." It was believed that the Cards' promising first-base prospect, Joe Hague, would thus have more of an opportunity to develop with the trade being made, as it was imagined that Torre would be spending some time as a catcher as well. "I have a lot of respect for Mr. Devine," Torre told the St. Louis press upon his arrival in town. "Before he asked me anything about money, he told me I'd play every day with them— mostly at first base, but filling in behind the plate sometimes. . . . You certainly can't have any complaints when you get traded to a club like the Cardinals." Then, thinking further about his turn of fate and all those who may have had a hand in it, Torre added, "Maybe this is one of the pleasant benefits of having a sister who is a nun." Torre, apparently trying to pull a random figure out of the air for dramatic effect during his press conference, claimed to have batted .145 against St. Louis in 1968 but actually had struck the .200 mark (eleven for fifty-five).

Torre would be, in one sense, the actual replacement for Maris, as he would don the famous number 9 formerly worn in St. Louis by Maris as well as long-time Cardinal great Enos Slaughter. Half-jokingly, Torre said he hoped that the slender single-digit jersey number would help hide his weight, which had been an issue with the Braves. In progressing through his professional baseball career, he had lost the boyhood fat that showed him at 240 pounds while only fifteen years old, growing up in Brooklyn. However, over the winter he had allowed himself to balloon back over 220 pounds—something he promised Gussie Busch he would keep in check. Torre then put himself on a special diet before the 1969 season and had most recently lost 30 pounds, which he said was in preparation for the hot St. Louis summers (but, as he was asked by a local writer, aren't Atlanta summers quite hot as well?).

In addition, with the speed of his new teammates in St. Louis such as Brock, Flood, and others (as opposed to his slugging, lumbering former comrades in Atlanta), Torre was predicting that, as a Cardinal, he would be near the top of the National League charts in runs batted in. He was not alone in this opinion, for in a preseason poll of the Cardinals players that was taken every year by Broeg, seven had picked Torre to lead not only the team but the entire league in RBIs for 1969, while six had selected McCovey and five had forecast Dick Allen of the Phillies. The going-away choice among the Redbirds for the league batting champion, meanwhile, was defending winner Rose. "He's got a good hitting park," McCarver explained about the Cincinnati native, who played in front of family and friends in the Queen City in hailing from the city's west side. "He's a switch hitter who hits to all fields and he can run." Rose, at a circuit-best .335, had been one of only five players in the National League to hit .300 or better in the offense-starved campaign of 1968; by 1970 he would equal Musial and Gibson's St. Louis feat by becoming the first $100,000-a-year player in Cincinnati history, as Howsam had been generally successful in continuing the penny-pinching tactics he had learned from Rickey in St. Louis.

While the Cardinals were shaping up in Florida, hitting the sports headlines back in St. Louis that March was the news that forty-year-old Joe B. Hall had been hired as the new basketball coach at St. Louis University. Hall had been the freshman coach for the past four seasons under the famed Adolph Rupp at the University of Kentucky (for whom Hall had played in 1949) and was now taking over at SLU for Joe Brehmer. Rupp, who was the winningest coach in college basketball, would face mandatory retirement from UK in three years because of his age, and Hall would leave SLU after the 1971–1972 season to return to Lexington and succeed his mentor.

On the same day as the Torre-Cepeda trade on the seventeenth, the director of the Major League Baseball Players' Association, Marvin Miller, met with the entire Cardinals team to update them on the union's progress in the collective bargaining negotiations. The American and National leagues were splitting into two divisions each for 1969 (which simply created more work for sixty-two-year-old traveling secretary Leo Ward, who in March 1969 was recovering from a stroke). Regarding the new divisional setup, the issue for the union was that there was nothing in place in the current agreement to provide for the non-pennant-winning divisional winners to get a share of the postseason revenue. Miller, however, wanted to go further; he was looking to preserve the "first-division" concept, in doing so proposing that the top three teams in each division share in the playoff money.

When Miller was asked about the status of the reserve clause by one of the Cardinal players in the room—the long-standing codicil in baseball that held a player bound to his current team until traded or sold—he responded only by saying that the concept was "inequitable in its impact and not as essential in its present form as management says."

Miller, in fact, was in the process of renegotiating nearly every aspect of the current bargaining agreement—even the number of exhibition games that a team should play over the course of the preseason and regular season (within a few years, all midseason exhibition games would be gone, a relic of the pretelevision days in which clubs would permit far-reaching towns to experience big league baseball—at a profit for the teams, of course, on scheduled days off on the teams' calendars). In fact, he had already convinced the New York Mets to even boycott a planned May 8 date to play against the United States Military Academy at West Point, as Miller complained that such contests now needed the approving vote of the Players' Association before they could take place. A graduate of economics and labor relations from New York University in 1938, Miller was in the process of making yet another grab at the owners' pot of gold since taking over the union in 1966.

While dealing with the strange new behaviors of the players, the presence of Miller roaming around the Cardinals' spring training facilities in St. Petersburg also did nothing to brighten the mood of Busch. The annoyances served only to heighten his disgust with what he was now viewing as money-zealous, ungrateful prima donnas, and by March 22 he could mask his anger no longer.

As the team was about to depart the locker room for workouts that morning, Busch appeared at the door with other brewery executives and instructed all to remain in the room and have a seat. With a few members of the media present as well, Busch shut the door and started in on a hollering tirade, the likes of which had never been heard publicly in his tenure with the organization. He changed topics frequently and abruptly during the fifteen-minute rant, venturing from salaries to work habits to the proud history of the organization. Most of the players were dumbfounded as the yelling continued, glancing around the room at each other in disbelief when the boss's look would dart in the other direction for an instant. The most upset was Curt Flood; although Busch's speech was directed at the team as a whole, the greatest one-on-one wedge developing between owner and player—and perhaps the most surprising, given the amiable history between the two—was between them, as Flood would long resent the clubhouse tirade. "The speech demoralized the 1969 Cardinals," claimed Flood later. "The employer had put us in our place. Despite two successive pennants, we were still livestock." Flood would also recollect that Busch tried to accentuate his remarks by trading Cepeda "a few days later," but the trade had actually occurred five days before the speech. It was certainly not one way in which the feelings were changing, for there had been signs starting to surface to the owner that Flood was not the same person he had embraced more than ten years earlier, when the outfielder was acquired by the organization in a trade with Cincinnati. And in the coming weeks, other events would surface that would even further distance the two men.

However, as far as most of the St. Louis sportswriters were concerned, the owner's outburst was actually met with *approval*—something they felt not only Busch had a right to do, but was *necessary* to jolt the team out of a building lethargy, complacency, and focus on money that was obvious to them. It had to be done before it was too late, they reasoned, with the regular season about to begin in two weeks. "The brewer-sportsman has a fine track record when it comes to civic responsibility and contribution and the rights of others," wrote Broeg two days after the incident. "It's about time some of the wealthier athletes did too. . . . [A] player doesn't have to be a star to appreciate the sheer joy of playing a boy's game for money, a fact that never seemed to escape Stan Musial." Then as Broeg's typewriter charged on, Cepeda's personal financial troubles came to his mind, as well as other moments in which Busch had helped his employees—and Flood was certainly no exception. "The fact is that over the years, [Busch] has played wet-nurse to players, advancing them money without interest, bailing them out of problems and practically holding their hands through situations that grown men could be expected to avoid or, at least, handle on their own."

What was later revealed as the main purpose behind Busch's address to the team was what he felt to be a *transgression of loyalty* to the organization. Whether in brewing beer or playing baseball, allegiance had always been paramount for Busch, and in return, he felt that he consistently rewarded it when displayed. He always believed that he paid his employees well—both inside and outside the physical plant of the brewery—and, in turn, expected a degree of commitment in return. For example, he had been perhaps the first owner to personally pay for chartered flights for his team, while other clubs were scurrying through airports to catch commercial routes. With this type of special treatment, Busch felt, an equal level of dedication on the employees' part was required. Busch believed that the fans in St. Louis had proved their faithfulness to the team, and he commanded those in the Cardinal organization to show them the same respect. As a gesture to the fans in this sentiment, Busch had always kept the price of the bleacher seats at the ballpark just one dollar, a cost that remained in effect many years after other teams had soared far beyond this figure for similar seats in their ballparks.

Even Devine, his long-trusted general manager, had once lost his job due to what Busch perceived as infidelity. In early 1964, the idea was planted in Busch's mind by certain brewery advisers that Devine and then field manager Johnny Keane were attempting to craft personnel decisions for the team behind his back (in later years Whitey Herzog—who served in both field manager and personnel roles for the Cardinals—said that Busch gave him free rein in decisions about players and that all Busch wanted was to be told of a move before it hit the newspapers). Enraged, Busch immediately began making arrangements early in that season for both men to be fired, replacing Keane with Leo Durocher and Devine with Rickey, the latter of whom had already returned to St. Louis for another tenure with the ball club in a consulting capacity (Rickey, in fact, had made it clear to Devine privately that Rickey was hired to be *more* than a consultant and to actually have the final say in roster moves). Soon, Durocher would be seen coming and going from the Busch estate several times that August, presumably in negotiations with Gussie for the field manager's job.

As fate would have it, Keane would lead the Cards to a late-summer pennant charge with the newly acquired Brock in the outfield in a trade with the Cubs and ultimately go on to defeat the vaunted Yankees in the World Series. A master of public relations, Busch then knew he could not fire the men—or, at least, not Keane. No sooner than in the postgame press conference immediately after the World Series victory, Busch was heard praising Keane's qualities. But in one of the rare moments in which Busch was outmaneuvered in the "boardroom," Keane suddenly announced—with live cameras rolling on the faces of both men—that he was leaving the Cardinals to manage the Yankees, the club he had just defeated for the title. Looking to salvage some degree of victory for himself in the wake of this embarrassment, Busch still showed Devine the door (and Branch Rickey would pass away just over a year later, on December 9, 1965, approximately a month after suffering a heart attack in the middle of a speech he was delivering in Columbia, Missouri, in conjunction with his election to the Missouri Sports Hall of Fame).

Thus, even though Devine had been long forgiven and rehired, even veteran newcomers such as Pinson had become questionable in the minds of the administration when the team returned to its practices for the final two weeks of spring training after the owners' concerns were vented. Pinson, still envisioned to take the place of the retired Maris in right field, had injured his groin in early August 1968 with the Reds. It was an injury that would limit him to only 130 games after averaging 155 per season and more than 650 plate appearances in his first ten years in the big leagues. His average had also dropped to .271, but the Cardinals were confident that he would bounce back. An Oakland native, Pinson had been tutored in the Bay Area by the same mentor, George Powles, who had helped groom Flood in his baseball skills. Pinson, in fact, was convinced that Powles had literally saved him when, long ago, another boy threatened Vada with a knife. "It was at that moment that Coach Powles came into my life," he recalled. "He stepped between us. With his back to the kid with the knife, he gave me hell. He said I was a fool, charging the kid with the knife. 'Two wrongs didn't make a right,' he insisted, and I realized I was learning something."

Primarily a pitcher by the time he got to high school, Pinson would soon chase down fly balls in the same McClymonds High School outfield as Flood and another star, Frank Robinson. When his prep days were finished, Pinson signed with the Reds and scout Bobby Mattick for two thousand dollars in 1956 (three years earlier Robinson had also signed through Mattick with the Reds, and by 1956 he was starting in the outfield as a twenty-year-old rookie in Cincinnati). Flood also inked with Cincinnati, but once Pinson became a full-time outfielder, he quickly outdistanced Flood in the race through the Minor Leagues, and Flood was dealt to the Cardinals. Now, coming full circle many years since their childhood days in Oakland, Flood and Pinson were excited to join forces in the pasture of Busch Stadium.

Late in March, Pinson would catch his foot under a fence in a game at Bradenton against the Pirates. Initially, it was feared that Pinson had broken his ankle, but X-rays were negative and he was allowed to continue his spring regimen. It was the only hurdle for the newcomer in his baptism as a Cardinal, as Pinson was hitting a blistering .450 by that time.

As part of Broeg's poll, the Cardinals almost unanimously forecast that the addition of the steady Pinson had done the most to ensure another pennant claim in 1969, with the Torre-for-Cepeda acquisition being considered an even draw. In addition to Pinson, Mike Shannon had also posted a strong exhibition batting average of .396, while Brock had finished the spring in fine fashion as well with a .365 mark. It had been a point of emphasis in Florida for Brock to improve his contact, as he had struck out in nearly one of every five plate appearances in 1968 (improvement in this area had indeed been evident, as he fanned only five times in sixty-three at-bats in Grapefruit League play).

There had not been many teams who had come close to the Cardinals in the National League the past two seasons, and despite the discord perceived by some in town, more of the same was expected from the outside with the advent of divisional play in 1969. "It is conceded that St. Louis will dominate the [Eastern] division and that the Chicago Cubs ought to finish second," predicted Leonard Koppett of the *New York Times*. Displaying no confidence in the hometown Mets, Arthur Daley, another writer at the *Times*, held the same view. "The East is the personal property of the St. Louis Cardinals," he warned, "perhaps the best and deepest club to be seen in the preseason tournament. It is impossible to pick against them." The Cubs indeed appeared to pose the greatest threat to end the Cards' reign, as a three-year rebuilding job by Durocher was starting to come to fruition.

With high batting marks in St. Petersburg, Schoendienst left camp feeling the offense would score plenty of runs. Instead, he was ironically more concerned about the pitchers—even after their dominant 1968 campaign—as he wondered if the slow arrival in St. Petersburg back in February of Carlton, Washburn, and Briles would have an adverse effect down the road. "Infielders, outfielders, and catchers can get ready in a hurry for the regular season," Red noted. "But there's no way for pitchers to get in enough work unless they report on schedule." Timely in their arrivals or not, the lack of innings pitched by the established starting pitchers in Gibson (fourteen), Carlton (sixteen), and Briles and Washburn (thirteen each) was glaring. In comparison, all four had pitched twice as much in spring training of the pennant-winning season the previous year. "None of the starting pitchers reported until he was two weeks overdue," Broeg worried, also pointing out that the March weather in Florida had not cooperated. "And when it came time for the regulars to pitch, that's when cold weather turned wet."

As the preseason drew to a close, Busch and Devine were still concerned about stabilizing the roster; thus, they turned to a face from the past. Longtime first baseman Bill White, an all-star in five seasons with St. Louis in the late 1950s and early 1960s, was obtained in a trade with Philadelphia on April 3. White had already sold his house in St. Louis and looked for a permanent place to live in Philadelphia after having been given a television broadcasting job by the Phillies, but was later talked out of retirement by the front office; soon after, he was dealt to St. Louis. When he made the deal for White, Devine had envisioned his use strictly as a pinch hitter and an occasional rest for Torre at first base. "Bill fits the bill," he laughed. "If he can't do it [pinch-hit], I don't know who can. He knows the pitchers in the league." White, receiving an approximate salary of fifty thousand dollars, put Devine over that imagined one-million-dollar mark in contracts he had negotiated for the 1969 Cardinals. "I had my best years in St. Louis," White commented about the deal, "and I'm very fond of Bing Devine. Wherever I go, I like to be an asset—and I haven't been the last two seasons in Philadelphia." White's decline in production had prompted the Phillies to move their slugging third baseman, Allen, over to first base.

At the beginning of April, the Cardinals caravan from Florida found itself heading back toward St. Louis at the same moment another progression was making its way west from Washington, D.C., in the direction of the Gateway City. Former president Dwight D. Eisenhower had passed away from congestive heart failure at Walter Reed Hospital on March 28. After lying in state before fifty thousand mourners in a simple military casket in the Capitol Rotunda, his body was transported by train to his hometown of Abilene, Kansas, for burial. The procession would become a thirteen-hundred-mile, thirty-hour journey to his resting place. Harry S. Truman—the beloved Missourian and one of two living former presidents, along with LBJ—was at one of his favorite retreats in Key West, Florida, when Eisenhower passed and was unable to attend the services for his own health reasons (Truman himself would pass away three years later). While stopping in St. Louis on April 1, Eisenhower's car was halted at Track 2 in Union Station, with viewers able to pay their respects from the west side of the terminal on Twentieth Street. Afterward, the funeral train would roll west out of St. Louis toward Kansas, as the Cardinals would shortly follow behind—for they would play their final exhibition game on April 6 against their new in-state rivals, the expansion Kansas City Royals.

The Royals were one of four new Major League teams in 1969, joining the Seattle Pilots in the American League, while the Cardinals would have to contend with new National League entries in the San Diego Padres and Montreal Expos (the Pacific Coast League, incidentally, had been paid an indemnity of more than a half-million dollars from the Major Leagues as a result of placing franchises in Seattle and San Diego). As a result, each league would now be divided into two six-team divisions, as opposed to the traditional one list of ten teams in viewing the standings. While still geographically in the western half of the National League franchises, the Cardinals were placed in the "Eastern Division," where their primary opponents would be Montreal, Chicago, Philadelphia, Pittsburgh, and the New York Mets, the latter an expansion club themselves seven years earlier as a National League replacement for the fleeing of the Dodgers and Giants to the West Coast. Although not experiencing a winning season in their short history—including a modern-era record of 120 losses in their first campaign in 1962—the Mets had slowly gained respect among their new divisional rivals. They had posted a 73-89 mark in 1968, their best yet, thanks to one of the most promising young pitching corps ever seen. "The Mets aren't going to be making as many mistakes as they used to," Schoendienst warned. "They've always had outstanding pitching for a couple of years .... [Tom] Seaver's one of the three best pitchers in our league. And don't think they're not going to score some runs." The division of the leagues and dilution of talent through expansion, however, were thought by most to weaken the imminent overall quality of the Major Leagues.

The Cards returned from Kansas City to begin the regular schedule on April 8 at Busch Stadium, with a gala spectacle in order. As was tradition, the team encircled the stadium in an open motorcade with Caray as the emcee, standing at the microphone to introduce each passing carful of VIPs. When the parade was finished, Major League Baseball Commissioner Bowie Kuhn presented the club with its 1968 National League pennant, as team representatives then subsequently transferred the flag to four fans who had been previously selected at random. The four chosen ones strutted proudly as they marched the flag out to the pole in center field where it was hoisted to the top (in the early days of the ballpark, the flagpole at Busch Stadium—as was the case in the old Sportsman's Park—formerly stood within the field of play). Moments later, Musial—who had thrown out the first pitch in the first of the two exhibition games in Kansas City—offered another first pitch in advance of the singing of the national anthem by Washington University graduate student Jeral Becker. Gibson then took the mound, looking to further his remarkable 1968 numbers.

The pregame laurels, however, were the final happy moments over the next few days. Whether a carryover from the disastrous final two innings of the 1968 World Series, the off-season contractual distractions, a lack of overall focus in spring training, the verbal undressing from the owner, or other factors, the Redbirds started their 1969 campaign by being swept at home by the Pirates in three straight games. The Pittsburgh team was sporting a new look, counting on rookie infielders Richie Hebner and Bob Robertson to supply some fresh offense in the lineup. While Hebner would be pushing the .400 mark by mid-May, it was Robertson who had particularly impressed the Pirates' hitting coach, Bill Virdon, a former Cardinals outfielder. "That kid is capable of hitting 40 home runs a year if he's swinging right," Virdon said. In the opener, Gibson had labored through the ninth inning to a 2–2 tie in the opener against Steve Blass, striking out ten, but the team wound up losing in the fourteenth inning. Blass, eager to get going with the season himself, had shown up at Busch Stadium more than two hours earlier than the rest of his teammates to the Pirates' practice session the day before. "I just can't wait," the pitcher said. In the year of the pitcher in 1968, no one in the National League had a better winning percentage than his record of 18-6, and Blass was looking for the success to continue. "I got up at seven o'clock this morning and couldn't fall back asleep. So I decided to go to the ballpark." Despite the three losses, Pinson made an immediate splash, gathering two hits, including the Cards' lone extra-base hit, a double in his initial St. Louis at-bat in the first inning to score Flood.

Before his first game with St. Louis, Pinson had received some good-natured hazing from his new teammates that is normally reserved for rookies. Someone had written a message for all to see on the locker room chalkboard:

Q: Who was 2-for-22 in the World Series?
A: Vada Pinson with the Cincinnati Reds in 1961.

When Pinson later discovered the culprit to be little-used catcher Dave Ricketts, he had ample ammunition for a reply. He chose the following fact:

Q: Who went 3-for-22 last year and got an extra $2,500 for each hit?
A: Dave Ricketts

(The approximate per-player loser's share for the Cardinals in the 1968 World Series was $7,500; Ricketts was three for twenty-two in the regular season and one for one in the World Series.)

Whereas Pinson had started well, the other new Redbird in Torre had gone only one for fourteen in a St. Louis uniform, while his counterpart in Atlanta was already paying dividends for the Braves. On April 11 (the day before Torre would snap his poor beginning with a three-for-four effort), Cepeda single-handedly downed the Reds with a homer for Atlanta, his first for his new club. Additionally, Cepeda had now produced the game-winning hit for the Braves in three of their first four wins. And by the end of May, the organization would present Cepeda with a new tractor, as he was voted the team's Player of the Month with a .338 average and fourteen RBIs for May.

Given their production in the spring, it was surprising that a lack of offense was the chief factor in the slow start for the Cardinals in 1969. After a 1–0 shutout at the hands of the Cubs in Busch Stadium on April 16 (a game in which Shannon and Chicago second baseman Glenn Beckert endured a violent collision on the base path), Schoendienst stayed in his office in the locker room long into the night and was surprised when veteran equipment manager Butch Yatkeman—who had started working for the Cardinals as a batboy in 1924—told him it was already past midnight. Uncharacteristically for Red, he was already getting the lineup card ready for the following day, as he felt the batting order needed drastic changes. The first move was to relieve Brock in left field with the rookie Hague, as Lou—one of the hottest March hitters—had begun the season at a paltry .100 mark with four hits in his first forty trips to the plate. Javier, another of the winter holdouts, was at .207 and was replaced with Huntz, while McCarver's .189 gave way to putting Torre behind the plate, with Bill White making an unexpected start at first base.

The bold moves by Schoendienst would not help, as the Cubs shut them out the next night as well, riding the four-hit pitching of Bill Hands and Phil Regan to a 3–0 win over the Cards. The confident Cubs were flying high behind their colorful leader in Durocher, off to their best start of a season in nearly thirty-five years at 9-1 (soon to be 11-1 after two more games in Montreal), while the defending champs were struggling at 4-6. Several of the veterans for St. Louis, in fact, were grumbling that the lineup changes were entirely premature. Among them was Flood, who even took his complaints to the St. Louis media when Schoendienst elevated some of the young players to higher spots in the batting order.

On the fourteenth, the Cardinals had the "privilege" of playing the first regular-season Major League game outside the American borders. They were in Quebec to take on the Expos in their temporary home of Jarry Park, a shoddy, Minor League–quality stadium north of downtown. Plans had been made to construct a magnificent new structure for the team in the center of the city, but fulfillment of the idea was still years away. Montreal politicians insisted that the playing conditions at Jarry Park be made as fine as possible, but that still left Flood and other Cardinals concerned for their safety. "I've played on some bad diamonds, but this is the worst," the outfielder continued to moan about his circumstances as he took a tour of the grounds the day before the opener. "I pray I don't get killed out there tomorrow." Expos general manager Jim Fanning resembled an event planner of a banquet hall preparing for a wedding reception, as he was seen scrambling around the park the day of the first game, organizing folding chairs that had been added for extra seating in open areas of the ballpark and correcting items that were actually fixable. As with Flood, things did not seem quite right on the field to home plate umpire Mel Steiner, either; thus, to be sure, he took out a tape measure and made certain that the distance from home plate to the pitcher's mound indeed showed a distance of sixty feet and six inches.

A few days later, Durocher—bringing his Cubs to Montreal for the first time—insisted that Fanning repaint the white seats that were behind home plate to a different, less distracting, hue. Despite Fanning's agreement, the Cubs took the field for their first game against Montreal to notice that the seats were still white, which served to disguise the baseball against the background, as Cubs third baseman Ron Santo claimed he could not see the ball off the bat. Reports of the field's condition were no better from the Chicago media men covering the series. "The infield was soft and lumpy," described George Langford of the *Chicago Tribune* after taking a stroll around the diamond. "The crust of the infield was puffed up and gave the sensation of walk-ing on balloons."

The quality of the National League playing surfaces, however, would become the least of Flood's concerns. Just over a week later, on April 27, he would be ac-cidentally spiked on the base path by Mets shortstop Bud Harrelson, an injury that would be slow in healing and impede his play for several weeks. As part of the treatment for the gash, Flood was given a tetanus shot; on the morning fol-lowing the administration of the shot, Flood overslept—the result, he claimed, of aftereffects of the injection. Consequently, he missed the team's annual ban-quet given in its honor by the St. Louis Advertising Club—an event that did not begin until noon. Devine, however, was of the opinion that Flood had been out on a drinking binge the prior evening to cause the absence, a habit for which Flood had gained a reputation. After Flood had even failed to phone the restau-rant as a courtesy, Devine then informed him upon his arrival at the ballpark that missing the banquet would cost him a $250 fine. Some attributed the out-fielder's recent behavior to his trying to sort through other personal troubles in the spring of 1969, for Flood's older brother Carl was involved in a holdup and shooting in a jewelry store in St. Louis. The story, naturally, was pasted all over the local and national news, complete with rolling film of the incident re-corded as Carl Flood was in a long standoff with police after the robbery. Carl, like George Powles, had been one of Curt's mentors while growing up on the tough streets of Oakland, and Curt felt a duty to stand by his side, especially at this moment. Busch, however, was upset that Curt had not informed him of Carl's arrest before the story got to the papers—which, in fairness to Flood, was a virtual impossibility with the live coverage of the situation.

By May 4 the Cards were 1-12 at home and were already seven games be-hind the Cubs. "When blame is assessed," Devine said bluntly of the sloppy start, "you should blame the front office—and start at the top." In pointing to himself as a culprit, Devine's reserves that he had newly integrated into the 1969 Cardinals were batting a combined .095 (six for sixty-three), with only one pinch hit in twenty-four at-bats—and the one was provided by a regu-lar starter in Pinson. Broeg was no more sympathetic. "Since August 2 [1968], which amounts to nearly half a season, they've been a second-division ballclub overall, and a last-place team at home." Up until that date in 1968, the Cards had played 71-36 ball in running away with the National League; after that date and into the 1969 regular season, they were a sickly 36-44, as barbs about their high salaries and lazy ways continued to persist. "Some of us," Broeg added of those in the St. Louis writers' bloc, "overemphasized the strength and perhaps the pride and dedication of the Cardinals.... [T]he Redbirds, frankly, just don't seem as sound as they did before." Furthermore, it was not just the local press that was noticing the downturn. "They [the Cardinals] are almost hopelessly behind the Chicago Cubs," the *San Francisco Chronicle* announced conclusively as early as May 20. "They are trying to go up on the down escalator."

Meanwhile, further trouble in the standings lurked from an unexpected source—the once-lowly Mets, who by the twenty-first had risen to the .500 mark at 18-18 for only the second time in the franchise's eight-year history. "This club is going to be a contender," predicted Seaver, their durable young ace off the mound. "There is no doubt in my mind."

To shake things up in the Cardinals, there was talk of summoning prodigy pitcher Reuss to St. Louis, who was continuing to dazzle at Tulsa. The pitching would nonetheless return to form, with Carlton truly emerging as a top-shelf starter for the first time in 1969 and chosen by Schoendienst as the starter for the National League All-Star Game in July. Later in September, he would strike out nineteen New York Mets, tying the Major League record, with the feat being the sixth and final time on the year in which Carlton had recorded double-digit strikeouts in a single game; Gibson himself would turn the trick eight times in 1969 (the record-tying game, ironically, was supposed to be Gibson's turn in the rotation, but Red had decided to give Gibson an extra day's rest). But with the departure of Cepeda and Maris, the Cardinals' lack of a home run power source at the plate was truly glaring. Flood, though not normally a home run hitter anyway, by May 20 had gone 145 games without a long ball, a stretch dating back to the previous June 7.

So now, more than ever, the team found it necessary to win with speed on the base paths, and to do so, they turned to the master in Brock, who would be successful in his first twenty-one stolen-base attempts in 1969. He had become the premier technician at the craft, always using exactly thirteen steps in going from first to second on a steal. And unbeknownst to teams around the league, he was also able to read the bone on the right forearms of catchers to see if the middle finger was being put down in the sign to the pitcher—evidence that a breaking ball was on its way to the plate, and thus, an easier pitch on which to swipe a base. After his tremendous start, Brock ran into a twenty-one-year-old catcher for the Cincinnati Reds named Johnny Bench on May 30, a man who while only starting his second full year in the big leagues was drawing comparisons to the best in history at the position. When Brock darted for second base in the fifth inning at Busch Stadium, Bench let loose a howitzer shot that nabbed the elite base stealer by a good ten feet. After the game, the young receiver called the throw "one of my greatest," an opinion shared by Cincinnati coach Vern Benson, who would join the Cardinals' staff the following year. "That's the farthest I've ever seen Brock thrown out," Benson uttered, shaking his head in disbelief. The St. Louis dugout was impressed as well. "Bench compares with the best I've ever seen," said assistant coach Dick Sisler, who had been in professional baseball since 1939. "How can anyone throw harder?"

The Cards could not seem to get their footing in an up-and-down 1969 summer. Gibson was still the workhorse of the pitching staff, and his team always looked to him in the biggest games. In an epic clash on July 4 in Busch Stadium, he battled Cubs ace Ferguson Jenkins into extra innings when a rare occurrence took place—one that proved Gibson was indeed human after his superhuman effort in 1968.

With the game knotted at one run apiece in the tenth, the first four Cubs hitters in Don Kessinger, Beckert, Billy Williams, and Santo reached base on hits against Gibson and scored the go-ahead run. Emerging slowly from the dugout, Schoendienst trekked toward to the mound and took the ball from the big right-hander in favor of left-handed reliever Joe Hoerner, as the Cubs had taken a 3–1 lead, which would later stand as the final score. It marked the first time Gibson had been removed from a game without finishing the inning for the first time in two years, spanning sixty straight starts (later, on August 16 at Atlanta, Gibson would become the third pitcher, along with Walter Johnson and Rube Waddell, to strike out two hundred batters in seven different years; by 1970 he would be alone with eight). Two weeks later, he would join Carlton at the All-Star Game in Robert F. Kennedy Stadium in Washington, Gibson's seventh selection.

At a dinner the night before the All-Star Game, Gibson was able to meet Jackie Robinson for the first time. Spending a long time together, they reviewed the civil rights actions and baseball highlights of the past tumultuous decade. As Gibson and Robinson were swapping stories, the Cardinals were in the midst of a torrid run—a record of 30-9 over July and August—which had put them back in contention to defend their pennant after a slow start. The Cubs had maintained between a six- and eight-game lead for the majority of the summer, but by late August had begun to crack. The Redbirds' rally had galvanized support in the city, as Harry Caray led the cheers in singing his attack song, "The Cardinals are coming, tra-la, tra-la." However, most were convinced that Chicago had too much talent to lose the chase—especially *Chicago Tribune* writer Robert Markus. "The only team with enough talent to take the Eastern Division away from the Cubs is St. Louis," Markus wrote in his column on July 11. "But St. Louis is too far behind to do it."

Yet even as the Cubs were beginning their noted collapse in which they would go 8-17 in September, the two-time incumbent champion Cardinals still could not catch the Mets, surging forward even harder than Schoendienst's men. Gil Hodges's crew shocked the baseball world in posting a 23-7 record in the season's final five weeks after winning twenty-one games in August as well. In fact, from the time the rains had been falling on the Woodstock music festival up the road in northern New York in mid-August, the Mets would finish the season by winning nearly four out of every five games, with a 38-11 mark in their last forty-nine games. The New York outfit had been so charmed that victory even emerged in Carlton's nineteen-strikeout performance against them in Busch Stadium on the Monday night of September 15, as Ron Swoboda managed two home runs off the left-hander to prove the difference in another 4–3 Mets win.

The Cubs had just been in St. Louis before the Mets' arrival and were still seeking to reclaim the top spot from the New York club while standing at only three games from the lead as their series with the Cards concluded on Sunday afternoon the fourteenth. The Cardinals and their fans, having long faded out of the race at nine games back, had approached the three-game series with their rivals from the north as their own "playoff" for 1969. The final duel on Sunday in front of forty-four thousand onlookers featured Gibson against Cubs southpaw Ken Holtzman, a native of the University City area of St. Louis in a battle that one local writer said "had a World Series atmosphere." With the stands shaking from thunderous ovations all day long, the two great hurlers took the contest into the tenth inning in a 1–1 tie—just as Gibson and Jenkins had done on the Fourth of July—with each starter refusing to be removed. In the bottom half, Gibson led off the inning in being permitted to bat for himself (suggesting that he was going to take the mound for a possible eleventh inning as well) and grounded out. Brock next stepped to the plate in the leadoff spot and promptly won the game with a homer to right, his first since July 16 and what would be his last of the season with more than two weeks left to go. In an instant, the isolated blow had furthered the Cubs' demise in both winning percentage and morale, as Holtzman had now received a total of four runs of support from his mates in his four starts against the Cardinals on the year. "A disconsolate group of Cubs looked downhearted as they slowly walked off the field to their gloomy clubhouse," noticed veteran reporter Harry Mitauer of the *St. Louis Globe-Democrat.* It was one piece of satisfaction the St. Louis club could take with it throughout a tumultuous season, one that closed a successful decade for the franchise.

Promise was also there for the future, as the youngster Simmons secured one of the Cards' last wins on October 1 with a ninth-inning triple. In the stands watching the game at Busch Stadium was a Baltimore Orioles scout. "We'd like to take Simmons off the Cardinals' hands any time," the scout said, as the young man from Michigan was fast becoming the hottest backstop to enter pro ball since Bench a few years earlier.

Even so, there was much disappointment with what had occurred with the Cardinals, dating back to their early-season complacency that caused the slow start. "The 1969 team was clearly a better team than the Mets, who went on to win the division," assessed Halberstam, "but it was an embittered team that played well below its potential." Gibson, in fact, pointed out that the Cards' staff had better statistics than the famed Mets pitchers of 1969 in terms of ERA, thanks mostly to him (2.18) and Carlton (2.17). Reuss would do his small part as well, as the heralded prospect made a shining Major League debut against the Expos in Montreal on September 27, permitting only three hits and two walks over seven innings in securing the win (this in spite of Reuss and the Cardinals overcoming two rain delays that had each lasted nearly an hour). The 1969 season also marked the first time that the Cardinals' pitching staff notched 1,000 strikeouts in one year (1,004).

But contributing greatly to their fall from the top of the standings was that the Cardinals had not taken part in the relative rejuvenation of offense around baseball in 1969. During the season the other nine teams in the National League averaged 139 more runs scored than each had plated in 1968; the Cards scored only 12 more and had crossed home only slightly more than even the feeble expansion clubs in Montreal and San Diego.

In the end, the stunning Mets had taken it all by defeating Atlanta in the inaugural National League Championship Series and the Orioles in the World Series. To get to the final round, New York had to get past Cepeda's Atlanta Braves in the NLCS, a team that had sprinted in a mad dash to the finish line as well, winning ten of its last eleven games on the schedule to overtake the Giants for the Western Division crown. "I've never seen a ball club, any ball club, play like this one did the last month," shouted Cepeda proudly in the locker room after clinching the playoff berth—reminiscent of his "money trunk" dances in the Cardinals' clubhouse the previous two years. "Not San Francisco, not St. Louis, not anywhere." In the midst of a raucous celebration in Atlanta's Fulton County Stadium, fans set off firecrackers on the field after the game and even tried to push their way into the Braves' dressing room to join in the celebration.

Gibson had noted that, in effort occasionally to get something going offensively for the team in 1969, he had started trying to steal more bases, swiping a lifetime high of five on the year at the age of thirty-three. He would jam his knee on one of his slides, however, which altered his pitching motion and placed more short-term stress on his arm. Like Sandy Koufax, he also was battling an arthritic elbow through which he would fight for four more starts after his matchup with Holtzman, including his twentieth victory of the year on the season's final day against the Phillies on October 2, leaving the Redbirds with a record of 87-75—lodging them in fourth place behind the Mets, Cubs, and Pirates, the latter of whom had jumped ahead of the Cards by a game in the waning days of the schedule. After their dismal start at home at the beginning of the season, the Cards had at least rebounded to finish above .500 in Busch Stadium (42-38), powered by their 17-5 mark in St. Louis in July. Critics pointed out, however, that they were 6-12 against the Mets overall on the summer.

And unlike Halberstam, Caray's partner in the broadcast booth, Jack Buck—who saw the team every day—did not think the Cardinals were necessarily a better ball club on paper. The influence of society's youth counterculture, Buck felt, had weakened the team. "After the 1968 pennant year, the Cardinals were not a good ballclub. The world was changing because of drugs, civil rights actions and the anti-war movement, and baseball players were caught up in all those activities just like everybody else from their age group." Buck thought that the team had become spoiled, and as an example, he noticed when all the players rudely sent back a meal on a team flight they thought was not good enough for them. "They should have been with us in the Depression, or later in the Army," Buck said of his own experiences. "In the Army, we went a couple of days without *anything* to eat, including rations. The ballplayers' behavior shocked me. The stewardesses cried as they picked up the trays. I wouldn't do that to anybody."

Among those in that age group who had disappointed was Washburn, who had been just as promising a pitcher as Carlton in coming through the Cardinals' system. Washburn had fallen to a stark 3-8 record in 1969 and was soon traded to Cincinnati, just a year removed from a season in which he followed Gibson as the most dominant pitcher on the staff, having even thrown a late-season no-hitter against the Giants. It was yet another deal that Devine orchestrated with his former St. Louis counterpart in Howsam, as the two had consummated the noteworthy Pinson trade before the season. Back in the winter, Devine knew fully that the man with which he was parting for Pinson, Bob Tolan, could easily become Pinson's equal as a player—and in his first full chance to do so with the Reds in 1969, he took a major step in that direction. Tolan in 1969, in fact, would even break up Brock's run of four-straight stolen-base titles. He also posted 24 bunt hits among his total of 194 for the season, the high for his career that would finally end in 1979. "When I told Bobby he was going to be a regular," Cincinnati manager Dave Bristol said, "one of the first things he did was practice his bunting in the batting cage." (In only a few weeks Howsam would fire Bristol and replace him shortly with young first-time big league manager George "Sparky" Anderson. Anderson, a former employee of the Cardinals' Minor League system, had received a call from Howsam about the Cincinnati job just as Anderson was in the offices of the California Angels, in the very process of putting his pen to ink on a contract to be an assistant coach with the Angels.)

Thus, some gambles paid off for the Redbirds in 1969, while some did not. They had seen their emotional leader in Cepeda leave the team in spring training. Now, as a new decade approached, they discovered that not only was their entire team evolving all the more, but so was the very game itself. And at the center of it all come 1970 was Curt Flood—a man who went from a virtual recluse to a polarizing figure overnight.

3 "A Well-Paid Slave Is Still a Slave"

I'm not mad; I'm disappointed. Instead of a sport, this is now a real headache.

The fans, I'm afraid, will react to this later. . . . [W]e have to take a stand for the good of baseball.

I hate to be the sucker to do it, but I'm willing to do it.

—August A. Busch Jr., March 11, 1970

The moves made in 1969 had not been good enough to keep the Cardinals on top, as Devine was ordered by Busch to continue the overhaul, and in no uncertain terms, the message was sent that no one's job was safe. Bing subsequently directed his assistant Toomey—whom Bob Broeg once called a "reformed sportswriter"—to make one important phone call on October 7, 1969.

The phone ringing on the other end of the line was at the home of Curt Flood in St. Louis. After Flood picked up, the conversation with Toomey would last less than a minute, but it was one that sent shock waves around the baseball world. Toomey had quickly and frankly informed Flood that he was "being transferred" to the Philadelphia Phillies. In an instant, the shape of the Cardinals from the stalwart teams of the 1960s had started changing.

Flood thought he would have time to contemplate the prospect of switching teams and cities, and the more he pondered the idea, the more he did not like it. After getting the news from Toomey, Flood later in the day reportedly picked the phone back up and called Devine directly, telling the general manager that he did not wish to pack up his career and his other local pursuits after twelve years in St. Louis and move someplace else. "He told me that was my business, and goodbye," Flood would state curtly in a courtroom in May when questioned about that particular conversation. Shortly thereafter, Flood then received a form letter in the mail, standard for such a transaction and dated the following day, October 8—identifying him only as "Player No. 614"—which informed him of his "release of transfer from one National League club to another." Flood knew that the ball club was well aware of his mounting personal troubles; nonetheless, he had felt that St. Louis was his adopted hometown, and he wished to remain there. He had no desire to move farther east to Philadelphia, farther away from his original roots in Oakland. Thus, as Flood stewed on his prospects, he decided that if it was inevitable for him to be forced to leave St. Louis, he should at least have a say in his destination. Getting wind of Flood's reluctance, Phillies general manager Joe Quinn clandestinely increased his contract offer to the outfielder up to one hundred thousand dollars for his services. It was a simple courtesy, as it was not required to finalize the deal, but Flood was still not in the mood to move (and the new figure, ironically, was what Flood had been seeking from the Cardinals all along).

So instead, not yet having reached thirty-two years of age, Flood chose to quit the game. In a prepared statement, he said through a spokesman that he had decided to retire from organized baseball, effective on October 8, and would remain in St. Louis where he could devote full time to his business interests. Some were comparing it to the situation of Jackie Robinson, who in December 1956 refused to report from the Brooklyn Dodgers to the team to which he was traded—the cross-town rival New York Giants—and instead decided to retire.

Outfielder Byron Browne, Joe Hoerner, and McCarver—the latter two being other key components of the St. Louis machine from the 1960s—were also part of the trade in being dealt to the Phillies. McCarver was, like everyone else at the time, unaware of Flood's intentions. He, unlike Flood, had been nothing but a Cardinal in his professional career to date. Therefore, the catcher was also sorry to depart the Gateway City, but ready and willing to take on his new responsibilities. "I really hate to leave St. Louis because I enjoyed playing there," he began with nearly the same initial sentence with which Flood answered. "The fans were as good as any fans you'll find anywhere in the big leagues. . . . [M]aybe Curt Flood and Joe Hoerner and I can make the Phillies a live team again. They've been going bad for quite a time." Hoerner, perhaps the finest reliever from the Cardinal pennant-winning teams, had been long sought by Philadelphia.

After a few days, Flood changed his mind once again and decided he did not wish to retire after all. But he knew that returning to the Cardinals was an impossibility; thus, despite more than sixty years of historical baseball precedent to the contrary, Flood was convinced he could not be traded without his consent. Two weeks after he met with the Players' Association's executive board in a consultative move—the specifics of which were not released—Flood sent the following letter to Bowie Kuhn on Christmas Eve, 1969, in which he not only already considers himself a "free agent" but instructs Kuhn to let the other teams know that he is available for open bidding:

December 24, 1969

Mr. Bowie K. Kuhn
Commissioner of Baseball
680 Fifth Avenue
New York, New York 10019

After twelve years in the Major Leagues, I do not feel I am a piece of property to be bought and sold irrespective of my wishes. I believe that any system which produces that result violates my basic rights as a citizen and is inconsistent with the laws of the United States and of the sovereign states.
It is my desire to play baseball in 1970, and I am capable of playing. I have received a contract offer from the Philadelphia Club, but I believe I have the right to consider offers from other clubs before making any decisions. I, therefore, request that you make known to all Major League Clubs my feelings in this matter, and advise them of my availability for the 1970 season.

Sincerely Yours,
Curt Flood

Thus, in baseball's very last act of the 1960s and two days before the dawn of a new decade, Kuhn responded to Flood with his own letter on December 30. He began his statement by assuring Flood he was sympathetic with his position. Nonetheless, as an attorney himself, Kuhn added he did not envision the player having a legal standing to make the challenge.

Undaunted, Flood yet set off on his personal crusade, willing to spend the entire 1970 season away from baseball—the first such move by a player, at least in Bob Broeg's memory, since Edd Roush of the New York Giants had boycotted the entire schedule in 1930.

Two weeks after receiving Kuhn's response, Flood filed a federal lawsuit on January 16, 1970, which claimed the reserve clause—the long-standing professional baseball policy that held a player's roster status bound to the discretion of his original club—violated federal antitrust legislation, and he sought four million dollars in damages, which he presumed to be his lost wages. His teammates did not know what to tell him.

"You'll never get another job in baseball," McCarver told Flood over the phone upon hearing of his intentions.

"I know that," Flood answered.

The initial hearing of his suit was quickly denied in early March by federal judge Irving Cooper. "It would have allowed him to negotiate with the clubs," according to Marvin Miller, as the MLBPA membership was generally behind Flood in his fight. "He would in effect have been a 'free agent.' He would have been like a human being in America, who has a skill and wants to be paid for it." The ruling left Flood deflated, saying that the decision "means I've lost my one chance to play ball this year"—even though, ironically, the Phillies were still waiting for him with open arms. Both Flood and Judge Cooper, however, each figured it was only the "first inning" in what would be a long, drawn-out contest in a thorough review of the viability of the reserve clause. With nothing to do in the short term, Flood decided to go abroad, landing in Copenhagen with a desire to paint and write "long philosophical letters" to Gibson, according to the pitcher. Before leaving, he was asked by Howard Cosell in a television interview how he could be unhappy with his current ninety-thousand-dollar salary—not exactly slave wages, Cosell pointed out.

"A well-paid slave is still a slave," Flood responded.

It had indeed been a tumultuous first year for the new commissioner, Kuhn, who in time would find himself engulfed in a gathering storm between employers and employees in his business. In addition to straining to get Miller and the owners together on a new collective bargaining agreement, Kuhn had also gone on his own personal crusade to "clean up" baseball in 1969—albeit on quite a different topic from what Flood had in mind. Recent problems had surfaced in the National Football League related to gambling connections with active players, and Kuhn was determined to see that such improprieties were not afoot in Major League Baseball. To this end, he felt it necessary to prod two prominent club officials—Atlanta Braves president William Bartholomay and Oakland Athletics owner Charles Finley—to relinquish their holdings in wagering enterprises, even though such holdings were in order with the law. When Kuhn learned that government investigations revealed that both men held stock in certain Las Vegas casinos, he felt compelled to act.

But perhaps the most startling episode within this issue—and one that Kuhn planned to handle boldly—was the situation of Tigers pitcher McLain. After becoming the last thirty-game winner in helping lead the Tigers into their 1968 World Series victory over the Cardinals, McLain won another twenty-four in 1969 before being suspended indefinitely by the commissioner's office for association with organized gamblers headquartered in Flint, Michigan. The alleged activities were said to have taken place back in 1967, when McLain was believed to have contributed nearly six thousand dollars to a local bookmaking operation. In early 1970 records would show that McLain owed the Internal Revenue

Service nearly ten thousand dollars, which resulted in the government seizing his furniture that sat in a house outside of Detroit that he owned and was currently renting to a friend (McLain, meanwhile, was living in the Tigers' winter home of Lakeland, Florida, while serving his suspension). As a result, he would be forced to sit out for the first three months of the 1970 season. The pitcher would run into further problems before the year's end, as Mayo Smith was being replaced as Detroit's manager by Billy Martin—just two seasons removed from Smith's championship season. "I think McLain has been punished in a substantial way," Kuhn announced in handing down the ruling, "and I think the good name of baseball has been vindicated." The story, naturally, had been the recent focus of barstool discussions at the old Lindell Athletic Club, a tavern near the Detroit ballpark in which Tiger players would often be seen after games and which was considered one of the first true "sports bars" in the country. "He should be barred for life," said an unsympathetic Ed Flanagan, a construction worker who pushed his helmet aside on the countertop to grab his beer in disgust, spilling part of it. "He's not setting a very good example for the young kids coming up behind him." The "AC," as the Lindell had been called, was located at the corner of Cass and Michigan avenues and would be a fixture for Detroit fans for nearly forty years from its opening in 1963. Strangely enough, it was also the focus of an earlier gambling investigation by NFL commissioner Pete Rozelle in that very year, a situation in which Rozelle forced Detroit Lions player Alex Karras to sell his shares in the bar.

McLain would ultimately return on July 1, 1970, to face the Yankees in Tiger Stadium, greeted by the largest Detroit home crowd—53,863—in nine years, including all the 1968 World Series games in the city against the Cardinals. He took the mound and began firing pitches into the catcher's mitt of his old battery mate, Freehan, as if nothing had ever happened—even though Freehan had publicly disparaged McLain in a recent interview. In surrendering three home runs in a five-inning stint, McLain ducked inside the clubhouse after his performance and oddly waited for the game to end with a bucket full of ice water by his side, which he intended to throw on the sportswriters whom he anticipated would be pestering him shortly (instead, he accidentally hit Tigers trainer Bill Behm when the moment came). He would continue to pitch ineffectively, appearing in just fourteen games for Detroit in 1970 as his personal and professional life would take further downturns. By September he was suspended by Kuhn once again—this time for the brief remainder of the season—as allegations surfaced of McLain's carrying an unregistered handgun on his person.

By no stretch, however, was this the only headache with which the commissioner was having to deal heading into 1970. Soon, he was compelled to call pitcher Jim Bouton of the Houston Astros into his office. Bouton stood before the angry commissioner for two hours, attempting to explain the meaning of certain passages of Bouton's new book, *Ball Four*, excerpts of which had been advanced to *Look* magazine (one of the magazine's writers, Leonard Shecter, had coauthored the book with Bouton). Within the manuscript Bouton became one of the first ever to divulge the sacred, concealed "dark side" of the Major League locker room and nightlife to the general public. Bouton, in fact, went so far as to disclose personal information about his former teammates—most notably, those with whom Bouton cohabitated in his years with the starch-imaged Yankees. In doing so, Bouton had clearly ventured into uncharted journalistic and athletic territory. His manuscript met with the rage of players on every roster in the Major Leagues ("Did he forget most of us have wives?" one responded on condition of anonymity, who apparently had something to hide). And while Bouton presumably received a thorough tongue-lashing from the commissioner, Kuhn decided that the matter should end there. "I advised Mr. Bouton of my displeasure with these writings," he revealed, "and warned him against future writings of this character. Under all the circumstances, I have concluded that no other action was necessary." In return, Bouton stated that "I have no plans to write any more books," but also added that "I am absolutely not sorry for writing *Ball Four*."

Also on Kuhn's plate was the possibility of a one-day players strike, a subject broached a year earlier by Gibson on *The Tonight Show*. Naturally, the proposed stoppage had come on the advice of Miller and resulting from the union's wishing to see an increase in the minimum salary and a return of the regular-season schedule to 154 games, the figure that had stood until the addition of eight games each year since 1961. Fortunately for most, the 1970 season would begin on time and would be uninterrupted in the early going; however, by the middle of May, the union would turn down the owners' offer for the next renewal of the collective bargaining agreement. The proposal had been to increase the minimum salary from $10,000 to $12,000 (and up to $13,500 by 1971), which was struck down on a vote of 505–89, with Quinn's Phillies being the only team with a majority in favor of the deal. After this vote would occur, Miller then hinted that a one-day walkout was now a distinct possibility, with such an act probably taking place on a Saturday on a nationally televised network broadcast of a significant game. By season's end, even the umpires from both circuits were threatening to boycott the league championship games and World Series if their own postseason pay was not augmented.

While McCarver, Browne, and Hoerner were of course the first teammates to learn of Flood's intentions, the other Cardinals were naturally stunned by the news of the situation. Still, they also reveled in the fact that a bona fide power hitter was coming to the team as a result of the transaction. With Flood refusing to join the Phillies, it was likely that the Cardinals would need to surrender another player off their roster as compensation in the future. But as for now, the trade would send second baseman Cookie Rojas, pitcher Jerry Johnson, and slugging infielder Dick Allen to the Redbirds, the latter of whom was the prime target in the deal for Devine. "We felt we needed a power hitter for the ballpark," the general manager said in retrospect years later. "Busch Stadium is a big ballpark. We had never come up with a power hitter, and for a lot of reasons Dick Allen was available, and we decided to take our chance."

The downside to the acquisition for the Cardinals, however, was Allen's well-known erratic behavior, mostly a proclivity to go missing for days at a time. The stories of Allen's past had grown into an urban legend of its own, including a rumor that he urged the Phillies management to have his widowed mother placed on the team payroll. When this leaked to the press, public sentiment in Philadelphia turned on Allen almost instantly. The first wave of sustained rage from the Philadelphia fans toward Allen seemed to arrive in 1965, when a fight in the batting cage with teammate Frank Thomas resulted in further scorn from editorials in the sports pages in town. Two years later, he was cited by the IRS as owing nearly nine thousand dollars in back taxes. And twice in 1968—in spring training and then again in August—Allen went AWOL, leaving the Phillies with no information on his whereabouts. Finally, Allen most recently had been suspended for twenty-eight games and fined five hundred dollars for his off-field conduct in the middle of the 1969 season, and by August would say that "I have no intention of returning here," in reference to the City of Brotherly Love. When he arrived to the Cardinals in the spring of 1970, he added to that thought: "If it had meant my life, I wouldn't have gone back to Philadelphia another season. I expect to be booed, but not stoned. . . . Philly isn't a bad town, but when you've taken the abuse I took, it's time to move on." Back when the trade was announced, Allen could not contain his eagerness to join the Cardinals; anxious to get going, he wanted to settle in and "get a place somewhere, even if it's in the YMCA, and concentrate on baseball. . . . I'd rather work on a farm and earn $100 a week than play for the Phillies."

Thus, before making the trade, Devine—who back in 1963 and 1964 had been chosen by his peers as baseball's best general manager, even though he was soon to be dismissed by Busch for the first time—had consulted long hours with Schoendienst, as Devine knew that Red would ultimately be the one having to contend with Allen on a daily basis. "If you want to make the deal, go ahead," the field manager advised Devine. "But understand I'm not going to try to make over Dick Allen." In Allen's long, checkered history in Philadelphia, the Cardinals had naturally come across his personality from time to time. As recently as May 1969, he had interestingly challenged one of his counterparts in the trade, Hoerner, to come out of the dugout and fight in the middle of the game, a prospect at which Hoerner simply laughed. This was on Sunday, May 4—the same weekend in which Allen had been fined another thousand dollars by the Phillies for being late to the Saturday game the night before and missing altogether the first game of the series on Friday night. "I don't know Allen," Schoendienst continued in his assessment in trying to rationalize the trade. "I've never spoken to him. I know his reputation, of course, but I don't know any of the background of what went on in Philadelphia. . . . [H]e will start here with a clean slate." As a gesture of good faith to show that he had curbed his gambling habits, Allen, before coming to St. Louis, sold four of his beloved five thoroughbred horses he owned. "I bet a few dollars here and there," he confessed, "but it's working with them, exercising them—just being outdoors—that I love." Like with Flood, however, alcohol was another matter; while he attempted to hide the problem, Allen was not shy to admit he would sometimes partake in that activity as well. "I'm no angel," Allen openly characterized himself on the topic of drink. One of his favorite hangouts in St. Louis would soon become a local joint on Franklin Avenue. "I've taken a nip here or there, but not to excess. Truthfully, I've taken a couple of belts at times before I went on the field, just to calm down. . . . I hope the fans judge me as a ballplayer who wants to play a hard, winning game."

While the St. Louis management and media were putting a positive spin on things, emotions were naturally mixed around the clubhouse about the trade and the comings-and-goings of all those involved. "I was enthusiastic about the idea of acquiring Allen," Gibson admitted, "[and] was happy to have Rojas on our side . . . and was sickened by the thought of Flood and McCarver leaving us. Those two guys struck right at the heart of what the Cardinals had been all about for the past decade. . . . [W]ith them being gone, being a Cardinal would never mean quite the same thing." Before they had become teammates as a result of the trade, the fact that Allen was a black man had not excluded him from the wrath of Gibson from the mound. "We played in a time when black people were supposed to stick together," Allen would reflect. "So I asked Gibson one time why he always threw at the brothers. He said, 'Because they're the ones who are gonna beat me if I don't.'" As time went along over the course of the 1970 season, Gibson would support his new teammate by trying to deflect some the overly curious newspaper writers away from Allen in the clubhouse.

The Flood-Allen trade has long been discussed in baseball circles as a watershed moment in the establishment of free agency and the recrafting of bargaining tactics of the Players' Association; however, it can also be viewed as an important landmark in the evolution of Gussie Busch as an owner. The great irony of the Allen acquisition was that Busch was discarding a player whom he had thought was a "company man" in Flood (but having fallen from grace in the past year) and essentially replacing him with a player who might have been regarded as the least such "company man" as existed in the big leagues at the time—this while Busch was simultaneously lamenting the poor attitude of the typical modern player. The Allen deal, it could therefore be argued, signified at least some willingness on the part of Busch to tolerate the new behaviors of the young generation. Thus, while Busch was fully aware that Allen's sometimes confrontational attitude had finally worn out its welcome with management and fans in Philadelphia, he nonetheless gave Devine clear permission to pursue the slugger.

With spring training getting into full swing in March 1970, the latest issue of *Sport* magazine quoted Flood as apparently satisfied with the money he made in St. Louis, calling his twelve years in a Cardinals uniform "good and happy years for me. . . . [M]y salary climbed close to the $100,000 mark, the highest any ballplayer who wasn't a pitcher or a home-run hitter ever had received in baseball." In the article, however, Flood went on to criticize the beneficent hand of Busch and his clubhouse rant of a year earlier, saying that the speech "destroyed the intangible this team had—its unity and feeling of pride in being part of the Cardinal organization. We never got over that."

As a result, even just twelve months removed from Busch's speech in the locker room, preseason exercises for the Cardinals in 1970 had the strangest atmosphere ever recalled by those in the organization. As evidence on paper of the great change taking place, the only positional starters beginning 1970 from the pennant-winning clubs of just two and three years prior were Shannon, Brock, Maxvill, and Javier. And although Busch may have originally figured he got a "steal" from the Phillies in light of Flood's decision to retire, they were initially unable to come to contract terms with Allen—who was still absent from their spring training camp by mid-March, as was Carlton once again, who was coming off his best season to date and sought to more than double his $24,000 salary. It was a matter with which the owner did not wish to involve himself, as once again Busch left the issue of salary discussions with players to Devine and Toomey. But by March 10, perhaps fearing a lessened return on his investment, he had tolerated enough of the two holdouts. "We will not negotiate further," Busch came out and said. "We've made up our minds that the offer we made to Allen is the one we're going to stick with. He's going to report or he's not going to play with the Cardinals." Allen had originally put forward the salary figure of $140,000 for discussion, which he later reduced to $125,000—the latter of which would have equaled Gibson's (and, in having been given to Gibson, was the most ever paid to a Cardinal pitcher to that time). In reality, Busch did not wish to pay him more than Lou Brock's annual salary, which at the time stood at $85,000, and was hoping for something closer to the $75,000 that Allen was carrying over from the Phillies. Carlton, meanwhile, had originally asked for $50,000 but was now willing to consider $40,000—which was still $10,000 more than Busch was willing to pay him. When Carlton still refused to sign his contract the following day, an ever-angering Busch responded by saying that "I don't care if he ever pitches a ball for us again." But ultimately, Cardinals executive vice president Dick Meyer would get Carlton to sign on March 16 for $80,000 for two years, with a slightly larger portion being paid in the second season—the first multiyear contract for a Redbird since Ken Boyer had received such a deal nearly a decade prior. The two-year agreement—something never afforded to Gibson, Brock, Flood, Shannon, McCarver, or any of the other Cardinal stars during the '60s—was believed to be a satisfactory compromise for both sides. However, the multiyear deal was not even seen as a good thing by *Carlton,* who upon further deliberation actually disliked the knowledge of having his 1971 salary dictated in advance. Once Carlton was under contract, Busch added that Allen's demands were all the more ridiculous in light of the fact that he had yet to even don a Cardinals jersey.

Even more incredulous to the owner was that some of those Cardinals already in uniform also wanted large increases in salary. This may have been understandable a year ago, some figured, in wake of the team's success in 1968—but how could they honorably make the same requests after the team's fall in 1969? The owner would have no more of it.

It was at this point that Gussie Busch uttered a statement that proved two things: To him, the game had changed irrevocably. And so would his approach in dealing with players. "I'm not mad; I'm disappointed. Instead of a sport, this is now a real headache. The fans, I'm afraid, will react to this later. I can't understand Allen. I can't understand Curt Flood. We have to take a stand for the good of baseball. I hate to be the sucker to do it, but I'm willing to do it."

Change was indeed coming to baseball, in the negotiating room, in the locker room, and on the playing field—literally. On the same day that the owner was voicing his latest frustration, back on the banks of the Mississippi River the first spools of Astroturf were being rolled out on the floor of Busch Stadium. But even this effort was not without its own labor difficulties, just as with the players who would tread on it, for the groundskeepers had initiated their own strike in the previous weeks.

Still, good news (and Allen himself) arrived at the Redbirds twenty-four hours later on March 12. Coming to an agreement on his pay, Allen showed up at Al Lang Field in St. Petersburg to an empty facility, as the Cardinal regulars were already up in Lakeland for an exhibition game with the Tigers. Present in St. Pete, however, was Devine, waiting eagerly with pen in hand to finalize the player's commitment. When the team returned and practice resumed at the Cards' training facility on the thirteenth, Allen—who had turned twenty-eight just a few days earlier—was unconcerned with being late, letting everyone know that he had not "been on time for spring training in six years" anyway, asserting that "I think three weeks is enough to get ready. I like to spend my birthday (March 8) at home with my family and then think about playing ball." As expected, Allen starting raising eyebrows equally with his offensive skills as with his commentary; specifically, he was exhibiting the most raw hitting power and strength that anyone had seen in a St. Louis uniform—ever. Wearing long, thick sideburns in the style of the day, they seemed to whip around as rapidly as his swing with each pitch in the cage. He was also wielding what virtually amounted to a tree trunk for a bat—the likes of which very few players had used in the Major Leagues since the 1930s, and heavier than anyone on the Cardinals ever remembered having donned, including the monstrous stick formerly waved by Orlando Cepeda. "He swung that big ol' forty-two-ounce bat like nobody I'd ever played with," Gibson in fact recalled. Just days after the trade was announced back in October 1969, Broeg was already predicting that Allen would likely break the Cardinals' then team record of home runs in a season of forty-three, set by Johnny Mize in 1940. Broeg's reasoning was that the last two home run sluggers with personal baggage and turmoils to arrive in St. Louis—Cepeda and Maris—found the comforts of the Gateway City much to their liking. Added Phillies scout Johnny Ogden, who had been in big league ball for more than forty years, "Allen has got as much power as anybody who ever played this game, and he hits with more power to the opposite field than any hitter I ever saw."

Allen, however, was not personally supplying all the power to the long drives he was showcasing in the batting cage. For 1970 an experimental ball called the "X-5" was being used once a week in practices and games in spring training, supplied by Spalding Sporting Goods. The ball was designed to be 5 percent livelier than the one used in previous seasons, in an effort to generate more base hits (similar to an effort launched in early 1934 and other seasons to increase fan interest). Therefore, it only added to the jaw-dropping cannon blasts that Allen was launching over the wall. Soon, pitchers began to complain of an increased fear of injury from the exit speed after the ball's contact with the bat. And when four Chicago White Sox hurlers were hit with line drives on March 18, American League president Joe Cronin had seen enough. "The commissioner has had his little experiment, and now he should call it off." Kuhn did indeed order an end to what was termed the "Rabbit Ball Trial" near the close of March, as research had shown from the exhibition games in which the ball was used that teams were scoring nearly twice the number of runs they had plated in the same exhibition weeks of March 1969. Kuhn stated that any further plans for using the ball would be discontinued.

While new faces such as Allen's were becoming customary to appear around the Cards' spring training camp in 1970, at least one old familiar face had returned as well. After a five-year absence, former star third baseman Boyer was finally back in a Cardinal uniform—as manager of the organization's Class AA Minor League team in Little Rock. Boyer's pitching coach at Little Rock for the season would be Arkansas native Dick Hughes, a sixteen-game winner for the world champion Cardinals in 1967 who did not make the Major Leagues until the age of twenty-nine, after nine years in the minors. Hughes, however, could not overcome arm injuries, and his playing career was over by 1968.

By the same token, it also took some time for the absences of St. Louis mainstays Flood, McCarver, and Hoerner to sink in and become normal. "Flood just may have played his last big league ball game," Broeg had advised his readers back on March 6. The veteran writer, however, was shedding few tears in light of the player's actions. "Over the years, the Cardinals have helped him, above and beyond the call of contractual obligations, with financial and personal problems of which he must still be aware, yet did not choose to mention or acknowledge. . . . [T]his is what happens when sports ceases to be the Fun-and-Games Department." To further complicate matters, Kuhn had suggested on March 12 that he might need to soon step in and order someone off the St. Louis roster to be sent to Philadelphia if the Cardinals had not decided on a compensation player to give the Phillies by the opening day of the regular season.

The dealing of Flood also naturally left a gaping hole to be filled in the Cardinals' center-field slot. And while the acquisition of Allen had provided for one necessity of power in the batting order, Flood's departure left another vacancy on the offensive side as well. Pinson was also gone, having turned out to be a disappointment in 1969, with his average dipping to a career-low .255. Pinson, like fellow Oakland native Flood, had also been traded in the off-season—in November 1969, a month after the Flood deal—which brought sixth-year outfielder Jose Cardenal to St. Louis from the Cleveland Indians in his place. When Pinson would finally end his career with the Kansas City Royals in 1975, he would finish with 2,757 hits—at the time, the most ever for a player not elected to the Hall of Fame.

Cardenal, a speedy player who also carried a little bit of pop in his bat despite weighing only 160 pounds, had in Cleveland equaled or surpassed the production of Pinson in St. Louis and along with rookie Leron Lee was given the first shot at the center-field job in Busch Stadium. "He's a real good center fielder," affirmed Cards reserve outfielder Vic Davalillo, who had earlier played with Cardenal in Cleveland. "He can go back on a ball and come in. He's got a good arm and he's fast and smart, a base-stealer like Lou Brock. I think he'll do the job because he's a fastball hitter and the National League is a fastball league." As Lee was primarily a corner outfielder (as was fellow newcomer in the outfield in Carl Taylor, arriving from the Pirates as part of a trade that sent the rising pitcher Giusti to Pittsburgh), another option Schoendienst was considering was to move Brock over to center. This theory would potentially inject more power—and protection for Allen—into the lineup if third-year player Joe Hague could prove he was ready to take over in left.

A two-sport athlete at the University of Texas, Hague quit the football team when Coach Darrell Royal tried to keep him from playing baseball in the spring. "I wasn't enjoying it anymore," Hague said of the gridiron in Austin. Leaving football behind also meant that Hague was losing his college scholarship, but he quickly regained the funds after he proved his worth for UT baseball coach Bibb Falk, being named to the All-Southwest Conference team three years in a row in 1963, 1964, and 1965. Briefly playing alongside All-American linebacker Tommy Nobis at Texas, Hague had been a top football defender at that position in coming out of high school ball in El Paso. He had spent much of his childhood on the road, traversing the country in growing up in a military family, with his being a master sergeant in the U.S. Air Force. After signing with St. Louis scout Fred McAllister for ten thousand dollars in 1965, Hague lost twenty pounds from his football playing weight (leaving him at two hundred) and would proceed to pound out sixty-six home runs the next three years in the Cardinals' Minor League system. Used primarily as a pinch hitter in limited duty for St. Louis in 1968 and 1969, Hague was now seeking a regular spot for the first time in the 1970 campaign. He had to fend off the challenge of Lee, the Cardinals' first-round pick in the 1966 draft, who was batting .353 in Grapefruit League play by mid-March (while Hague stood at .273 at the same juncture).

Meanwhile, the Phillies seemed to be hardly missing Flood, as they were convinced that second-year man Larry Hisle could fit quite smoothly into their own future plans for center field, having played 139 games at the position in his rookie year of 1969 while socking twenty homers (not lasting long in Philly, Hisle would later become the property of the Cardinals for only one month after the 1972 season, going from the Dodgers to St. Louis and then to Minnesota in a pair of trades in October and November that year). Lee and Hague were each mentioned as possible compensatory replacements to Philadelphia for Flood's failure to report; with Allen now in the Cardinals' camp, a decision on the matter—either by the Cardinals themselves or in a directive from Kuhn—was coming in the very near future. A rumor even circulated that the Phillies were also seeking Mike Shannon as the replacement, with the intent of offering veteran infielder Tony Taylor to the Cardinals as a gesture in return. Ultimately, the Phillies were asked to choose from a list of ten Cardinals Minor League prospects. In scouring the list, both Quinn and manager Frank Lucchesi arrived upon the same name they wanted: Guillermo "Willie" Montanez, a left-handed hitting outfielder and first baseman. Flood's attorney, Allan Zerman, then joined the tiring hot-stove discussion on the issue and considered

Montanez—who at the time had played in only 8 games in the big leagues—an insult to his client. Lucchesi had managed Montanez when the player was in the minors as a seventeen-year-old in 1965, and the skipper was convinced of his potential. In addition to Montanez, the Cardinals issued the Phillies a number-one draft selection as extra compensation as well. Over the next decade, Montanez would develop into a slick-fielding, hot-dogging player around first base with a capable bat for the Phillies as well as several other teams.

Shannon had indeed been on the Phillies' short list, but a devastating personal issue soon surfaced that would have nullified such a move in any event.

In spite of the off-season departure of McCarver, the catching position for the Cardinals would not be immediately open to Ted Simmons, for the youngster had to fulfill a military obligation that was originally projected to last until at least the eighth of May. (The Cardinals, meanwhile, were surprised in spring training to see McCarver wearing uniform number 2 for the Phillies—Schoendienst's number with the Cards—instead of his familiar 15 that he donned for years. "When I came over, they asked me if I wanted 15, which had been Richie Allen's number," McCarver said laughingly ["Richie," incidentally, was an alternative first name for Allen, which had been developed by the press—and one that Allen disliked.] "I said, 'No way,' and funny thing, they believed me.") For the time being, the catching chores were given to Torre, who had served at the position extensively for the Braves (in addition to 17 games for the Cards in 1969). To fill Simmons's spot, rookie catcher Bart Zeller would be promoted to the parent club from the Little Rock roster. Zeller, a twenty-nine-year-old from Park Forest, Illinois, and alumnus of Eastern Illinois University, had batted .271 in 110 games in the Texas League in 1969—his seventh year of professional baseball without, to that time, having ever tasted the big leagues for a stint in the "bushes" that was nearly as long as Hughes's had been. Zeller had actually held the title of "player-coach" at Little Rock, being talked out of retirement from the Minor Leagues four years earlier by the Cardinals. At that time, Zeller had felt compelled to quit baseball and support his wife and two daughters by taking a high school teaching and coaching job. The pull of the game was too strong, however, and Zeller and wife agreed to give the Minor League Baseball life one more try. Zeller would be yet another unfamiliar name of the opening-day roster studied by Cardinals fans in 1970, as a never-ending parade of drama was marching through the organization, with all waiting for the next catastrophe to strike.

It struck Mike Shannon. While everyone knew that Simmons was a star in the making in St. Louis, the playing career of a local legend appeared to be simultaneously coming to an abrupt end as a beloved member of the Cardinals' family had been beset with stunning illness. The St. Louis native Shannon had reportedly contracted glomerulonephritis, discovered during routine examinations given to the players at the outset of spring training. "The condition, a defect of the filtering function of the kidneys, might reverse itself," announced team physician Stan London to a group of reporters who all were likely hearing the name of the disease for the first time. "But, even so, I believe it could be mid-season or later before Mike would be in physical condition to play ball." (Being frank and most realistic about his situation, Shannon admitted to the press that "there is an extreme possibility I might die of it.") Shannon spent a month in a Florida hospital during March for his initial treatments and then another month at Jewish Hospital in St. Louis in further recuperation after the regular season began.

Thus, the team was now again scrambling to fill yet another position left vacant from the departure of one more of their stars of the 1960s. When news of Shannon's condition first came to light, Schoendienst's first thought was to now move Torre back to third—only recently having been anointed the new catcher in Simmons's military absence—and put newcomer Carl Taylor behind the plate, who had batted .348 in part-time duty for the Pirates in 1969. The intent of the idea was to accommodate Allen and keep him from having to switch back to third, so as not to disrupt his offensive production—even though Torre himself was currently struggling with his hitting in posting a .125 mark at that point in spring play. Other possibilities considered for Shannon's replacement at third were Allen's coarrival in St. Louis in Rojas and longtime Cardinal utility player Phil Gagliano. Rojas, an accomplished and able player, had five years earlier earned a spot on the 1965 National League All-Star team. He had first entered pro ball with Cincinnati back in 1962 but was quickly dealt to the Phillies so that the Reds could make room at second base for Pete Rose. Now coming to the Cards with Allen, "Cookie" was yet another individual who assured St. Louis fans they would be pleased with the new the slugging first baseman. "Richie gave 150 percent when he was on the field with the Phillies," he told reporters. "Now, it seems that he's giving 200 percent. I never saw him not hustle."

Third base was quite foreign to Rojas, however, as he had almost exclusively played at second and was thought to be needed to fill that spot in Javier's place, later if not sooner (as it would turn out, Rojas would spend only half a season in a Cardinals uniform, being dealt in June to the Kansas City Royals and his roster spot subsequently taken by a Minor League pitcher named Alan Hrabosky). Javier was once again enduring a rough spring training, but this time, it was nothing of his own doing. In the course of two weeks he had been involved in an automobile accident, had been struck by a ball in practice for which he needed seven stitches woven above his eye, and had to return briefly to his home in the Dominican Republic to attend the funeral of his grandfather. Even Javier's longtime partner in double plays, Maxvill (who himself was fighting for his own job with Huntz, as Maxvill's legendary soft hitting had sunk even further, to an abysmal .175 in 132 games in 1969), was taking turns at second base in Javier's absence.

After a few days of juggling ideas in contending with Shannon and Simmons being out for a while, Schoendienst finally thought it best to keep Torre behind the plate and relent to moving Allen to third. Thus, Allen, who had spent all winter assuming that he would be mostly playing at the more comfortable (to him) first base position, was thus quickly thrust into a place where his defensive liabilities had been one of the objects of the Philadelphia fans' scorn for much of the past seven years. The decision would also move Hague into a starting role at first base—regardless of whether the coaching staff felt he was ready for an everyday job. With Hague, Allen, Cardenal, and Gagliano listed as likely new opening-day starters, the Cardinals' lineup was suddenly unrecognizable. Furthermore, on the pitching side, Carlton (because of his contract squabble) would have to start the regular season out of the bullpen in order to strengthen his arm for starting roles, something that he should have been doing with a timely arrival to camp. But even with the team's 10-13 record in the Grapefruit League amid all the experiments, the manager figured a winning formula would ultimately be discovered. "Allen's been throwing a lot better from third base than he has in the six years I've seen him," a pleased Schoendienst noted a few days after the switch. But Allen would add in an unsure tone, "If I *can't* throw, now's the time to find out." Allen claimed that damage to the ulnar nerve in his right hand from an automobile accident in 1967 had caused circulation problems in his throwing arm, especially when cold weather struck, and although April in St. Louis would be an improvement over Philadelphia, Allen knew he would still be forced to endure chilly temperatures in late spring regardless of the location. In exclusively playing first base for the first time in his career in 1969 for the Phillies, Allen had grown accustomed to not having to make many throws at all.

Joining Shannon and Simmons on the inactive roster to start the year would also be the precocious pitcher Jerry Reuss—further making Carlton's lack of readiness a problem—who after his magnificent one-game debut in late 1969 appeared primed to jump right into the Cardinals' starting rotation for 1970. The reason was that Reuss, like Simmons, first had to fulfill a six-month military tour and would not be activated by the Cardinals until the end of May.

Amid all the changes, switches, and vacancies on the club, all knew they could count on one thing—the dependability of their number-one starting pitcher. Bob Gibson appeared to be in regular form on March 19 as he pitched seven scoreless innings in a 3–1 exhibition victory over the Minnesota Twins. Still, for the first time since taking over as manager in 1965, Schoendienst was planning on giving Gibson four days of rest in between starts for 1970 as opposed to the usual three to which the pitcher had been accustomed (although this strategy had been used by the manager with Gibson at certain points in 1969 as well). And when a nervous writer saw Gibson wincing in pain and grabbing his right elbow in the locker room after the win over the Twins, it was feared that even the mainstay of the team had been felled as well. "Sure, it hurts," Gibson spoke up when he saw the concerned look on the writer's face. "It always hurts. I can't remember a time since 1963 when it hasn't hurt during a game or right after it." His easygoing nature with the soreness was desperately needed in light of all that had already occurred, as the loss of Gibson was inconceivable.

And nothing could lessen the spirits of showman Allen, who on March 21 belted his fourth homer in as many spring games as the Cards beat the Red Sox in Winter Haven. Many years later, in 1998, another new Cards first baseman, Mark McGwire, started the regular season with four homers in four games as well (although McGwire had finished the last part of 1997 in St. Louis), and like with McGwire, the simple change of a uniform for Allen appeared to kick-start his career, as his average was a sizzling .461 in socking the ball all over Florida. As a team, the Cards would drop seven of their last eight contests in Florida to finish with the 10-13 mark, in addition to a 9–2 win over the University of South Alabama before heading north—a team coached by former Cardinal player and manager Eddie Stanky, now in his second season at the school.

As one of the chief challengers to the Cardinals over the past several years, the Chicago Cubs had seen the 1969 campaign be a particularly bitter disappointment. Many had felt the Cubs had placed the most talented club on the field, but collapsed down the stretch in bowing to the torrid pace of the Mets, who overcame the nine-and-a-half game lead of Chicago in mid-August by playing nearly .800 ball for the season's final six weeks. Nonetheless, the Cubs players felt stronger as a result of the downfall. "We're together because of it," Ron Santo let all know as the team got ready for the new season. Yet it was apparent that Cub followers were not ready to forgive or forget—even in the team's faraway spring oasis in "sociable" Scottsdale, Arizona, as it was called by their legendary slugger, Ernie Banks. On March 29 Santo had endured several innings of verbal abuse from a jilted Cubs fan sitting in the lower seats near the dugout who had been calling him "pizza belly," among other things. By the sixth, Santo had heard enough. With the Cubs preparing to bat, the perpetrator continued his assault in regard to the team's demise in the past season and proceeded to fire sixteen cents in coins at Santo, just as the player had emerged in sight near the on-deck circle. Forgetting himself, Santo tried to leap over the railing to get at the heckler but was restrained by his teammates—first by Banks, then by three others. While the fan was immediately ejected from the stadium after launching the missiles, it was nonetheless a clear indication that at least some of the Chicago faithful were now expecting more than just second-place finishes in the future. Still, other Cub fans came to the defense of Santo and the rest of the team. "Those are white-collar fans who can afford the box seats who boo him," the heckler was described by one of the famous Bleacher Bums from Chicago, a self-described "blue-collar" type who had scraped together enough cash to make a spring trip to Arizona to follow the team. "We call them 'box seat bushers.' The blue-collar guys, as we are, like him. If they get on him like that this year, we're gonna go over there and bust some heads." "Busting some heads," in fact, was precisely how the 1969 season ended at Wrigley Field—as the Bums literally hung from the outfield wall after the final Cubs home game on October 2. When the final out was recorded, they lowered themselves onto the field and ran amuck, jumping on top of the dugouts in a chaotic scene as security personnel attempted to restore order.

Everyone knew—including Santo's tormentor—the third baseman was an emotional player anyway, as Santo had a reputation for passionate play and for his famous clicking of his heels after Cub wins. No one was more aware of this fact than his manager, Durocher, who actually wanted to see a bit more stoicism from Ronnie. "I wish I could get Santo to be like Billy [Williams] and Ernie [Banks]," he pondered. "When they strike out, they just come back to the dugout, put down their bats, take off their hats, sit down and never say a word. "It doesn't hurt their play," Leo continued about the other stars on the team. "But Ronnie gets so mad—the next time he goes to bat, he's like this, . . ." Durocher said as he twisted his fists together, displaying Santo's stress after making an out.

On May 12, 1970, the thirty-nine-year-old Banks would hit the five hundredth home run of his career; the following day he would get the lone Cub hit off the Mets' Gary Gentry in the eighth inning. The five hundredth homer came off Atlanta's Pat Jarvis, a man always miffed by the fact that his favorite team, the Cardinals, never signed him. Jarvis was signed by a Detroit scout who saw him strike out eighteen batters in the all-star game of the Clinton County League. "The Clinton County League, a collection of small town Illinois teams, has produced several major leaguers over the years—including a freckle-faced infielder named Red Schoendienst of Germantown and Tom Timmerman of Breese, who is now pitching for Detroit," Dick Kaegel of the *Post-Dispatch* pointed out. As a batter, Jarvis had been the first strikeout victim of Nolan Ryan in 1966. But in addition to surrendering the epic home run to Banks, he would also surrender himself years later, being brought up on corruption charges while serving as the sheriff of DeKalb County, Georgia. It was a position Jarvis held for nearly twenty years after being elected in 1976 with no previous experience in law enforcement.

By the time Harry Caray was involved in his collision as a pedestrian with the car in front of the Chase Park Plaza in November 1968, fellow Cardinals radio man Jack Buck was already considering leaving the team. Buck's salary was locked at $20,000, but due to the contract he had with Busch, he was not permitted to do any outside work. As an example of this policy, Buck specifically recalled a college football game he had broadcasted in Illinois for which he got paid $750; afterward, he had to immediately hand the money over to the marketing department at Anheuser-Busch. With such limitations appearing likely for the foreseeable future, by late 1969 Buck was getting ready to pack his bags and seek work elsewhere. It was at this very juncture, however, when Caray "blew his job," as Buck put it, and the number-one microphone in St. Louis would finally open up for him.

Urban legend around St. Louis has always circulated the idea that the incident was an intentional hit on Caray, citing a longtime feud between him and Gussie Busch. While the dispute was publicly described as being money related, several people in the brewery had alleged that a love affair had been occurring between Caray and Busch's daughter-in-law (phone records obtained by detectives, hired by Busch, displayed numerous calls between the two). Caray himself, however, later quelled such rumors by explaining the incident in his own version—that the driver had been a disoriented Vietnam veteran, only recently back from the war, and who had gotten engaged that afternoon and was thus distracted in his driving. While healing at Busch's estate in Florida, Caray was prodded by the detectives about the accident, and soon allegations began to snowball about the alleged affair. Regardless of the veracity of the rumors, Caray was instructed by Busch not to talk to the media about their problems— but he did anyway, as in a local interview he outlined the personal friction for which Busch fired him. Caray would philosophize many years later in his autobiography that, when one is accused of having an affair with an attractive woman, one does not admit it—but that one also does not deny it if one is as ugly as he considered himself to be.

The bottom line: Jack Buck was finally the main man in St. Louis baseball broadcasting for 1970. A native of Holyoke, Massachusetts, Buck also had previous broadcasting stints at Columbus and Rochester before starting with the Redbirds in 1954. As his own new sidekick, Buck suggested the Cardinals hire the recently retired Red Barber, the famed old voice of the Reds, Dodgers, and Yankees who had always been "sittin' in the catbird seat." The brewery made Barber an offer, but he turned it down. Barber told Buck by phone, "I'd love to do it, Jack, but my wife would kill me if I got back in it." Many years later, Schoendienst would call Buck the best interviewer with whom he had ever dealt. "Another reason Jack stood apart from the rest of the broadcasters was he possessed another unique skill—he *listened* when somebody was talking. A lot of guys will have all their questions planned out in advance, no matter what your answers are, and that results in a bad interview. Jack never did that—he waited and listened to what you had to say, [and] then asked an intelligent follow-up question." Buck was truly a natural at his job; if he told the listeners that he would "be back in a minute" for a commercial break, he could put down his microphone and instinctively pick it back up fifty-eight seconds later, ready to go once again.

Buck was always gracious in waiting for his turn, as he had it made clear to him by Harry that Caray was the number-one man in the booth. An example of this atmosphere was during the Cardinals' World Series appearances in 1967 and 1968, a time in baseball when the two participating teams in the series were each permitted one announcer for the national broadcasts, and, naturally, the long-tenured Caray was selected by the Cardinals in 1967. In 1968 Caray became upset when Buck suggested that the Cardinals propose to the league offices that two announcers from St. Louis—one for television and one for radio—be allowed to do the World Series broadcast. Considering it an assault on his power, Caray was initially threatened by the idea, refusing to agree. He later relented, as Buck was permitted to do the radio call with Pee Wee Reese while Harry handled the television side. It was representative of the long road of subservience Buck had to endure, having been Harry's second in command since 1961 (in addition to the two first being paired together from 1954 to 1959, at which point Buck had been replaced for one year in 1960 with St. Louis native Joe Garagiola when Milo Hamilton left the broadcast team). "He didn't want me to get the job in the first place," Buck said of Caray when Jack first arrived at the Cardinals. "He wanted the Cardinals to hire Chic Hearn, who at the time was a broadcaster in Peoria, Illinois [and who would go on to fame as the Los Angeles Lakers' radioman]." Buck, however, was not alone in being alienated by Caray; Garagiola and Buddy Blattner (who had done national broadcasts as well) were also made to feel to be in second-fiddle roles only, as Caray incessantly reminded them of his popularity in town.

Having fun and doing a variety of jobs for KMOX radio in St. Louis, Buck would bide his time and hold his ground in his own subtle way, and along the way playfully jab back at Harry when the occasion allowed. Such was a time in 1969 when Buck, in roasting Caray at a luncheon speech, introduced him by saying, "What nice things can I say about Harry that you haven't heard from the man himself?"

It was indicative of an underlying friendship the two men would ultimately develop and strengthen throughout the later portion of their careers, punctuated by a lengthy on-air conversation to which they treated fans during a Cubs-Cardinals rain delay in the late 1980s after Harry had long moved on to work in Chicago. The rain-delay moment—when many stations of Major League teams simply play a rerun of a sitcom—became a great dialogue of two veteran sportscasters' views of the modern state of baseball, what they felt was wrong with the game, and what should be done to fix it. Harry did most of the speaking and all of the interrupting during the discussion, as Buck would occasionally glance toward the camera with an understanding smile coming from the side of his face. The smile told of several things: that Buck was once again respectfully giving way to the man who had been the Cardinals' lead broadcaster for so many years, that Caray was enjoying himself in that very role one final time, and that fans should truly stop and listen to what Caray had to say.

The conversation was also a small example of Caray's tendency to issue unabashed, unapologetic criticism of poor play in the field through the microphone, characteristic of his time with the Cardinals until his departure after the 1969 season. It was a style that had made Caray popular among his listeners in St. Louis and beyond—but had also worn on Busch by the end of 1968, and to some it had became another factor in the decision for a change in the radio booth. Caray's candor, however, was something that Buck believed was a strength. "I wonder if Harry would be able to get a job in today's marketplace," Buck wrote in 1997. "Today's announcers have become too vanilla and too commercialized. There is no room today for controversy created by the broadcaster. Teams will not hire an announcer who is going to be controversial and create problems." In Buck's opinion of their last few years together, there would never be a better time for baseball announcers. "The 1960s was a golden era for broadcasting," he continued. "I was quoted a few years ago as saying I thought the quality of baseball broadcasting had dropped a peg, but now I think it's down two or three pegs. Almost anything is acceptable now in the big leagues." With Caray moving on to Oakland in 1970 for one season with the A's before commencing a long stretch on both the North and South sides of Chicago, the lion's share of the Cardinal airwaves now finally belonged to Buck.

Buck, the new lead announcer, would be gazing down upon a new playing field at Busch Stadium. With the 1970 regular season approaching, the laborers' strike had been resolved, and the artificial surface at Busch Stadium was fully installed by the beginning of April, covering 113,000 square feet on the property. At this first installation of the surface, the entire dirt infield would remain, while the new rug would be placed only in areas previously occupied by grass (in the coming years the all-dirt infield at Busch would be replaced with larger areas of artificial turf, leaving dirt only around the pitcher's mound and the "sliding pit" areas around each base and home plate). First used in Major League play in Houston's indoor Astrodome in 1965, the carpet had certain assets that could not be matched by natural means, as its proponents claimed. "Wherever there is artificial turf, there have been fewer ankle and knee injuries," assured Edward Bock, president of the St. Louis–based Monsanto Company that developed the Astroturf formula patented by Monsanto workers

James Faria and Robert Wright. Bock explained to league inspectors that the turf would be laid on the field in straight strips fifteen feet wide, rolled down side by side against each other and stretching in straight lines from southwest to northeast (that is, from the home plate end of the ballpark in Busch Stadium toward the outfield wall). Even with the sections bordering each other, Bock convinced observers that the seams in the carpet would be unnoticeable. What was the exact formula for laying a perfect artificial surface? "The installation is just over eleven and a half inches in depth," Bill Beck of the *Post-Dispatch* explained to his readers after taking notes from Bock on the tour. "Three inches of crushed rock, seven inches of asphalt, three-fourths of an inch of pad and five-eighths of an inch of Astroturf"—all at cost of $3 per square foot installed, at 1970 prices.

In addition to the Astrodome, Monsanto had secured deals to provide surfaces for fifty other collegiate and professional athletic venues by the end of 1970. But over that time, it had also seen competitors emerge in its field—even for the local contract in Busch Stadium, which was originally figured to be naturally given to Monsanto. Among the companies vying for the job at Broadway and Clark Street was the Minnesota Mining and Manufacturing Company, commonly known as "3M," looking to underbid Bock's firm. In the four years since the Astrodome had opened, the entire concept of the development and marketing of artificial surfaces had changed. "Astroturf now looks like grass," noticed Broeg about the recent improvements in looking at samples of the 1969 model as compared to the original product from earlier in the decade. The 3M Company had developed its own line called "Tartan Turf," which had already been purchased by the University of Wisconsin, University of Tennessee, and Michigan State University, as well as Three Rivers Stadium, the new home of the Pirates and the NFL's Steelers in Pittsburgh, which was set to open in late May. Tartan Turf—which was softer and more comfortable on which to play than Astroturf, while the latter offered a look that more closely resembled grass—would also make an appearance in Chicago in the early 1970s when the NFL's Bears moved from Wrigley Field to a new lakefront home at the venerable Soldier Field, a park district–owned stadium hosting mostly high school and college all-star games before the pros' arrival. Bock envisioned a day in the future when his Astroturf went far beyond the confines of the athletic field and would be used in many aspects of everyday life by ordinary people who were simply looking for a durable household texture. "The possibilities are limitless," he said, "especially considering the round-the-clock utility of any Astroturf-covered area under urban circumstances where land is scarce and at a premium." Bock had started working for Monsanto in 1941 after quitting graduate school, making $130 a month at his first job with the company before gradually rising to the top position over the decades. In the spring of 1970 at the World's

Fair in Osaka, Japan, further exhibitions of synthetic athletic fields of the future were on display. Even Stan Musial, a knight of the old-style game, fancied the possibilities for batters with the Astroturf revolution. "Anybody who hits the ball on the ground has a better chance now, particularly if he can run," he said. "Those early years when I hit the ball more often to the left or right of the shortstop and could really run—I'd have loved it [playing on an artificial surface]. . . . [I]t probably would have meant 30 or more [team batting-average] points to the 1942 Cardinals, who were really fast and seldom struck out." Ultimately, the carpet would become the hallmark of the speed-oriented Cardinal teams to play in the Busch Stadium over the next twenty years.

And as promised by the owner, the seats surrounding that new playing surface at Busch Stadium would be kept at reasonable prices for 1970. While the cost of a box seat ticket would slightly rise to $4.00 apiece, it was also announced that general admission tickets remained at their 1969 rate of $1.50. In addition, bleacher seats would still be only $1.00—and would be distributed on a non-reserved-seating basis, continuing the tradition of fans lining up at the outfield gate adjacent to Broadway long before the turnstiles opened, hoping to get a front-row view just above the outfield wall.

Part of the reason that an artificial surface was decided for use in Busch Stadium was for reduction of the wear and tear accumulated from housing a professional football team in the same ballpark. For decades old Sportsman's Park on Grand Avenue had endured the presence of not only two Major League Baseball teams during the summer (at least until the Browns left town in 1954) but also the football Cardinals in the fall, who had moved from Chicago in 1960. Installation of the Astroturf at Busch Stadium suggested that pro football was there to stay in St. Louis, for Bill Bidwill, the owner of the football club, had only recently dismissed rumors that his team was planning to jump to the American Football League and perhaps another city. "This is strictly speculative," Bidwill said of the individuals circulating the story. "We're in the NFL, and we intend to stay there."

The Cardinal players got an early tour of the new turf on Sunday, April 5, as the team arrived back in town earlier than planned when an exhibition game in Kansas City against the Royals was canceled. They were stunned by the speed with which the ball traveled on the carpet, leading Sisler to be eerily prophetic about the future of St. Louis baseball long before the names of McBride, McGee, Coleman, and Van Slyke would arrive. "You're going to have to have fast outfielders for Astroturf, and fortunately we do have speed in our outfield," he pointed out. "There's no way to keep those balls hit between outfielders from going to the wall." Added another assistant coach, George Kissell, "The defenses will have to be better than ever. If an outfielder misjudges a flyball and comes in too far, the ball has a good chance of bouncing far over his head." Kissell also predicted that the level turf would *help* outfielders in at least one way—in the ability to aggressively charge base hits in readying one's self to throw, something that the unpredictability of uneven grass and dirt could not provide. But as for those defenders who play much closer to the hitter—which initially frightened Musial when he moved to first base after years in the outfield—Kissell also concluded sarcastically that "you'll never see an infield play *in* again," due to the terrifying speed at which ground balls would be batted. And Gibson added an interesting view about Astroturf from the pitcher's perspective after practicing on it for the first time. "I don't have to be as good a fielder as I used to be," the winner of four-straight Gold Gloves would say, "because not as many balls come to me—they bounce over my head."

And suddenly now, with Shannon's health situation, among those Cardinal infielders who would have to adjust to the accelerated missiles on the new turf was Allen—the reluctant third baseman by default.

Wednesday, April 8, was opening day, the mark on the calendar on which all teams and their fans begin with hope anew. For the Cardinals, play would begin north of the border, as they had another early-season date in frigid Montreal for the second year in a row with forty-degree temperatures causing painful reverberations each time the batter struck the ball. The Cards' owner, meanwhile, was convinced that his club would surge toward the title once again when he conducted a speaking engagement back in St. Louis a week later. "I'm going to make a prediction—and I've been wrong a few times, but not many," Gussie Busch announced to the annual "Welcome Dinner" thrown for the team by the Knights of the Cauliflower Ear in the Chase Park Plaza. "We're going to win the pennant and the World Series in 1970." Busch seemed on track to put the bitterness between him and the players behind him, and to this end, the new slugger he had acquired pitched in immediately. Allen slammed two doubles and a spectacular homer in backing Gibson and the rest of the Redbirds to a 7–2 season-launching triumph over the Expos, beating pitcher Bill Stoneman and manager Gene Mauch—the man who ironically had cultivated Allen as a player from his rookie season in 1963 until Mauch became Montreal's first skipper with the expansion franchise in Canada in 1969. "Allen is a great athlete, and his teammates and the St. Louis fans will love him," Mauch said of his former player after the game. "He's a team man." When asked by the writers if the long home run Allen hit was a pitch that had "gotten away" from Stoneman, Mauch paused for a moment, and then responded, "That ball got away from *everyone.*"

Over in the visitors' clubhouse, Allen sent reporters interested in his reactions over to Javier (who had driven in the game-winning run), as the new star quietly celebrated by reading an inspirational letter from his mother that had just arrived. In addition to his fine day at the plate, Allen was not required to handle a single play at third base in that first game—which, he admitted, was fine with him. It was part of a hot start for the Cardinals that included seven wins in their first nine games, their only losses coming against the defending-champion Mets and two of their pitching aces in Seaver and Gentry. In just ten days, Seaver would enjoy perhaps his finest day ever on the mound, tying Carlton's recently set Major League record of nineteen strikeouts—including a new mark of ten in a row at one point—in toying with the San Diego Padres on April 22. Gibson hated being compared to other pitchers from his era, but most of all to Seaver, even though the two men held tremendous respect for each other. "Why should I worry about Seaver?" he finally had to tell reporters when another matchup between the two had arrived on the calendar and the newspapermen wanted to know his feelings. "He can't beat you. It's the hitters who beat you." Seaver was nine years Gibson's junior, and in listening to discussions of his replacing Bob as the top gun in the National League, he responded in kind. "Beating Gibson doesn't mean I replace him," Seaver said. "I have to beat the Cardinals, not him. The writers talk of Seaver-Gibson, but this is still a team game. There are 18 men on the field."

When the bespectacled Allen was introduced to the crowd before the Busch Stadium opener two days later on April 10 against the Mets, the overwhelming roar of the 47,568 in attendance moved him to tears as he tipped his batting helmet—a piece of equipment that Allen would uniquely don over the rest of his career while playing *defense*. The standing ovation lasted more than two minutes. Standing near Allen was the Cardinals' starting pitcher on the evening, George Culver, when the thunderous noise greeted the new player. "I got chills when Allen got that ovation," Culver said. "They have good fans here. They respect talent." Dal Maxvill could remember no new player in recent history, including Maris and Cepeda, who received such a welcome in his initial St. Louis appearance. And Allen could recall only one such similar greeting in all his years in baseball—the final day of the 1968 season, after which he had hit three home runs against the Mets (strangely enough, that reception did not come in the Phillies' home park but rather in Shea Stadium in New York).

Later, when he came to the plate for the first time in his new home, Allen heard "boos" from the home stands, as would be heard in future years when men named McGwire and Pujols were in the batter's box. The "boos" were being directed at the opposing pitcher (in this case, Jim McAndrew of New York) because of Allen's being walked on four straight balls as the recovering Shannon listened to the game on the radio from his bed in Jewish Hospital. "I feel that I'm right there," Shannon said of the experience. It had been a long time since he had been able to listen to a ball game, and he had no clue at the time that the medium would one day be his next calling. "I see everything developing [from the game descriptions of Jack Buck]. I put myself into the situation.

I think about who the hitter is." Culver, admittedly stiff in not having pitched since his last spring training assignment twelve days earlier, was wild in the early portion of the game but righted himself to win 7–3 (the only victory in the series for the Cards), as new starters Cardenal and Lee were the batting stars with three hits each, while Allen was shut out. The excitement of the packed house in downtown St. Louis was motivational for the victorious Culver, as it had been for Allen, as the pitcher had spent the past two seasons with the Reds before coming to the Cards in a deal for the injured hurler Washburn. "I didn't see that many in the park in three or four games when I was with Cincinnati," Culver observed about the fervent St. Louis fans, who had ascended up the long ramps toward their seats to peer curiously down upon the strange new artificial playing surface on the stadium floor as the season got under way. Culver and Mike Torrez were two new starting pitchers within a rotation that had been nearly as overhauled as the batting order, having replaced Washburn and the ailing Nelson Briles, while Reuss was also absent, pending his military obligations. Torrez and Reuss were the young gems in the organization, two imposing pitchers, each standing more than six foot four on the mound. While Reuss was serving in the army, Torrez solidified his own status on the big league roster with a one-hit performance against the Expos in Busch Stadium on April 15—his eleventh straight win (dating back to a fine audition in 1969) after having beaten them in Montreal the week before as well. Witnessing the 10–0 drubbing of his Expos team was Dick Williams, the St. Louis native who was back in town in the role of hitting coach for Mauch and the Expos. He continued to be impressed with the reshuffling job that Devine and Schoendienst had done with the new Cards roster. "I've got to think the Cardinals are a stronger and better-balanced club than the 1967 Cardinal team we played in the World Series," said Williams, who faced his hometown in the championship round that year as the manager of the Boston Red Sox. Soon, word was out around the league that the Cardinals had fully restocked their talent cupboard. Added veteran Chicago Cubs relief pitcher Phil Regan when he saw them the first time, "The Cardinals weren't hungry last year. They're hungry now."

The quick spring out of the gate had boded well for the Cardinals in the past, as similar strong beginnings to the 1967 and 1968 seasons had led to National League pennants and one World Series title. Schoendienst's other years at the helm—1965, 1966, and 1969—had conversely produced poor records at the start of the year and, coincidentally, no postseason berth. But with the Cubs on a mission to fight back from their 1969 late-season free fall, they proved their conviction in the season's tenth game on April 21. That day they tied the Cards for first place with a 7-3 record, as Gibson was beaten in Wrigley Field in a game that included a three-run homer by Billy Williams, as Gibson uncharacteristically permitted seven earned runs in just over six innings of work. Gibson always claimed Williams to be one of the toughest hitters he ever faced, calling him "my number one nemesis." He held the sweet-swinging Cub in the highest esteem, even though the numbers of their individual duels would bear out otherwise; Williams had batted only .203 against Gibby since 1964 (in faring well against other stars of the era over that time, Gibson had limited Hank Aaron to only a .210 mark, Tony Perez to .090, and Allen himself to only .097 before the latter joined the Cardinals, according to research conducted by Bill Leggett of *Sports Illustrated*). It was also the second time in his three starts on the young season in which Gibson had been driven from the mound, something that had been such an extreme rarity in recent years. Could it be that the reports out of spring training were true—that Gibson had a dead arm?

To prove otherwise, Gibson would proceed to strike out fifteen Cincinnati Reds in his next start, the greatest assurance he could issue to let everyone know things were okay. "Nobody better ever say that Gibson is over the hill," said thirty-six-year-old Sparky Anderson, who at this point had been on the job as the Reds' manager for only two weeks. "He's still got to be the best pitcher in baseball. . . . [I]f he's over the hill, I feel sorry for guys who are supposed to be at their peaks."

Maxvill was equally perplexed at such notions that Gibson was in decline and suggested that the man be afforded a break every so often. "What's wrong with Bob Gibson?" he asked incredulously. "Yeah, I can think of a couple of things: every once in a while, he gives up a hit that scores a run. And something else bad about him: he can't walk on water. Out in Frisco after a rain, I saw him try it. He just sloshed through it like me."

The victory against the great right-hander was also Pyrrhic for Chicago, coming at a great cost, as workhorse catcher Randy Hundley tore ligaments in his knee in a collision at home plate. He would be lost to the Cubs for the next three months, dealing a damaging blow to completing their penance from their sins of 1969 and their long-sought pursuit of a championship.

Allen proceeded to sock three more homers in those first nine contests, leading Cardinal followers to believe the club had found an even more productive version of Cepeda. But despite his expected achievements at the plate, Allen was still not particularly enjoying his new slot on defense. "Hurry back—they're eating me up at third," Allen would laughingly tell Shannon in phoning his hospital bed, in the hopes of speeding his recovery.

Schoendienst, it had appeared, had indeed found the right formula from the angst he was suffering toward the end of spring training, deliberating upon the "spare parts" needed to craft into a regular lineup. The absence of Flood, while naturally glaring at first, was ultimately noticed less and less as the new center fielder, Cardenal, had posted an early nine-game hitting streak and was still batting more than .400 by the third week of April. The reason, according to him? The expansion of his American diet. "When I came to this country from Cuba to play baseball, I couldn't speak much English," Cardenal explained. "So I ordered ham and eggs or hamburgers all the time. I couldn't say anything else to eat in English." All the burgers and eggs must have made him strong: even though he weighed his slight 160 pounds, Cardenal was discovering that his typical thirty-three-ounce bat was too light for him—so he switched to one of the thirty-six-ounce clubs that Cepeda had left behind in the equipment room. Cardenal still continued to "choke up" on the larger bat, but nonetheless credited the new stick for allowing him to meet the ball at the proper moment as opposed to swinging too early. He had also been encouraged to switch batting styles by Sisler, who dissuaded Cardenal from trying to be a home run hitter even though Jose had once belted seventy-one dingers over the course of just two Minor League campaigns. In addition, he was showing off the speed on the base paths and in the outfield of which Davalillo spoke. The gift of speed, Cardenal claimed, came from having to tiptoe through the broken glass around which he and his boyhood friends had played ball on a sandlot in Cuba—often in their bare feet.

Part of Schoendienst's successful new formula was that Allen was playing the best third base job he had ever issued in his career, in spite of his disinclination to be there. He kept it up until Shannon finally returned to the active roster on May 14, when he entered a game against the Pirates at Busch Stadium in the eighth inning as a pinch hitter. He was greeted with a standing ovation from the crowd—albeit only around ten thousand for the Thursday-afternoon affair. Shannon had been cleared by doctors to begin working out a couple weeks earlier, and thus relieved *a truly relieved* Allen at third base in the top half of the ninth, who despite his relative success at the position was openly happy to move back to first base. And with Shannon appearing to be healthy and soon ready to reclaim the spot on a regular basis, Devine was prompted to trade the veteran utility infielder Gagliano to the Cubs two weeks later. In the move, the general manager was able to bolster the relief corps by adding Ted Abernathy from Chicago—although Abernathy would be packaged in another deal to Kansas City by July.

"If I had gone on and played," Shannon said about his physicians' forbidding him from starting his season back in April,

> I might have really damaged the kidney. I might never have played again. It might have taken my life. I'll trade a few weeks for the rest of my life any time.
>
> You do what the doctors tell you, and you have faith. People say it must be awfully tough, just sitting around doing nothing. But sitting around is what I have

to do to get better. It's like having a pulled muscle—you sit around and relax un-til it heals. You do what you have to do. After that, it's up to the Man upstairs. He's running the show, let's face it . . . I may never play again. I don't know.

Unknown to Shannon at the time was that his playing days were indeed num-bered and dwindling more quickly than anyone imagined.

The same evening in which Shannon appeared in his first game back, anoth-er player's return was celebrated up north in Milwaukee—that of Hank Aaron, coming back to the city of his greatest production, as the Braves collectively also came "home" for the first time in five years for an exhibition game against the newly formed Brewers of the American League. Four days later in front of the biggest Cincinnati crowd in twenty-three years, Aaron would become the ninth player to reach his three thousandth hit. "Why, he might even assault the unbelievable," Broeg wondered about Hammerin' Hank. "Babe Ruth's career home run total—714." Answered Aaron, "I'd need a 50-home run season in the next year or two, and I'd have to play longer than maybe I can. I feel I can go on for another two or three seasons, but I wouldn't just want to hang on if I wasn't productive." Seventeen months later when Aaron would reach 639 ca-reer homers by the end of the 1971 season, he then grew more optimistic about the possibility of catching the Babe. "I'd sure like to get it [the record]. It's the most prestigious of all records. It has stood for a long time and I think that only Willie [Mays] and I have a shot at it. No one else in the immediate future ap-pears to have a chance." Mays was actually ahead of Aaron with 646 himself by the end of the 1971 season.

The Brewers had brought the big leagues back to Milwaukee for the first time since 1965, when the city had coaxed the Seattle Pilots franchise to relocate to the Midwest after only one year on the West Coast. Milwaukee fans met the team with open arms, having purchased more than a thousand season tickets the day they went on sale as the old radio station WEMP—the same one that broadcasted the Braves when they were in the city—would be given the play-by-play rights once again. The City of Seattle, however, had not given up the team without a fight, for William Dwyer, the special assistant to the Washington state attorney general, was in the process of filing an eighty-two-million-dollar antitrust lawsuit in federal courts against the American League and the owners of the franchise. This had been done in spite of the fact that baseball officials, as compensation for approving the move, had promised a new team to Seattle (in addition to the aforementioned indemnity for Pacific Coast League consider-ations) as soon as expansion would take place in the American League. Dwyer's suit, interestingly, was flung at the same fortress that Flood's action was trying to penetrate—the desired dismantling of the half-century immunity that big league baseball held from antitrust legislation (specifically, in Flood's case, the reserve clause). Even the governor of Washington, Dan Evans, had joined the fight. "I think the leadership in the American League and the league owners that have led us to this sorry state of events can't be condemned too much for the way in which they treated this area," he said. "I think the best comment is to hope the people of Milwaukee are treated better than the people of Seattle and the State of Washington were treated."

After getting two hits in seven tries against the Cubs in starting assignments the next two nights, Shannon's batting average would plunge into the .100s over the next three months as his physical condition worsened, leading toward a breaking point that would arrive in mid-August.

4   Nephritis

I believe older players of our day were more concerned with the image of the game. Now, everybody is so outspoken. They say and do things without regard for whom it hurts.

—Stan Musial, 1970

Just over a week after Shannon's return to the lineup, Allen on May 23 was challenging for the National League lead with a .317 batting average. In addition, in returning across the diamond to the first base bag with Shannon resuming his duties at third on an everyday basis, he would go from May 4 to June 10 without making an error at *any* position he played. Not even a pitch to the head from the Cubs on May 16 could thwart his progress. After observations from physicians that night, he was released from Jewish Hospital—three days after Shannon had been discharged from the same facility—and still in his game uniform at two o'clock in the morning, he found himself in the hospital parking lot with no ride. With Allen's car still parked at Busch Stadium, he then had to phone clubhouse manager Butch Yatkeman for a lift.

The success of the new slugger could not keep the team from struggling after its fast start in April, and various degrees of improper off-field behavior were seen by some as a chief cause. Like Gussie Busch, Schoendienst was becoming frustrated with the ever-increasing, ever-mystifying lack of respect for the game that several members of the team were displaying. Yet some in the media—even the ever-supportive Broeg—had suggested that Red himself should be more accountable for the players' actions. "If I were going to criticize Schoendienst as a manager," he wrote in the midst of one especially bad stretch of player misconduct in 1970,

"I'd urge him to run a tighter ship." Certainly, Schoendienst was by no means tolerant of misbehavior. As an example, when four Cardinals had missed the team's curfew at its hotel in Cincinnati in early May, the manager personally levied fifty-dollar fines against the guilty parties. "Managers don't make rules on major league clubs—the players do," Schoendienst had originally said back in 1965 when he was first hired as the field boss. "If the players show they need a lot of regulations, I'll issue those regulations."

In Schoendienst's view, the transgressions at the Cincinnati hotel had contributed to the team's dropping both games to the Reds. The trip along the Ohio River was part of a five-game losing streak that had suddenly sent them into fifth place with a 10-14 record, far removed from their first-place start during the initial weeks of the season. It also led to additional vocal outbursts at the team from the normally reserved southern Illinoisan. Red hollered at the club in the visitors' locker room as the team moved on to Atlanta, where Gibson was once again inexplicably pounded by an opponent for seven runs, with his season ERA now soaring near five a game. This time, he had permitted ten hits in five innings of work, and it was the fifth time in six starts in 1970 that he had been knocked out of a contest after completing 80 percent of his starts the year before. To those who witnessed Schoendienst's tirade, Red's tone was not unlike that of Busch in his infamous spring training speech of 1969. Ed Wilks, covering the trip for the *Post-Dispatch,* granted that the moral material with which the manager was working was not of the same cloth to which Red, his old roommate Musial, and other old-timers were accustomed. "Schoendienst [is] dealing with a different breed of baseball players than the pros he had as teammates through 19 years as a major leaguer."

Another writer for the paper concluded, "Behaved or misbehaved, the Cardinals have missed their chance to take charge in the Eastern Division of the National League." The words were clicked out by Bob Broeg on his typewriter back home in St. Louis, where disappointed sports minds had instead recently turned their attention to the local Blues of the National Hockey League. In only its third season of existence, the team had fought its way to the Stanley Cup finals in each of those three years under their gifted young coach, Scotty Bowman. After having lost in the final round to the famed Montreal Canadiens in 1968 and 1969, the St. Louis team was now battling another "Original Six" team, the Boston Bruins, for the 1970 league title. Despite raucous, fanatical support from their followers at home in the old St. Louis Arena, the Blues dropped the first two games of the series at the grand old rink near Forest Park and another at Boston, and then struggled to stave off elimination by taking the Bruins to overtime in Game 4 at the Boston Garden on May 10. Forty seconds into the extra time, the year's most valuable player, Bobby Orr, took a give-and-go pass from teammate Derek Sanderson and blew the puck past St. Louis goalie Glenn Hall to win the series. A second after the puck crossed the goal line, a United Press International photograph displayed Orr flying through the air, his body parallel to the ice with his arms nonetheless raised unconcerned in celebration, having been tripped in jealousy by a Blues player. In time, it would become perhaps the most famous hockey photograph of all time. Although reaching the league finals for three straight seasons, the Blues had lost all twelve of those games in the championship round.

The St. Louis baseball team, meanwhile, had been considerably less exciting. The frustration of Schoendienst was manifested individually by Allen, who, though not committing any egregious personal acts to date, was nonetheless now starting to show signs of the unpredictable pattern of behavior he had established in Philadelphia. Allen was the one of the preeminent examples of the counterculture that was coming to the fore in baseball in 1970, after it had emerged more rapidly among the youth in general society earlier in the 1960s. While still a young man at twenty-eight in 1970, Allen had been in the Major Leagues since the age of twenty-one. Thus, he had developed himself as a professional in his chosen craft through the duration of the sixties, and to some in baseball, he was one of the sport's representatives of that very same youth counterculture in America (seen in different forms with men such as Belinsky, Flood, Ken Harrelson, and other outlandish—or, in Flood's case, at least obstinate—players of the era). Such players, along with their fellow youth, challenged the thresholds of society alongside other demographic groups of the young in America in the 1960s.

Furthermore, the societal turmoil that Jack Buck was noticing had not eased with the advent of the 1970s. "There were times when I didn't enjoy being around that group of players," Buck admitted about the 1970 season. "Once at O'Hare Airport in Chicago, we got off the plane and walked through the terminal. The players were carrying music boxes, wearing sandals and T-shirts. One of the players was wearing Levis without undershorts and had a hole in the seat of his pants. I remember thinking, 'These are the Cardinals?'" It is open to speculation why Busch—who had always demanded conformity to company policy, both inside and outside the brewery—permitted such activity to go on. Schoendienst, meanwhile, felt as if his hands were tied. "When you asked a player to do something," Red reflected upon the changes in the relationship between player and manager in the 1960s and early '70s, "there were guys who wanted to know why, and you didn't have the automatic power that a manager was used to having. The word that seemed to be forgotten, and still is forgotten today, is *discipline*."

While the 1960s had witnessed multiple systemic changes to the sport of baseball (in terms of organizational structure, player-management interaction, and other areas), popular music had already been transformed within the decade as well, culminating with the landmark Woodstock music festival in upstate New York in August 1969. With the 1970 Major League season only a few days old, a final punctuation on the music era arrived with the disbanding of the most recognizable of popular groups. It was made public on April 10 by lead singer and guitarist Paul McCartney that the Beatles would no longer stay together, with McCartney and other members planning on pursuing their own solo careers immediately (by May 8 the group's twelfth and final album—*Let It Be*—would be released to the public, and by December, McCartney would be in court in London to pursue the rapid dissolution of the group's legal partnership). Even so, other icons from the immediate past were also *reappearing,* for it was announced in September that Elvis Presley would emerge from his reclusion of no live performances after twelve years to commence a concert tour, beginning with a show at Veterans Coliseum in Phoenix (Elvis was hardly finished; a couple years later, more people tuned into his concert from Hawaii on television than had watched the moon landing in 1969).

Such music in the popular mainstream had been viewed by some as a peaceful, relaxing avenue of retreat during the turbulent 1960s. Nonetheless, it seemed that the nation could not release itself from the violence to which it had become accustomed in the past decade, a trail of blood that had been seeded in antiwar demonstrations and racial bigotry, and in early May 1970 as the Cardinals were trying to regain their supremacy of the National League they had enjoyed in the sixties, a reminder of an epoch of American history that the nation had wished to leave behind reared its head once again.

On May 4 a large throng of approximately two thousand students and townspeople had gathered on the commons of Kent State University in northeastern Ohio. It was an otherwise quiet Monday, with local baseball followers miffed about their Cleveland Indians being in last place, the team having no game that day, as they were about to begin a series in Chicago against the White Sox. The assembled group was protesting the recent turn of events in the nation of Cambodia, the latest area to be engulfed in war in Southeast Asia and one that had been the scene of an internal political coup in March. Also sparking the protest was the fact that, five days earlier, President Nixon had announced that American troops from the Third and Fourth Army Corps were soon to be crossing the border from Vietnam into Cambodia. Unrest had been growing in the college town for the past seventy-two hours, as other, smaller, demonstrations had occurred in which firemen had been pelted with rocks as they were attempting to extinguish a blaze ignited by a portion of one of the crowds. The events had prompted the local mayor, Leroy Satrom, to call upon Governor James Rhodes to dispatch the Ohio National Guard to the scene to keep order.

Around noon on May 4 the large group was ordered by the Guard commander to disperse. When it refused, a tear-gas canister was volleyed toward the protesters, but strong winds that day made the tactic ineffectual, carrying the gas off into the distance well beyond the crowd. Some of the students attempted to retrieve the canisters and fire them back at the Guardsmen, proving to be just as ineffective, as gas masks were being utilized by the unit. As the crowd began to drift threateningly toward the line of defense that the Guard unit had established, a command was heard from someplace to open fire. Nearly seventy rounds were released in the next ten seconds.

When the shots had finally ended, four students were dead, and nine lay wounded. Among those struck were innocent people merely passing by or observing the situation from a distance on campus. The Guard's adjutant general had claimed that a sniper was firing on the soldiers from a nearby rooftop, prompting the commence-fire order. Tragically, an incident strikingly similar to the Kent State event would take place just ten days later in another part of the country. State police in Mississippi would fire into a crowd of demonstrators at Jackson State University, resulting in the deaths of two students and twelve others being wounded.

The St. Louis region would soon learn it was not immune to such calamities, either. The trustees of Southern Illinois University at Carbondale, located one hundred miles to the southeast of St. Louis, voted on May 15 to shut down the campus in the wake of its own violence from students protesting the war in Vietnam. As in the Kent State situation, state police and the National Guard were called to the scene to restore order twice in the previous three weeks, as more than half of the twenty-four thousand students had already left the campus in fear for their own safety even before the order was issued. After a bomb had exploded inside a house in which three students were injured, many of the remaining students on campus and Carbondale residents alike began taking up arms in their own defense.

But in the midst of the domestic and international turbulence of the Vietnam War era, Major League Baseball in the United States went on—just as it had during World War I, the Great Depression, World War II, the Korean War, the Cuban missile crisis, and all the other periods of uncertainty. And often ballplayers—for some reason—were thrust into the debates of certain geopolitical events along the way. No one felt this pressure more than Bob Gibson, who had been viewed as a de facto "black leader" during the height of racial tensions in the late 1960s. Yet despite being greatly concerned with civil rights, Gibson was insulted by others' attempts to place him at the center of the issue simply because he was a black man. As an example, as he was getting ready in the locker room to pitch in what would become his historic Game 1 of the 1968 World Series in Busch Stadium, he was questioned by a newspaper reporter about a protest march taking place at that moment by the Black Muslims group in downtown St. Louis.

Gibson's simple response was, "I don't give a _____—I've got a ballgame to pitch."

Thus, it should come as no surprise that Gibson was business as usual on May 23, 1970, just days after the latest round of violence on American college campuses. With the Cardinals in Philadelphia for the teams' first meeting in that city since their momentous trade the previous fall, Gibson (as well as the former Phillie Allen) was once again probed by the media for his opinion of the recent events at Kent, Jackson, and Carbondale. And once again, he instead made it clear that he had no comment on these happenings and instead needed to focus on the job at hand. (To further add to his list of nuisances, Gibson and his teammates were forced to deal with the evacuation of their hotel in Philadelphia that same night, after the fifteenth floor had caught fire [the Redbirds had been staying on the nineteenth and twentieth floors]. Jose Cardenal, with help from Shannon and Javier [the latter of whom had taken quite some time to locate his glasses after waking up] banged on all the doors to rouse the other players and get them safely out of the building.) Gibby's job on this evening, in front of an unwittingly fortunate 12,333 in attendance at Connie Mack Stadium, was to go head-to-head against Jim Bunning, a legendary pitcher himself who was in his final full season in the big leagues. To his disappointment, Gibson would not find his old battery mate McCarver in the Phillies' lineup that night, as he had broken his hand on May 2 and would be lost to the Phillies in his first season in Philadelphia for the next four months. Gibson, however, never seemed to need any extrinsic motivation. He struck out the side in the Philadelphia first, making Tony Taylor, Denny Doyle, and Oscar Gamble his first victims. By the end of the night, he fanned sixteen batters—a career high in regular-season play, and just two days after Carlton had struck out sixteen Phillies himself—as he and his mates were victorious, 3–1, for Gibson's first win since April 26. All three Cardinal runs were courtesy of two home runs by Allen off Bunning in the third and fifth innings, with the Pennsylvania native gleefully sprinting around the bases each time, laughing along with the familiar derision he always received from the Philly fans. (In this, the final season at old Connie Mack Stadium, Allen was greeted by one banner that hung from a facade in the old structure that read, "How Do You Like Your New Babysitter, Richie?" Nonetheless, local reports were that most in attendance had cheered for Allen when he first stepped to the plate.) It had only been in the past week that Allen had been able to move back over to first base permanently with the return of Shannon, adding to the pleasure of his successful return to town. For Bunning, it was his sixth loss in seven decisions to date on the season, as the close of his own magnificent career was now quickly approaching. Still, the man who at the time had the second-most strikeouts in baseball history posted a valiant effort in his own right, whiffing seven Cardinals himself in a game that was authored in just over two hours by the two master craftsmen of the pitching mound. By August Bunning would become only the second pitcher ever—along with Cy Young—to have won at least one hundred games in each major league, as Bunning had spent nine years in Detroit before coming to the Phillies for the infamous pennant demise to the Cardinals in 1964.

Curt Flood, naturally, was nowhere to be found in Philadelphia, despite the presence of his old St. Louis friends in town for a few days. However, they were still thinking of him. As the Cards moved on from Philadelphia to New York to play the Mets, Flood's trial was concurrently proceeding in Gotham. As a friendly gesture, Gibson left tickets for him in case he wanted to attend the Cards' games in Shea Stadium.

In the Manhattan courtroom, Jackie Robinson, Satchel Paige, and Hank Greenberg were among the baseball luminaries from past eras who appeared in the gallery in support of Flood's case, as Bowie Kuhn, broadcaster and former Cardinals catcher Joe Garagiola, and others took the stand in defense of baseball. When Greenberg was called to testify, the former Tigers star charged that the reserve clause was "antiquated and obsolete" and recommended that baseball rid itself of it immediately. When Robinson spoke, he said that "anything that is one-sided in our society is wrong, and the reserve clause is one-sided in favor of the owners. It should be modified to give the player some control over his destiny." Marvin Miller also testified for Flood, describing his personal history of trying to renegotiate the reserve clause with the owners. When Flood finally took the stand, he was ordered by Judge Cooper to speak up so as to be heard, as the former player often sank his chin and mumbled as he referred to one of his baseball cards to cite his statistics over the years. Flood had retained Arthur Goldberg as his counsel (along with St. Louis attorney Allan Zerman and others), who listed an impressive résumé that included being an ambassador to the United Nations, a current candidate for the governorship of New York, and a United States Supreme Court justice—the latter place of which was where the fight was expected to ultimately end. "Whatever [Judge Cooper] decides, the losing side will appeal, and it may be two years before the appeals reach the Supreme Court," reported Leonard Koppett, covering the trial for the *Sporting News*. Indeed, it would be several weeks before any initial rulings were even made.

Ironically, as the testimony was taking place, Flood's company back in St. Louis—Curt Flood Associates—was being sued in U.S. District Court for $67,975 by Delmar Printing Company of Charlotte and by Midwest School Pictures for $150,000 for lack of cooperation on photo-finishing services.

Flood and the Redbirds were indeed missing each other, as the Cardinals were three games under .500 at 21-24, struggling to stay in the Eastern Division race. Such was the plight of the Oakland A's over in the American League West, trailing the front-running Minnesota Twins by eight games. But on May 28, the A's received a game-winning hit from new second baseman Tony LaRussa that gave them life. "LaRussa has done the job for us," Oakland manager John McNamara said after the game. "He's getting some base hits. We really brought LaRussa up [from the minors] for his fielding." Before 1970 LaRussa had played in only forty-seven games over the past three Major League seasons, but was now looking to claim the A's second base job on a permanent basis.

While the recuperating Shannon was showing an ability to play once again, the coaching staff was uncertain as to his durability at this point. Thus, Schoendienst decided it was Torre's turn to try third base—a position he had not played since his high school days twelve years prior. His availability for third came about as the result of Ted Simmons's return to the team at the end of May after a five-month military tour. Simmons would not turn twenty-one until August 9, but was nonetheless set to take over the regular catching duties after getting fifty-one at-bats worth of work (for a .371 average) at Tulsa. He assumed the role behind the plate for good on the thirtieth, a month after his wedding to the former Maryanne Ellison. Although most had always figured Simmons's defensive skills would need to catch up to his bat, he began his permanent stay in the big leagues with a surprising bang on the glove-work side of the game. In his first start against the Dodgers in Busch Stadium, Simmons gunned down two of the most noted Los Angeles speedsters trying to steal in Willie Davis and Willie Crawford. The next day, he (and the Busch crowd) was shocked when he caught the greatest Dodger base pilferer of them all in Maury Wills. There was, however, much more for the young receiver to learn, for throwing runners out stealing is hardly the extent of a catcher's defensive responsibilities. Despite the young player's potential, all were not happy with his initial approach in handling the pitchers. Gibson, for one, simply missed his old familiar confidant behind the dish in McCarver, and at first had difficulty in dealing with the young Simmons. "It was like the first day of school all over again," the pitcher complained—albeit understandably with Simmons's inexperience—about the rookie's first few attempts to manage a ball game on the field. "He had no clue about what I was trying to accomplish out there."

Years later Gibson would snicker in looking back on 1970 as he was getting to know Simmons. "I had to shake him off the first five or six pitches. Finally he called time, ran out to the mound, and said, 'Are you trying to give me a hard time?' I said, 'Ted, I'm trying to win the ballgame. You're just sitting back there putting fingers down." But with guidance from Torre (who would continue to make occasional appearances at catcher as well), Simmons would quickly get in tune with Gibby. And after a one-for-nine start at the plate, Ted's bat would come around as well—for over the next five games in early June he would go ten for seventeen, including his first big league home run on the seventh, and in doing so post a .423 average by that date.

It was during Simmons's emergence as the Cardinals' everyday catcher in early to mid-June (as well as the arrival at the club of rookie pitchers Al Hrabosky and Jerry Reuss from the minors and the military, respectively) that Flood's trial was winding down in New York, having been litigated for five weeks. A total of twenty-one witnesses had produced more than two thousand pages of testimony—including that of John Clark, a noted economist called to the stand by Major League Baseball and the team owners whose research showed a whopping 48 percent increase in the average player salary over the past five seasons. And on the day before the testimony ended, a new collective bargaining agreement was struck between the owners and the Players' Association, securing a three-year deal (effective retroactively from January 1 and running through December 31, 1972). It was, in essence, a compromise, with the players winning their sought increases in minimum salary and spring training travel expenses, as well as securing thirty days' pay for a player cut in spring training and sixty days' pay for a player cut during the regular season, but losing in their effort to have the 162-game schedule reduced. The decision on Flood's case, however, would not be completed until August.

With the Cardinals starting the day's play on June 22 a game under .500 at 31-32 in fourth place, they were nonetheless only four and a half games behind the Cubs in the tight National League East race. The elements had yet to come together to put the team over the top, and with Simmons getting more comfortable each day, Devine and Schoendienst felt that one more move might make the difference. To this end, summoned to the mound to start the first game of a doubleheader that day in Pittsburgh was Reuss, his first appearance of the year after fulfilling his own six-month military obligation. When Cookie Rojas was traded to the Kansas City Royals on June 13 to create an available roster spot, Devine and Toomey were struggling to choose between Reuss and Hrabosky—both relatively unproven commodities at this time—to take his place. Hrabosky, who had put up a 5-1 record at Little Rock, was selected. While envisioned initially as a starting replacement for the ailing Nelson Briles (suffering from a pulled hamstring), Hrabosky was immediately effective out of the bull pen—making him, Carlton, and fellow reliever Billy McCool the only left-handers on the pitching roster. Hrabosky had been born in Oakland but was raised near Anaheim and had worked at Disneyland while pitching for Fullerton Junior College. He had actually shown a greater passion for football than baseball in high school, but would receive twenty-five thousand dollars as the Cards' first-round pick in the January phase of the 1969 draft (later, in the June phase of that same year, the Cardinals also drafted a pair of young infielders named Bill Madlock and Russell "Bucky" Dent—but neither would sign with the team). Issued the jersey number 39 when coming to the Cardinals, Hrabosky only said, "I just hope I'm around longer than the man who used to wear it." He was speaking in reference to fellow pitcher Culver, who despite winning the home opener back in April had seen his ERA balloon to 4.61 and was thus dealt to Houston for reserve outfielder Jim Beauchamp.

As it turned out, number 39 would belong to the irascible little left-hander for many years. "Hrabosky has a good fastball and effective curve," reported the Cardinals' chief scout, Joe Monahan, upon the southpaw's arrival in the big leagues. Then, he made a point to add, "The most important thing about him is that he's a battler."

But while Hrabosky was soon seen as a natural coming out of the bull pen, the need still existed for another frontline starter. Thus, Reuss was soon added as well when Briles was officially put on the disabled list. It was the opportunity for which Reuss and Cardinal followers had long yearned, wishing to see what the talented, locally raised left-hander from Ritenour could do on a regular basis in the rotation. When Reuss joined the team at O'Hare Airport in Chicago for the flight to Pittsburgh, he took a seat on the plane next to Torre—who cruelly informed him that the person who had previously sat in that very seat (Briles) had won one game on the year and blown out his arm. But Reuss, who was a few months older than Simmons in turning twenty-one just three days earlier, would be undaunted for his 1970 debut. Sauntering to the mound in venerable Forbes Field, he rolled through the frightening names in Danny Murtaugh's batting order with stunning ease. His teammates would score five runs for him in the top of the second inning—just moments before the bottom half of that frame, in which he would freeze Roberto Clemente, Al Oliver, and Bob Robertson, fanning all three imposing hitters on called-third strikes. Reuss went on to weave a complete-game, seven-strikeout performance, a 6–1 victory over the Pirates that raised the Cards to the .500 mark for the first time since May 28. With Reuss apparently ready to join Gibson and Carlton as a regular in the rotation, it seemed imperative that the other promising young starter, Mike Torrez, continue to develop in the absence of Briles, Washburn, and Hughes, men who had quickly fallen from memory after being key components of the recent pennant-winning years. However, after an impressive 10-4 record in his first full big league season in 1969, Torrez would never again reach double digits in victories in a Cardinal uniform.

The win by Reuss was also one of the final games at old Forbes. After the Cardinals would leave town in a few days, the Cubs would play the last contest in the quaint stadium adjacent to Schenley Park and east of the downtown area on June 28. As soon as Santo grounded out to end a 3–2 Pirate win, a throng of souvenir seekers stormed the field, led by a pack of young boys who ignored the public address announcer's warning of electrocution as they climbed to the top of the scoreboard to rip down the placard numbers. The same group of boys then returned to the grandstand, happily assisting ladies seeking their own mementos by ripping the box seats right out from their rusting bolts and proudly presenting them. Club officials watched angrily from above, considering the unfolding scene to be disrespectful of the place that had been home to Pittsburgh professional baseball since 1909. From a visiting team's perspective, it was good riddance; many of the veteran Cardinals wept no tears about the departure of the old yard in the Steel City. "I'm not sorry to see the park go," said McCool, who had pitched in the National League since 1964. "I wish I put a bomb under it." Claiming that torn cartilage in his knee was caused by a divot in the Forbes turf, McCool was not the only St. Louis player who had wanted to be the one to swing the ax. "Forbes Field was my worst park," added Torre. "I couldn't see the ball good there. Bad lights. Too many shadows. And the only time I broke a finger was there—I broke it when I took a throw from Felipe Alou in infield practice." Torre also recalled a night long ago at the dimly lit park when, while catching for the Braves, he could not see a knuckleball coming from Phil Niekro, and the pitch got by him for a passed ball to allow the Pirates to score the winning run in that particular game. The spacious pasture had also been the site of Lou Brock's first inside-the-park home run, and the second base area was the spot where a portable grandstand was once placed in 1932 so that Franklin Delano Roosevelt could make a presidential campaign speech.

As time for the old ball yard in Pittsburgh was winding down, writers in the press box at Forbes Field had been reminiscing about the notable hitting displays that had been seen there over the years. A recorded total of seventeen home runs had cleared the famous grandstand roof in the right-field corner in the sixty-one years and forty-seven hundred games in which Forbes was in use (the area also was the lone portion of the stadium where bleacher seats were located, with the center- and left-field areas left open for partial views of the stadium from Schenley Park). Six of those blasts had been accomplished by their most-feared contemporary, long-ball slugger Willie Stargell, in whose honor the roof had been named "Stargell's Stoop." His final such blow back in late April had snapped a one-for-twenty-seven slump he had experienced at the start of the season.

In time, the stadium would be razed and the space used for a new building at the University of Pittsburgh, where the old home plate remains encased in glass in its original position for viewing today. Soon, the new Three Rivers Stadium would open on July 16, 1970, at a final cost of fifty-five million dollars, a ballpark that stood imposingly on the riverbank across from downtown. The new stadium was located on a plot known as Exposition Park—the grounds on which the Pirates had previously played, strangely enough, before moving to Forbes in 1909. Despite the massive acreage and impressive view the new facility would encompass, Three Rivers actually held a smaller playing area for baseball than Forbes (as the new ballpark would have an outfield wall twenty-five feet closer to home plate in the power alleys and forty-seven feet closer to home plate than at Forbes Field). And by June 1971 only three home run balls would reach the upper deck in the new ballpark—and all three had been slugged by Stargell.

As with the opening of the other new ballparks of the era, various temporary inconveniences were experienced in Pittsburgh—such as the sixteen-month labor struggle in getting parking lots and garages constructed near the stadium. Until this impasse was resolved, most of the fans had to walk across the bridges from downtown or take ferry boats to get to the games, as no spots were initially available adjacent to the building. Later, walking or boating to the game would instead become recreational options as the construction problem was relieved.

While Reuss kept the Pirates' powerful lineup in check that particular day in Pittsburgh, he would lose his next decision in bowing to a 5–0 shutout at the hands of Ferguson Jenkins and the Cubs in Busch Stadium on July 1, which snapped a tortuous twelve-game losing streak for Chicago—one shy of the club record and one that seemed to have sent Leo Durocher's team into yet another apparent collapse. When the streak had begun on June 22, the Cubs were four and a half games in front in the National League East; by the streak's end with their beating of Reuss, they were now the same margin *off* the lead. Reuss, meanwhile, would not be victorious again until July 30, but yet had proved he had the "stuff" to remain at the Major League level. Being such young rookies, he and Simmons also had to continue to learn the milieu of being part of a Major League team on a day-to-day basis. As an example, when Reuss missed a sign while batting in one particular game, Gibson "fined" him five dollars (part of a locker room kangaroo court, with the money from such infractions going toward a team party at the end of the year). Dal Maxvill, offering to serve as counsel to Reuss as his "attorney," suggested an appeal—but no one knew what the appeal process was, so the decision stood.

West from Pittsburgh down the Ohio River, another new National League park had opened two weeks earlier on June 30 in the form of Riverfront Stadium in Cincinnati. It was cut in the same circular, multipurpose design as Busch and Three Rivers (and, by the beginning of the 1971 season, Veterans Stadium in Philadelphia as well). The Atlanta Braves ruined the event for the Reds and their excited Cincinnati fans by beating the home club 8–2, as Hank Aaron homered in the first inning off Jim McGlothlin—the second safe hit ever in the new yard in following teammate Felix Millan, who had singled in front of him. "It looks like I've found a park I can hit in," Aaron said after the game. "I like the Reds' new park—but then, of course, I may think differently tomorrow." Like in Pittsburgh, stadium workers in Cincinnati were still fine-tuning the system, such as the operation of the scoreboard (the two Atlanta tallies from Aaron's homer at first failed to register—a prelude of a long evening of more graphical errors, cold hot dogs from gas lines not properly broken in, and other minor inconveniences).

Four years later in the same stadium, Aaron would belt an even more memorable home run. But in two weeks, Riverfront Stadium would see a full array of celebrities in hosting the Major League Baseball All-Star Game on July 14, which marked the first time in thirteen years that fan voting had decided the starters. Previously, the players from each league had made the choices—and difficulties were present in this process at various ballparks as well, as many notable players (such as current National League batting leader Rico Carty) had been left off the ballots distributed to fans at the games. When the game arrived, it was a matchup that featured a classic beginning with Tom Seaver facing Jim Palmer off on the mound and finished with a classic ending with Pete Rose bowling over Cleveland catcher Ray Fosse at home plate for the win—the eighth victory in a row for the National League in the annual affair. The collision would give Fosse a shoulder injury that, he claimed, would ultimately curtail his career, as some questioned Rose's fervor in a game that did not count in the standings. Rose, however, was unapologetic, confirming that he played hard no matter the situation. And while the press attempted to concoct some sort of personal antipathy between Rose and Fosse as a cause of the event, all were surprised to learn that Fosse and his fellow All-Star Cleveland teammate, pitcher Sam McDowell, had actually spent the previous evening at Rose's home in Cincinnati, laughing and sharing stories from their particular associations—long before interleague play became a reality in the majors—into the early hours of the morning of the fourteenth. Rose, however, would feel some ill-effects from the collision as well, as a bruised leg muscle from the incident would cause him to miss the first-ever game at Riverfront's "cousin" at Three Rivers in Pittsburgh. The Reds were the visiting team in the opening of that new park two days later on the sixteenth, as Pie Traynor, the Hall of Fame third baseman for the Pirates, got things started that evening by throwing out the first pitch.

The fervent Rose counted everything—especially his base hits—and usually knew all of his statistics by heart. "Ty Cobb holds the record for the most years getting 200 or more hits—nine," he would randomly point out a few months later before the start of the 1971 season. "Wouldn't it be something to break a record set by him?"

One difference among the new stadiums in St. Louis, Pittsburgh, Philadelphia, and Cincinnati is that the latter three, unlike Busch, would each have an artificial surface from their inceptions. As usual, the heat of the infamous St. Louis summer was gripping the city in mid-1970, and the Cardinals, in playing their first season on Astroturf, were only now discovering the discomfort of a relentless sun beating down on the synthetic field. "The next time we have a day game," Maxvill suggested to the readers of the *Post-Dispatch* in July, "watch the outfielders. They'll keep lifting their feet and hopping around." Maxvill was the players' representative on a new ad hoc group formed by Kuhn, called the "Artificial Turf Committee," which also included Devine and which would examine the assets and liabilities of the various surfaces over time. Maxvill's point was understandable, for while standing on the rug was perfectly comfortable during night games, one could literally see the heat rising during afternoon contests at Busch from the floor of the stadium (additionally, pitchers from both the Cardinals and visiting clubs were complaining that the completion of their necessary running drills on the turf was hurting their knees). Some were even projecting that the additional heat rising from the carpet would aid the travel of balls hit in the air. Officials from the turf's manufacturer, Monsanto, quickly pointed out that the official city temperature in the downtown area was typically four to six degrees hotter than other parts of St. Louis, which added to the effect that some thought was being caused by the Astroturf. Nonetheless, it caused one to wonder how Casey Stengel may have further accentuated his comments about the park's "holding the heat well" at the 1966 All-Star Game—even when the ballpark held cooler grass beneath the toes. And when Dick Allen first came into contact with the turf back in early April, he had uttered one of his most memorable phrases. "If a horse can't eat it," legend had Allen stating, "I don't want to play on it."

Completing the first overhaul of the five-year-old stadium, the Civic Center Redevelopment Corporation would complete its renovation of the ballpark's public address system by the end of May 1971, two years in the planning, which greatly improved the audibility of the stadium announcer in the upper deck and bleacher sections.

One of his fellow managers with whom Stengel had to battle back in the 1930s—former Gas House leader Frankie Frisch—had been serving as a guest analyst on some of the Cardinals' television broadcasts in 1970, and Frankie was getting ready to travel from his current home in Rhode Island to New York to help Casey celebrate his eightieth birthday at a party on July 30. During one of the broadcasts, Frisch was asked what he thought about Astroturf and the early complaints that players were lodging. He responded by saying that if the players felt that performing on it was so intolerable, they should consider the days when two big league teams played in the same ballpark in St. Louis—the Browns and the Cardinals—allowing the grounds crew at the old yard no time for maintenance, and thus leaving the playing surface granite hard. "The players should be happy to play this game on any field," he told the *Post-Dispatch*. "What if they had to play on fields like our old Sportsman's Park in St. Louis? The field there would be beautiful when the season opened, but two weeks later it was like a rockpile. They could water the field all day and the ground still would never get soft."

Able to pitch on all types of terrain, Gibson by July had doused any further talk of his supposed demise. He had reached his tenth victory of the year *even nine games earlier on the schedule* than in the unforgettable season of 1968, having rebounded from his poor start to the year to win ten straight decisions by July 5.

The following day, however, he and the rest of the team would go into a severe tailspin, losing seventeen of their next nineteen games. The slump was launched by an eight-game losing streak that included a four-game sweep at the hands of the Pirates in Busch Stadium that ended before the All-Star break on the twelfth, the final games for Pittsburgh on the road before opening their new ballpark. And on the night of the Three Rivers inaugural on the sixteenth, the Cardinals would post their longest losing streak in thirteen years, dropping their eighth in a row in bowing in Busch Stadium to the Braves and pitcher Pat Jarvis.

By the time the month ended, the Redbirds would submit an 8-21 record during July 1970. It was their worst month statistically in a quarter century, and perhaps the team's worst overall month ever, sending them to last place and thirteen games behind the lead. When they finally picked up another victory on the twenty-seventh after dropping yet another eight straight, Busch quickly said in defense of his middle management, "We should not lose sight of the fact that neither Bing nor Red nor his coaches can pitch, field, hit, or run for the players." Once again, tempers were flaring and player misbehavior was becoming more common, as even the mild-mannered Javier was suspended three games and fined $150 by the National League office for pushing an umpire. Even Javier and Maxvill, who had formed the impenetrable defensive middle of the infield on a pennant winner just two years ago, now incurred the wrath of Broeg's normally gentle pen. "The infield is probably the poorest the Cardinals have fielded since Frankie Frisch and Leo Durocher left the lineup at the same time," he wrote on July 13, the morning after the team had stranded thirteen runners in a 7–6 extra-inning loss to former teammate Dave Giusti (who was now 7-0 himself) and the Pirates. Before they would hit the bottom of the list in just a few more days, Broeg went on to lament the Cards' fourth-place standing in the Eastern Division at that particular time. "Chances are, the Redbirds are already dead birds in the 1970 race because it's extremely tough to sustain a long winning stretch when you're chasing three teams." Cardenal was doing a decent job in center field, but the absence of Flood had finally, after many years, unmasked the true defensive struggles of Brock in left. Brock, in recently passing his thirty-first birthday, had also recently passed the four-hundred mark in stolen bases in his career. But by the middle of the month, Cardenal was ahead of him for the team lead in that category, seventeen to sixteen—a sure sign to many that the glory days of the organization from the 1960s were now truly gone. With Cardenal having swiped seventy-six bases for Cleveland over the past two years, it seemed as if the base-runner baton in St. Louis was now being finally handed off by Brock. "Jose ought to lead the league in steals," Lou himself admitted, "if he keeps hitting the way he has, and if he keeps his strikeout total down. . . . Jose has a sneaky style, and he knows how to gamble with those leadoffs."

Yet despite the excitement that Cardenal, Allen, and the other newcomers were providing, it did not add up to victories in that horrid midyear stretch of 1970. Save for Gibson, the comprehensive pitching numbers were especially troubling. Carlton, as the most prominent example of the ineptitude, was leading the league in losses (fourteen) and did not win in July until the month's final day. And pessimism about the club's talent level was running so rampant, in fact, that some were predicting that a baseball "Dark Age" was about to be cast over St. Louis—at least according to Ed Wilks in his *Post-Dispatch* column on July 29. "How's this grab you: the Cardinals won't have a winner again for three, four, or maybe even five years," he declared. Gibson, too, decided it was the worst he had ever seen the ball club perform in his time in a St. Louis uniform. Willing to try anything to alter the course, Gibson even experimented with a knuckleball in July for the first time in his career. "We were so bad [as he recollected back to 1970] that I was booed during a game in which the Giants scored nine runs against me in the first inning," Gibson recalled in his autobiography (although no such game is on record anywhere during the 1970 season). Regardless of when the game had taken place of which he was thinking, it was clear in his mind *where* it had taken place. "It was the first time I had ever been booed in St. Louis." As he made his way to the dugout, Gibson still graciously tipped his cap to the fans, who perhaps then realized what they were doing, and to whom they were doing it. "They changed to cheers," he continued, "but that didn't wash the echo out of my ears. It stung badly." The myriad of moves made in the past two years had not only dissembled the pennant-winning teams, but the sum total of the replacements had not amounted to anything recognizable as a regular unit—let alone an effective one. By mid-July, Schoendienst had already used forty-seven different lineups through eighty-eight games.

Hope was provided in the win by Carlton on the final day of the month, snapping his own personal drought, which had been preceded by another victory by Reuss on July 30. And then, almost instantly, the two would launch a surge in which the team would suddenly win twelve of its next fourteen, instantly pushing them back into the divisional race. By the culmination of this run, Reuss left no doubt in establishing himself as a solid starter, with his most impressive outing to come at the end of the month in a two-hit shutout against Walter Alston's Los Angeles men in Dodger Stadium.

The roller-coaster season of 1970, however, would soon dip downward once again. Despite the quick ascension of Reuss to a prominent role on the team, another St. Louis native on the Cardinals' roster just as quickly found himself at the very end of his playing days just as the team was climbing back into pennant contention.

After dropping two games as part of the team's July slump, Gibson would right himself yet again from a second round of his 1970 personal doldrums to post a string of seven straight wins starting on July 28. In another sultry summer night down by the river on August 12, Gibson became the first pitcher to record two hundred strikeouts in eight separate seasons in beating San Diego 5–4—and do so in pitching *all fourteen innings of the affair.* August would indeed be the second resurgence on the year for the ace, in which Gibson would post a 6-0 record and a 1.68 ERA. He was aided by two hits off the bat of Mike Shannon, who after the game was complaining of sudden discomfort that felt frighteningly similar to his early-season bout with nephritis.

Shortly after returning to the hospital, Shannon was then forced to announce his retirement, being limited to a total of just fifty-five games in his final season. Immediately, he was offered a front-office job with the team, which he accepted.

Adding to the irony of the evening was that Gibson set the record by striking out another St. Louis product, Nate Colbert, in the second inning. Colbert is perhaps best known for hitting five home runs in a doubleheader, long after he had personally witnessed Musial perform the same feat in Sportsman's Park when Colbert was a child. Later in the evening, Colbert would touch Gibson for a homer as well.

And earlier that same afternoon, while Shannon was in the Busch Stadium locker room not knowing he was dressing for his final game as a Cardinal, his former teammate was also learning of the fate of his own future in the game. In New York, Curt Flood listened intently but disappointingly to the face that had become so familiar to him, Judge Cooper. Cooper had decided to uphold the legitimacy of baseball's reserve clause, which denied Flood's suit for free agency and, along with the immediate retirement of Shannon, was yet another sign that the great Cardinal teams of the 1960s were disappearing from view. In giving a summation to his full forty-seven-page decision, Cooper stated that "clearly, the preponderance of credible proof does not favor elimination of the reserve clause. . . . [It] is reasonable and necessary to preserve the integrity of the game, maintain balanced competition and fan interest and encourage continued investment in player development." Kuhn, meanwhile, displayed clear support in public for Cooper's edict, but also held out hope that Flood would somewhere, somehow, resume his Major League career. Miffed but undaunted by the developments, Flood and his attorneys promised to appeal—all the way to the United States Supreme Court if necessary. But an unsympathetic

Bob Broeg had read, heard, and seen enough of the maverick outfielder, as evidenced by the headline of his column two days later. "$100,000 a Year—What a Way to Be Mistreated," mocked the top of a page within the *Post-Dispatch* sports section on August 14. Many fans in St. Louis were also tiring of Flood's ongoing debacle, the former of whom appeared more interested in welcoming and honoring Willie Mays to St. Louis for his recent feat on the night that Broeg's article was released. Back on July 18, Mays had collected his 3,000th career hit, and the legendary Giant received applause rarely reserved for a visiting player in Busch Stadium. On a less celebrated note in that same game, his teammate Ron Hunt also broke Frank Robinson's National League record for being hit by pitch, as Hunt was plunked for the 119th time.

Rounding Labor Day, September 7, and heading into the final month of the season, the Cardinals unfortunately discovered that their surge in August could not overcome their horrendous July. The National League East would become a three-team race, with the Pirates leading the Mets by one game and the Cubs by two after games played on the holiday, with the Cards nine and a half back (on September 8, the Cardinals closed out yet another old National League ballpark, playing their final game in old Connie Mack Stadium in Philadelphia—and as a fitting tribute to the "good" old days, Allen angered his Philadelphia tormentors once again with an eighth-inning home run against his former team, his 34th of the year). Not wishing to repeat the collapse of 1969, Chicago manager Durocher chose to give days off to certain starting players on the Cubs—even Billy Williams, who would sit out a game on September 3, marking the first time in 1,117 contests he had done so, long ago having broken Musial's former National League record of 895. "I think the pennant means more to Billy and the club than any kind of a streak," Durocher reasoned. Leo soon took much abuse from the fans for ending the record—most coming from the same Bleacher Bums, ironically, who criticized him for supposedly "wearing out" his players the summer before. "If this helps him and helps us," Durocher concluded, "that's what counts." Williams, who consulted with Durocher before the game about taking a rest, had fully agreed to do so. "Sometimes a player can get so wrapped up in record streaks it hurts his club," he added in an understanding tone. From the rival city down the road in St. Louis, Broeg could not comprehend why his pen-scratching brethren in Chicago kept giving Durocher a hard time. "A strange phenomenon is the typewriter schizophrenia of Chicago sports writers. They want very much for the Cubs to win a pennant, yet hate like heck for Leo Durocher to be the manager of the moment." At sixty-five, Durocher was already receiving the maximum pension amount from Major League Baseball at the time—$1,945 a month—but was as fiery with the press, his players, and umpires as he had ever been, and showing no signs of wishing to retire.

Despite Durocher's youthful-like enthusiasm, a 9–2 loss to the Cardinals on September 17—the Cubs' home finale of the year in Wrigley Field—seem to take the rest of the life out of the team, as his pitchers were pounded for twenty-two hits on the Thursday before ABC Sports was getting ready to debut its new series titled *Monday Night Football*. In order to stay in the race (still positioned at two games behind the Pirates by the seventeenth), the Cubs would need to overcome the difference while closing the season with a fourteen-game, four-city road trip. Meanwhile, the skeptical and perennially jilted Chicago fans once again made plans for October that did not include watching postseason baseball.

It had been another grand year for the Cubs' Williams, as his smooth left-handed swing was compared by many Cardinal fans of Vic Davalillo, the Venezuelan-born outfielder who recently arrived at St. Louis in 1969. Davalillo had been a regular for several seasons in the American League, but had been relegated to spot duty with the Cardinals. Arriving in the United States in 1958 without being able to speak a word of English, the tiny five-foot-seven Davalillo quickly became a local favorite in Cleveland, signing autographs for fans every day and carrying candy in the pockets of his uniform pants that he happily distributed to children at the ball game as well. "Vic's a thinking-type hitter," praised batting coach Dick Sisler, "who has applied everything he learned over the years." In addition to a steady bat for the Indians, Davalillo had also been a Gold Glove–winning outfielder in 1965. Keeping himself in fine shape over the years, he was famous for regular intake of his "Davalillo Cocktail," a training beverage in which he would mix orange juice, milk, and egg yolk in a blender.

Davalillo also enjoyed other types of cocktails as well, and one episode of libation during the Cardinals' stay in Chicago in September led to a favorite story among the players. On the afternoon of Sunday, September 13, the Cardinals were playing the Mets in New York while the running of the New York City Marathon was taking place (the course, however, did not go near Shea Stadium, for unlike in modern times—in which the race travels through all five boroughs of the city—the first running of the marathon would stay within the area of Central Park). When the Cards departed La Guardia Airport that evening, the players looked forward to the off-day on Monday in advance of the series with the Cubs at Wrigley Field. With no responsibilities until Tuesday afternoon, the fifteenth, Davalillo was planning to make a visit to the renowned Rush Street area of Chicago, one of the famed entertainment districts on the north side of downtown. After partying well into the morning hours of Tuesday, Davalillo was barely able to get himself to Wrigley, still being nearly passed out from drunkenness as game time approached. A saving grace for Davalillo, he figured, was that he was rarely granted a place in the starting lineup by Schoendienst, and instead was more often utilized as a late-inning pinch hitter in certain situations. After straining to get into his uniform and make his way to the field, he went down the right-field line to hide on the bull pen bench. Davalillo was in such bad shape that his teammates had to carry him to the destination and disguise him underneath numerous warm-up jackets where the relief pitchers normally sat. There they propped him upright and held him in place by the weight of two teammates sandwiched on either side of him, similar to the antics in the movie *Weekend at Bernie's*. And of course, one of those crucial situations arose later in the game for Schoendienst to summon Davalillo as a pinch hitter, but he was nowhere to be found in the dugout when the Cardinals started batting in the top of the eighth. Sisler was one of the few who were aware of the player's condition and figured he had better be honest with the manager. After pausing a moment, he told Red, "You don't want Davalillo." Confused by Sisler's response, Red only insisted further. Thus, Davalillo was next seen stumbling his way down from the bull pen. He grabbed a random bat from the rack in the dugout without even looking at it, got into the batter's box, and with the first offering from Cubs pitcher Ken Holtzman took a violent, erratic swing. Davalillo spun in a complete circle and landed flat on his back, having started laughing in an inebriated stupor even before Holtzman had begun his windup. "*I told you* you didn't want Davalillo," Sisler repeated to Red as the second pitch was on its way to the plate. Davalillo promptly struck out and stopped laughing as he passed by the angry manager to the bench.

Yet over the course of the season, he would be sober enough to produce twenty-four pinch hits—which also produced twenty RBIs, five more than all Cardinal pinch hitters had mustered in all of 1969. The pinch-hit total also broke the existing National League record at the time (a record once held by Schoendienst, ironically), tied the Major League mark of Dave Philley, and remains a Cardinals' team standard to this day. It could have easily been etched in the records books that Davalillo actually *broke* Philley's Major League record; however, a pinch hit previously credited to him in 1970 had been later taken away by the official scorer. Back on June 7 when the Cardinals played the Padres at Busch Stadium, Davalillo posted two singles in the seventh inning—the first time in a pinch-hitting role for Gibson. When the Cards batted around the order in scoring seven runs in the inning, Davalillo's spot came up once again. The scorer decided that since Davalillo was now hitting in his own place for his second appearance in the inning—not Gibson's any longer—the second single he smacked would not count as a pinch hit.

Despite his jocularity, Davalillo also provided an extra dose of veteran stability to the club. A couple weeks earlier in San Francisco, he had diffused a locker room fight between Simmons and Carl Taylor, as Taylor misinterpreted Simmons's late arrival to Candlestick Park one day as a lack of concern for the team, as the two had nearly come to blows before Davalillo intervened. Simmons, who was juggling his off-days from baseball with army training duty, was surprised by the attack, as he had not been given a chance by the presumptuous Taylor to explain that the wake-up call system at the team's hotel had failed to arouse him that morning.

Schoendienst had been seeking some veteran leadership from Dick Allen as well, and the generally compliant slugger had been a pleasant surprise to all in St. Louis for most of the summer. As imagined he would, he had provided the imposing power bat in the Cardinals' lineup and had kept his average consistently in the .280s and .290s throughout the majority of the season. Through August, there was even talk resurfacing, as Broeg had earlier suggested, of Allen breaking Mize's team home run record for a season. However, late in that month, Allen suddenly came up lame with a pulled hamstring. At first he assured the fans it would not hinder him for very long. "What's that pirate's name—Captain Long John Silver?" he proposed in looking at things another way. "If I have to, I'll get out there on a *wooden leg.*" Even so, he would spend the next couple of weeks on the bench, with Schoendienst hesitant to even use him as a pinch hitter. The manager feared that the injury would be worsened by a sudden burst late in a cool evening, after Allen had sat cold on the bench the entire game. After returning to sock that homer in the final Connie Mack Stadium game in Philadelphia back on September 8, Allen then played in two more contests in Pittsburgh (in the midst of a long road trip) in which he reinjured the leg. And when the Cardinals got ready to return home a week later, Allen said he wanted to go back to Philadelphia, the place where he wished to have the treatment done on the hamstring. Instead, Devine and Schoendienst insisted that he accompany the team back to St. Louis and have the therapy completed there, in the presence of the team physicians. Privately, they were actually fearing that Allen would disappear to the racehorse tracks near Philly— something he was known to do—and thus, they wished to keep a close eye on him. In any event, the management could not corral him. Allen would fall off the face of the earth once again, not appearing in any games for the final three weeks of the season, a stretch of time in which few knew of his actual whereabouts. Very late in the season, Allen insisted on playing in one particular game at Philadelphia; his wife phoned Schoendienst and asked him not to put him in, but Allen convinced Red, and he played the game drunk—getting a homer, single, and a walk before Schoendienst took him out.

When Allen effectively vanished on September 11, the Cardinals were still mathematically in the division race at eight and a half games back. In the end, the team could not overcome his disappearance or its downturn in July, as it skidded into the finish line with a final record of 76-86 at the close of play on the first of October. The 76 wins left them 13 games out of first place— ultimately, the same gulf at which they found themselves after their horrid

July stretch—and was the lowest victory total for the team since the National League had gone to the 162-game schedule. The Pirates, in taking the National League Eastern Division, had done so by winning a mere 89 games, having left the door open so many times through which the Cardinals and other clubs could not mount a charge.

Beyond the disappointment shone the team's two brightest stars, who were able to add vibrant chapters to their storied careers. Brock, at thirty-one, had managed to set a Major League record with his sixth straight year of at least fifty steals and reached the two-hundred-hit mark for the third time in his career. Gibson (about to turn thirty-five by the end of the year) was the lone bright spot on the disappointing pitching staff, showing signs of his dominant 1968 campaign from two years prior with another remarkable year, listing a long sheet of accomplishments:

- He posted twenty-three wins in claiming his second Cy Young Award, pulling away from a tie with Dizzy Dean to become the first Cardinal pitcher with five twenty-win seasons (a total that likely would have been six by this time, had he not broken his leg in mid-1967—as would have Dean, interestingly, had Dizzy not endured a broken toe in 1937 himself).

- If Gibson could have beaten the Pirates in his last start on September 29, he would have been victorious against every team in the league in 1970—and that win would have equaled Dean's total of twenty-four in 1936, the most by a Cardinal since then.

- Gibson's forty-five career shutouts had him currently tied with Juan Marichal for the most among active pitchers.

- His 274 strikeouts were the most in Cardinal history in one season.

- He permitted only 13 home runs in nearly three hundred innings of work.

- He won the Gold Glove for the pitcher's position for the fifth year in a row.

- From the offensive side, he finished the year with a batting average of .303, having produced a .400 mark as late as July 7. In doing so, Gibson became the last pitcher to bat .300 and win twenty games in the same season.

His efforts, however, could not overcome the failures of the rest of the starting rotation, despite the fact it had given up the fewest home runs (102) in the National League and had successfully held down the star hitters of certain teams (Mays, for example, batted only .135 against St. Louis in 1970). Carlton, unable to build on his breakout year of 1969, could never rise from his early-season contract squabbles and wound up leading the National League in losses with nineteen—the most by a Cardinals pitcher in fifteen years. "Steve Carlton spent his holdout trimming trees at his father's home," Ed Wilks pondered in retrospect about the impediments back in March. "As it turned out, the Cardinal lefthander cut off the branch he was sitting on." Carlton blamed much of his woes on what he called his new "made-in-Japan" slider, a pitch he developed while the team was touring that country after the 1968 season and that he finally ditched in the last month of 1970. Instead, Carlton announced, he would focus on his curve as his primary breaking pitch in the future. The injury-riddled Nelson Briles had an ERA over 6.00, while the majority of the remainder of the starts fell on the shoulders of the youngsters Reuss and Torrez. Furthermore, no single reliever in the bull pen would reach double figures in saves, as Chuck Taylor led the way with eight (the traded Dave Giusti, meanwhile, had won nine games for the Pirates, saved twenty-six more, and had finished sixth in the National League Most Valuable Player voting). As Gibson remembered, "For a change, our offense was actually better than our defense in 1970."

Still, the job of batting coach Sisler would not be saved. Both he and Schoendienst's other longtime aide, pitching coach Billy Muffett, were shown the door the same day (September 29) that Red received a one-year contract extension at a rate of fifty thousand dollars, while Kissell and Benson were retained (in addition to bull pen coach Bob Milliken), with Ken Boyer joining the Major League coaching staff for 1971 as well. Muffett would be replaced by another former Cardinal relief pitcher, the forty-four-year-old and previous knuckle-baller Barney Schultz, who had spent the past four seasons as a mound tutor in the organization's Minor League system. Originally, the famous lefty Warren Spahn had been the first choice for the job but declined, instead deciding to keep his managerial post with the Tulsa farm club, which was close to his large cattle farm and in the hopes of holding out for a shot as a manager in the big leagues down the road.

As for the recently retired Boyer (who had played his final big league season with the Dodgers in 1969), the longtime Cardinal third baseman had always been viewed as a natural choice for a coaching position. "We had Ken in mind for the organization as soon as he was available after ending his playing career," Devine said about Ken's quick hiring to lead the Little Rock farm team in 1970. "He has impressed a lot of people with his work with young players." Added Schoendienst, "The young players at Arkansas liked Boyer. He'll have the same authority with the hitters that Sisler had."

With the exception of Gibson and Brock, proof now existed within the organization that there were no more sacred cows; the mystique of the pennants from the late 1960s would no longer count, as no job was safe. Maxvill, who had batted an anemic .175 in 1969, went into even further offensive infamy in 1970 by setting a National League record for the fewest hits in a season by a player participating in 150 games or more games. He had managed a total of 80 hits in 399 at-bats, landing him just over the .200 mark for the year. Since his defense was still superior to that of most shortstops in the league, he would be granted a reprieve and allowed to return as the Cardinals' regular at the position once again in 1971. And while Maxvill had survived another purge on the active-player roster, the dismissal of Muffett and Sisler—the product of clandestine meetings among Busch, Devine, and Schoendienst over the last three weeks of the season—proved that the executive committee was ready to make more bold moves to return the Cards to competitiveness for 1971. The next of these came only four days after the conclusion of the schedule, as another fallen star from another team would be brought in to save St. Louis.

In the midst of all the roster moves, Broeg decided that the general manager was not blameless in the team's 1970 breakdown. "Devine, whose adroit deals built the Cardinals into a championship contender, found himself in the same kind of slump as his field command and talent." Meanwhile, Schoendienst, who within a couple of months into the 1971 season would become the longest-tenured Cardinal manager in team history, was starting to feel the heat as well.

And Curt Flood was still nowhere to be found.

The face that launched over 3,000 strikeouts—the indomitable glare of Bob Gibson as he completes a pitch. *Courtesy of the National Baseball Hall of Fame Library, Cooperstown, New York.*

(*Above*) Red Schoendienst (at right, with former pitching coach Joe Becker) was a native of nearby Clinton County, Illinois, and already a devoted Cardinals man for three decades as the 1970s approached. *Courtesy of the National Baseball Hall of Fame Library, Cooperstown, New York.*

(*Opposite*) The desk of Cardinals general manager Bing Devine, a table from which the fortunes of the team would mostly ascend (and sometimes fall) from the late 1950s through the 1970s. *Courtesy of the National Baseball Hall of Fame Library, Cooperstown, New York.*

In the 1967 draft, the Cardinals selected Michigan schoolboy Ted Simmons with their first pick, seen as the heir to Tim McCarver at the catcher's position. *Courtesy of the National Baseball Hall of Fame Library, Cooperstown, New York.*

Following Simmons in the 1967 draft, St. Louis native Jerry Reuss quickly advanced from the campus of Ritenour High School through the Cardinals system to the major leagues. *Courtesy of the National Baseball Hall of Fame Library, Cooperstown, New York.*

(Opposite top) Cardinals' owner August A. Busch Jr. (left) meeting with National League president Warren Giles. By the 1970s, Busch had become frustrated with what he perceived as the greed and ungratefulness of many major-leaguers. *Courtesy of the National Baseball Hall of Fame Library, Cooperstown, New York.*

(Opposite bottom) Lou Brock steals another base in Busch Stadium while Philadelphia's Larry Bowa waits for the throw. *Courtesy of the National Baseball Hall of Fame Library, Cooperstown, New York.*

(Above) The talented Dick Allen, who while spending only one year in St. Louis was perhaps the most unpredictable Cardinals player since Dizzy Dean. *Courtesy of the National Baseball Hall of Fame Library, Cooperstown, New York.*

Hometown hero Mike Shannon, a prep football star who changed positions within the Cardinals for the good of the team before having his career cut short by illness. *Courtesy of the National Baseball Hall of Fame Library, Cooperstown, New York.*

"For the first two months of the season," Cardinals coach Ken Boyer said of 1971, "Joe Torre was as good a hitter as anyone I've watched." *Courtesy of the National Baseball Hall of Fame Library, Cooperstown, New York.*

Arnold McBride—better known as "Bake"—was a product of Westminster College outside St. Louis and would post a stellar rookie season in 1974. *Courtesy of the National Baseball Hall of Fame Library, Cooperstown, New York.*

By the mid-1970s, Al Hrabosky would develop into one of the dominant relief pitchers in the National League. *Courtesy of the National Baseball Hall of Fame Library, Cooperstown, New York.*

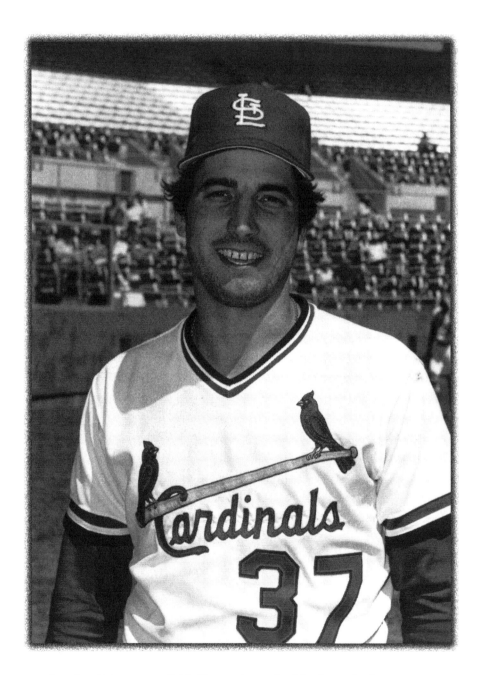

Late in 1974, a young Keith Hernandez arrived in the major leagues as a smooth-fielding, sharp-hitting first baseman. *Courtesy of the National Baseball Hall of Fame Library, Cooperstown, New York.*

Uncompromisingly focused and dedicated to his craft, Bob Gibson stated simply, "I owe the public one thing—a good performance." *Courtesy of the National Baseball Hall of Fame Library, Cooperstown, New York.*

5   "I'll Never Throw a No-Hitter"

After July [1971], I began to hold onto the wall after leaving the shower. I thought this was the kind of year you have once in your life, and I didn't want to slip and ruin it.

—Joe Torre

Part of Devine's plan to return the Cardinals to glory was to also return "small ball" as the team's offensive core and to discard the experiment of home run baseball in St. Louis. Thus, four days after the close of the 1970 regular season on October 5—but almost four weeks since he last appeared in a game for the Cards—Dick Allen was traded to the Los Angeles Dodgers for infielder Ted Sizemore and catcher Bob Stinson. Moving Allen was something that Broeg had accurately predicted and somewhat feared in his column just two days earlier. "If the strong man from Wampum, Pennsylvania is dealt for a middle-infield regular and perhaps bullpen strength," Broeg had forecast, "the Birds will be taking a calculated risk. . . . [C]an the Cards afford to give up Allen's power?" Still, the writer acknowledged the aging of the Cardinals' second base and shortstop positions as necessitating the deal. The arrival of Sizemore, coming off a .306 season in his second year as a Dodger starter, appeared to make Javier's numbered days dwindle in acceleration. Not helping Javier's own cause in this regard was that he was once again late to camp, not arriving until March 2. Moreover, looming larger within Javier's troubles was that he owed a significant amount of money to the IRS. "Uncle Sam says Julian owes $84,320 in back taxes," confirmed one national baseball publication in advance of the 1971 season.

With Allen packing his bags once again, Schoendienst was his usual thoughtful and philosophical self on the positives and negatives of the man. "He had a reputation of being a difficult player, but he played hard for me," Red assessed of the nomadic mercenary. "The only problem I had with him, and it was true throughout his career, is that he never seemed to play the last month of the season." In the end, Devine would reveal that Javier's age and the presumed continued development of Hague at first base were the primary reasons for making the deal. "We did produce power," the general manager admitted as a result of having Allen in the lineup in 1970, "but still finished worse than last year. Sensational bombers like Allen are good to have, but let's face it—the New York Mets moved the ball around and got the runs without too much power." (Despite Bing's assertion, the Mets ranked only ninth out of the twelve teams in the National League in 1970 in runs scored with 695, while the Cards were fifth with 744.) Allen actually heard about the trade secondhand while prepping for minor surgery at Jewish Hospital. At first, he was extremely angry; within a couple hours, he was disappointed; and shortly later, he found solace. "I wanted one season that I could play in peace," he reflected about being sent from Philadelphia to St. Louis, "and my wish was granted. . . . I never had rough words with any of the other players. In fact, we got along fine, in the clubhouse, on the planes, and on the buses." He also denied that he had been playing the horses—save, according to him, for a couple of visits to Fairmount Park across the river in Collinsville, Illinois. "I even kept away from the race tracks all season on the road," Allen added. "I went to the track only two times. I guess I won't last long in Los Angeles, either."

When a few reporters suggested that Allen had damaged the morale of the ball club, Devine disagreed. The general manager then fired back by asking, if this was so, why had the reporters not mentioned it until now, when Allen was traded?

Sizemore, the 1969 National League Rookie of the Year with the Dodgers, had batted eight for sixteen in Busch Stadium against the Cardinals in 1970, showing a strong favoritism toward the ground ball hits that the quick Astroturf could provide. "I ought to hit a lot more doubles in St. Louis than at Dodger Stadium," he predicted. Listed among Sizemore's talents was also being a good bunter—a strategy for which he was sometimes known to pull a special twenty-four-ounce stick off the bat rack. "They let the grass grow too thick in L.A. and you have to hit a bullet to get a ball between the outfielders," he added. He was a scrappy, hard-nosed player, who had been nicknamed "the Runt" by teammate Don Drysdale in Los Angeles. Prior to professional ball, Sizemore had been an All–Big Ten catcher at Michigan and, like Simmons, had done part of his growing up in the state (after having originally been from Alabama). He was converted to an infielder upon joining the Dodgers, a process that took nearly four years in the making in the Minor Leagues. While there, he was taught how to play second base by the same man who, ironically, long ago, had tutored Javier at the position in Monty Basgall (Basgall became a roving instructor in the Dodgers' Minor League system after having managed in the Pirates' organization, the latter of which was where Javier had started his career). After his stellar initial campaign, Sizemore had been limited to ninety-six games in 1970 due to a pulled hamstring suffered in spring training, an ailment that would hamper him throughout the season. In addition, surgery to remove bone chips in his wrist just before the start of spring training in 1971 would prove to be a major initial impediment in his time with the Cardinals as well. As he was leaving Los Angeles in early March—and just as John Wooden's Sons of Westwood were about to wrap up their fifth-straight NCAA basketball title at UCLA—Sizemore's last statement to local reporters was that he wished he had been traded a month earlier, as he and his family had only recently moved into a five-bedroom home near Disneyland.

Stinson, meanwhile, was imagined to be a solid catching prospect as a backup to fellow switch-hitter Simmons, as he had been the Dodgers' number-one draft choice for $40,000 in June 1966 after refusing to sign as a second-round pick of Kansas City twelve months earlier. After spurning the Royals, he again refused to sign even as a first-round selection of Washington in January '66, instead spending a season at Dade Junior College in Miami and holding out for what he felt he was worth. He impressed scouts from the very beginning of his high school career, in which as an outfielder he had once thrown out a runner at first base—*from left field.* Coming into 1971, the twenty-five-year-old had also proved himself a winner, having already been on three Minor League teams that had claimed league titles. "He's got everything," Boyer assessed. "Attitude, aptitude, and ability." Although not in the same physical mold as future Atlanta Braves MVP Dale Murphy, Stinson at the time (like Murphy) was considered equal an outfield prospect as a catching one, displaying excellent running speed in addition to his strong arm. In the event that Stinson would not be ready for the majors as a backup catcher, the Cardinals also acquired Iowa State University product Jerry McNertney from the Milwaukee Brewers, with Carl Taylor now being shipped out in a multiplayer deal. McNertney and Phil Roof had split time as the Brewers' starting catchers in the team's first year in existence in the Midwest in 1970 after the franchise moved from Seattle. Mc-Nertney, like Dick Hughes a longtime Minor Leaguer before ever reaching the majors, had now been in the big leagues since 1964. "I couldn't believe it," he recalled of his good fortune after first appearing at Comiskey Park that first year for the White Sox, "because I'd never been an all-star in high school, college, anywhere." In the end, the acquisition of McNertney was a fortunate one, for on March 13, Stinson would fracture his thumb in an exhibition game and thus would not be able to head north with the Cardinals to start the season.

For the first time in several years, the Cardinals would gladly avoid any major contract disruptions with the start of spring training in 1971. Gibson, now starting to do his own radio show and color commentary for Creighton basketball back in Omaha before coming to Florida, would be rewarded for his excellent 1970 season with a $150,000 contract, making him the highest-paid pitcher in baseball history. The negotiation process, which had taken place in October at the conclusion of the schedule, was amiable and surprisingly simple, lasting only a few minutes in Devine's office. "I mentioned a figure and Bob mentioned a figure," Bing summarized the process. "We weren't far apart, and then I called Mr. Busch. As a superstar pitcher and senior member of the club, Gibson deserves that kind of courtesy." After sealing the deal, Gibby ran into Toomey in the hallway coming out of the meeting with Devine. "We're with you forever, Bob—win or tie," he joked. In comparing the two greatest Cardinal pitchers in history (and the impact on the overall game that Gibson had made by the late 1960s), Dizzy Dean made $25,500 as his top salary in the midst of the Great Depression—and Dean's rate would be the highest figure for a National League pitcher for another fifteen years.

Another veteran coming off a strong campaign in 1970 and looking forward to even greater things was Joe Torre, who after having turned thirty on July 18 in his second season as a Cardinal had batted a career-best .325. Like Brock, Torre in 1970 had also cracked the two-hundred-hit plateau (his first time ever), as Joe also reached the one-hundred-RBI mark for the fourth time in his career. With Shannon presumably out of the lineup for good in 1971, Torre would have the personal luxury of settling into one regular defensive position at third base—being full-time at the position for the first time since high school—and would not have to jump from there to catcher to first base as he had done the season before. "I sometimes think Red believes anybody can play third," Torre had joked in a self-deprecating manner in the midst of the 1970 season. "I was happy to give it a try."

He and Javier had been the last position players to arrive in spring camp (with pitchers Reuss and Harry Parker rounding out the group, the former completing a college term and Parker a stint of military service; Parker, like Reuss, was a metro St. Louis product of nearby Collinsville and a starter on Collinsville High's 1965 state championship team in basketball). And the spring exercises were well into session by March 9 as the players were discussing the Joe Frazier–Muhammad Ali title fight from the night before, with Frazier downing Ali for the world heavyweight championship in Madison Square Garden. Most sportswriters were of the opinion that the defeat spelled the end for the former champ. "The 20,455 fans at the Garden and the 300,000,000 or so who watched on TV around the world must have their doubts that Ali can ever rise again," penned one. Others were decrying that the $2.5 million each that Frazier and Ali reaped from the fight was outrageous for their forty-five minutes of work. (The payday was especially savored by Ali, who was stripped of his title a couple of years earlier for his refusal of induction into the U.S. Army. Three weeks before the fight, the war had taken yet another turn as South Vietnamese troops, under American air cover, invaded Laos.)

The army for which Ali refused to serve was still, of course, drawing much of its leadership for tactical operations in Southeast Asia from the United States Military Academy at West Point. And on March 27, the academy was losing one of its own on-campus leaders. Bob Knight, who had posted a record of 102-50 in six seasons as the basketball coach, would leave the Hudson River area and be introduced that day as the new coach at Indiana University. Knight was replacing Lou Watson at IU, who had recently resigned before the team's final game, a move that "was precipitated by a protest meeting of players who complained they couldn't communicate with him and they 'weren't learning basketball,'" according to reports. In the process of building a stellar program at Indiana, Knight by 1974 would encourage one of his former players at Army, Mike Krzyzewski, to join him on the bench in Bloomington as an assistant coach. After two years in this role, Krzyzewski would return to West Point as the head coach himself, a post he would maintain until leaving in 1980 for Duke University.

Over time, Knight would develop a friendship with future Cardinals manager Tony LaRussa; in the meantime, the Cards had been spending most of spring training 1971 at the "August A. Busch Recreation Center," a four-field workout facility in the northeast part of St. Petersburg while going downtown to Al Lang Field for games and other practice sessions. During their stay at the Busch Center, they received a visit from Dizzy Dean on March 12, one day before the facility's namesake—Gussie Busch himself—was scheduled to make his first appearance at spring training. "Ol' Diz," as he liked to call himself, naturally wandered over to where the pitchers were working out. He noticed the grimaces that Gibson was showing on his face, being troubled by muscle spasms in his upper leg as he tried to loosen up—an ailment that had bothered him sporadically in past years. Starting life as a skinny sharecropper before entering the army and then pro ball, the sixty-one-year-old Dean had more than made up for his lack of early weight later in life. Settling into a sedentary broadcasting career, the former fireballing pitcher had ballooned up near three hundred pounds recently, enjoying daily helpings of peach cobbler and other fine cooking of his wife, Pat, at their home near Wiggins, Mississippi, Pat's home area where Dizzy had moved in retirement. Unable to stand only a few moments in the thick Florida heat, he retreated to the shade of the dugout and watched the modern-day Cardinals apply their trade. While watching, he dreamed of what-coulda-been with one other addition to the Gas House Gang's pitching staff in 1934.

"Me and Gibby," he blurted in his southern drawl, shaking his head in turning to a couple of other dugout observers. "What a pair we'd have made."

Although Gibson was turning thirty-six in the coming year (as few expected a repeat of his sensational year in 1970, the second best of his career), there was a greater positive feeling on the club entering the 1971 season. This was due to the emergence of more of the younger players—not only off the pitching mound but among the position players as well—giving the Cardinals a greater array of young talent than had ever been previously seen, particularly in the outfield. This fact was noticed by Brock, who himself was having another great spring halfway through the exhibition schedule with a .545 batting average—the same average that Hague, the heir apparent at first base, had posted by the same juncture. Still looking for improved contact, Brock in 1970 had finally ended his National League record of seven straight one hundred or more strikeout seasons—but only by the slimmest of margins, finishing with ninety-nine (he had also posted ninety-six whiffs in the season before the streak started in 1962). "In general, we've got the kind of depth we had back in '67 when we overcame injuries and won easily because our bench came through," he concluded. Additionally, the early work of young infielders Tom Heintzelman, Ed Crosby, and Milt Ramirez had been impressive, as had been budding outfielder–first baseman Cecil Cooper, signed from the Boston organization for twenty-five thousand dollars and who had led the Midwest League in batting with a .336 mark for Danville in 1970. As for all the up-and-coming outfielders, Brock felt that among Lee, Jose Cruz, and Luis Melendez, "I think all three of them could play regularly in the major leagues right now." Brock's list did not even include another speedy prospect in Jorge Roque. Melendez and Cruz perhaps had the least to prove, having respectively batted .306 and .321 for Tulsa over most of 1970 before their September call-ups to St. Louis. Interestingly, both young men had grown up in Puerto Rico idolizing Orlando Cepeda, and each was able to speak only very little English upon entering professional baseball in the States. Also added into the outfield mix in spring training were veteran backups Jim Beauchamp and Bob Burda, each having returned to the Cardinals after stints with other clubs since both had originally signed with St. Louis in 1958. Burda was another St. Louis native and, like Reuss, had attended the baseball-rich Ritenour High School in the city.

Thus, it was evident that there would not be enough spaces in the lineup card for all of the precocious young players, and as such, more than one of the talented youngsters would need to be returned to the Minor Leagues once again. Such demotions were decisions that Devine and Schoendienst did not wish to make, but were choices that others would have been happy to make *for* them. "I like Cruz the best of the lot," declared manager Preston Gomez of the struggling San Diego Padres, a team with little talent and a 63-99 mark in 1970. "But

Melendez is quite a ballplayer too. He swings the bat like a big [Jose] Cardenal. I'd take either him or Cruz right now. I wish we had something to offer the Cardinals." Another long-term possibility put forward by Devine was attempting to turn the versatile Melendez into an infielder through winter league training in Puerto Rico after the 1971 season.

But the primary reason there would be little chance for the youngsters to immediately show their stuff was due to the most prominent new veteran face on the roster. On the twenty-ninth of January, Briles and Davalillo had been dealt to Pittsburgh for Matty Alou, a man thought to finally fill the Flood chasm in center field and move Cardenal over to right (or perhaps Cruz, if he displayed himself ready). He had led all of baseball with an impressive 231 hits only two years earlier in 1969, far and away the most in either league. Alou was also one of the best bunters in the game, having even planted one for a hit as a pinch hitter in the ninth inning of the seventh game of the 1962 World Series against the Yankees, nearly seizing victory for San Francisco in what would be a 1–0 loss. His average had tailed off significantly in 1970, however, and it was the first time he had batted below .300 (.297) in five seasons. He was the second of three brothers to reach the Major Leagues from their home island in the Dominican Republic after inking his first professional contract with the Giants at the age of sixteen. "Felipe got $200, and I got $200," Matty said in comparing his signing bonus to that of his older sibling. "Jay was smart—he got $1,500." Ironically, it was Jay—officially known as "Jesus"—who wound up with the least-impressive big league career although posting solid numbers himself. Feeling growing pressure in the past year to provide for a bona fide replacement for Flood in center field, Devine was now confident that he had finally delivered. "Matty is as good with his glove now as Curt Flood was his last season [1969] with us," the general manager assured. "And he throws better than Curt did after Flood hurt his arm." In adding Alou to the lineup, the Cardinals now had—with Brock and Torre—half of all the batters in the National League who reached 200 or more hits the season before. A devout Catholic, Alou was said to have attended mass at least twice a week for his entire life.

With the emergence of the outfielders, even more youngsters such as Reuss, Torrez, Simmons, and Hague—each of whom had gained at least some big-league experience to date—were also expected to rise as leaders during the season. But while Brock and others were excited by this idea, the difficulty of predicting what would happen with the relatively unknown elements was troubling to other forecasters. "The Cardinals have their demi-dynasty behind them, and a long row ahead," a cautious Wilks warned folks who were seeking a return to the glory days of the 1960s. Additionally, new coaches had to be integrated into the system as well. For 1971, Schoendienst had decided to insert Benson as the third base coach, replacing Kissell. Benson had earlier been in that role when the Cards had won their 1964 championship against the Yankees, another team for which he had performed the same function in the past. "This is no means a reflection on George, who is an extremely smart baseball man," Red explained about removing Kissell, "but Benson was a very good third base coach for us and for the Yankees and Cincinnati." Schoendienst was also considering giving Kissell some time as the first base coach in order to free up Boyer to work with the hitters in the dugout while the Cardinals batted. The manager was once again rumored among some beat writers in National League cities to be on the "hot seat" entering the year and fully intended to keep his job—especially since he had just sent off his daughter, Mary, to the pricey St. Mary's College of Notre Dame in South Bend, Indiana.

With all the new faces, Schoendienst was also taking a lot of time in March to sort out yet another new-look batting order, trying to settle on a season-opening lineup from among all the new players. He was leaning toward the placement of Alou and Sizemore behind the leadoff man Brock, for while Sizemore was destined to be an outstanding number-two hitter, Schoendienst also envisioned Alou as adept at moving Brock around the bases. Ultimately, Sizemore was the choice in light of his tremendous bat control. "Batting second is a great challenge," Sizemore admitted. "You can do more things, and you have a lot more incentive when you're hitting behind Brock."

The schedule makers, meanwhile, had not done the Cards any favors for 1971; they would amazingly have no days off at home from April 9 until the All-Star break in mid-July, including no off-days whatsoever in the month of June—a fact dreaded by the players as they looked at the calendar.

The deal to bring Sizemore to St. Louis in Allen's stead had saved the front office some money, money that had been liberally spent since the pinnacle of the pennant years of the late 1960s. Part of the reining in of funds, however, was due to Gussie Busch's furthering disenchantment with modern players. Regardless of the reason, it was improving the Cardinals' bottom line.

Simultaneously, out east, there was a money crisis happening with the Major League franchise in Washington D.C., and Senators' owner Bob Short was looking for everything short of circus acts to bring fans back to the ballpark, in any manner possible. From this thinking came his idea to offer the Philadelphia Phillies three Minor League players in exchange for the right to negotiate a contract with Curt Flood, who was still in self-imposed exile in Europe and had published an autobiography titled *The Way It Is* while hiding in Denmark. With the new promise of a big payday, however, Flood was suddenly willing to make a quicker return from his "meditations" than originally planned (similar to the Ricky Williams situation seen years later in professional football, who in 2004 had claimed he had wanted nothing further to do with the riches of the National Football League only to return a year later). Short offered Flood

$110,000 to play for his franchise, the American League's Senators—the team's last year in the capital before moving to Texas to become the Rangers—and Flood quickly signed. Nonetheless, there was much debate about his readiness to play after the year-and-a-half layoff. "He's got a 25-year-old body," his former teammate Brock confidently claimed when he heard of the news. However, when the Senators' team physician looked at him, he said that "Flood has to have the oldest 33-year-old body I've ever examined." Wilks, perhaps in splitting the difference, claimed that "the bet in Washington is that Flood doesn't give the Senators half a season as a regular."

In any event, Flood made certain that his Washington contract stipulated that he was still opposed to the reserve clause and that his participation in league play in 1971 would not halt the pursuit of his case in the appellate courts. His autobiography, meanwhile, would stir up things locally in St. Louis about as much as Bouton's book had previously done so nationwide. In one excerpt from *The Way It Is,* he stated that "to be sure, black experience teaches that the American white is guilty until he proves himself innocent. No present reason exists to modify this axiom." Once again, Broeg—the local writer who had praised Flood's personal and professional qualities so many times over the years—was freshly disappointed in him. Back in 1968, Broeg had suggested to Flood that, in light of the manner in which the outfielder took care of himself, he might play until he was forty; now, Broeg did not hesitate to mention a topic rarely broached before—that he believed Flood's personal transgressions were a reason for his recent demise and that he was disappointed with Flood's attitude as written in the autobiography. "Flood penned what has to be a most discouraging sentence to all who think they've learned to accept a man for what he is and does, not for what he looks like. . . . [W]hether bedding, boozing, or playing ball, Curt is indeed curt. I never knew he was so damned unhappy." In Washington, Flood would join another wayward son in McLain, whom Short also summoned to the "act" he was building to draw more fans to the ballpark.

Thus, the roster additions made for quite a scene on April 5 in the nation's capital, where the Senators continued their traditional American League distinction of being the first to open the season (the same privilege was extended to the Cincinnati Reds in the National League, as they had been the oldest club). Taking the field for the first time in nineteen months, Flood jumped into the fray immediately, drawing a walk in the first inning while batting in the second spot and flying around the bases to score along with rookie shortstop Toby Harrah (making his Major League debut in the leadoff position) as part of a ripping 8–0 Washington win over Oakland. Flood would walk and score again in the second inning and added a bunt single in the fifth as part of the victory over the A's Vida Blue, a flashy left-handed pitcher who was starting his first full year in the majors. And while Flood and the Senators had gotten the best

of the colorful rookie on this day, great things were in store for the man who would ultimately have "Vida" stitched on the back on his jersey instead of his surname. "Blue is baseball's new boy wonder," it was written, despite the unsuccessful inaugural tussle with the Senators. "A pitcher with so much natural talent that he appears to have no limitations." The twenty-one-year-old Blue had already pitched a no-hitter and a one-hitter the previous fall in a foreshadowing call-up to the majors, and would strike out thirteen Kansas City Royals in his next start the following week in only six innings of work. "There's no telling how good he can become," his manager, Dick Williams, would claim.

Yet more attention was focused on the home clubhouse in the wake of the opener, as many were curious to know Flood's thoughts on his return. "I knew it would be hard to come back after the layoff, and I'm not out of the woods yet," Flood told reporters after the game. "I need to feel a little more comfortable at the plate and get acclimated in the outfield. . . . I'm just the same poor little colored boy. Nothing's changed." He had contributed to the Senators' first opening-day win in nearly ten years. Four days later, McLain would make his own Washington debut and beat the Yankees in ten innings by a 5–4 count, suggesting that the "good-heartedness" of the organization for sheltering personae non grata might pay handsome dividends for them over the course of the summer.

But instead, success for each of the new acquisitions turned out to be short-lived. Flood, still unhappy at his core and in the midst of a new eighty-thousand-dollar alimony and child-support suit from his ex-wife, Beverly, once again bolted across the Atlantic. He left the Senators abruptly, with no warning, and informing almost no one, as he attempted to gain control of his life in Europe for a second time. Before Flood left, Short had pleaded with him to declare bankruptcy (even though a destructive act in itself), but Flood ignored the advice. "If he had claimed bankruptcy," Short said after he learned that Flood was already in Barcelona, "they wouldn't have been able to touch his salary. If he claims bankruptcy now, he would be able to straighten himself out." With the former player nowhere to be found, the panicking Short enlisted the help of overseas news agencies and even the U.S. Department of State to assist in locating him. "I'm sure that if I found Curt and talked to him," Short added in desperation, "I could persuade him to rejoin our ballclub." But in the end, the second escape wound up being a permanent reclusion for Flood. About a week later, Short would arrive at his office with a telegram waiting for him on his desk: "I tried. A year and a half is too much. Very severe personal problems are mounting every day. Thanks for your confidence and understanding." Flood had played in his last big league game on April 25, hitting .200 for Washington in a total of thirty-five at-bats in three weeks of work. McLain's Major League life, meanwhile, would last only slightly longer.

Over the course of the summer of 1971, Philadelphia fans became less concerned about what they had missed in not having Flood play for them, for manager Frank Lucchesi had this to say about Flood's replacement sent from the Cardinals as compensation. "Willie Montanez is the best thing to happen to baseball in Philadelphia since the five-cent beer," the skipper said, adding that Flood's not reporting to the team had turned out to be a blessing. Lucchesi was speaking of the fact that Montanez—who the club was not sure would be ready for the big leagues so soon—was leading the team in nearly every offensive category, including hits (eighty-four), runs scored (forty-four), doubles (seventeen), triples (four), home runs (sixteen), and runs batted in (fifty-seven). By that time, he would also have the highest batting average out of any starting Phillies player at .281.

As the Cardinals prepared for their own 1971 opener, the second base job still belonged to the eroding Javier, as Sizemore was being given every opportunity to take the shortstop position away from Maxvill. Delaying a decision on the matter for Schoendienst was that each man was at the opposite extreme in both offense and defense, with Sizemore struggling to master the position and Maxvill continuing his notoriously poor hitting. The club had expected Sizemore to ultimately take hold of the spot once his injuries had fully healed (although the hand on which Sizemore had surgery would cause him problems for years to come, including being struck by two pitched balls in 1971 and tearing ligaments in the future as well). Meanwhile, Broeg cautioned readers to be patient with the team—especially in light of the fact that another relative newcomer, the youthful Simmons, was still learning behind the plate. "Even now, as the Redbirds open tomorrow [April 6] at Chicago, patience must be prevalent," he wrote. "Particularly in the assessment and understanding of Simmons in the equivalent of the quarterback position—catcher." It was conventional wisdom in baseball that a team cannot win a pennant with an inexperienced catcher taking over the job full-time, but the Cards felt that Simmons was worth the risk.

The thirty-nine-degree temperatures and biting wind on Chicago's lakeshore did not deter more than forty-one thousand spectators from showing up at Wrigley Field on April 6 as traditional rivals took to the field to open their National League seasons. A ceremony by the Chicago Fire Department before the Cubs-Cardinals game honored the victims and sacrifices of the Great Chicago Fire, taking place exactly one hundred years earlier on the following October 8. While other members of the department practiced on a controlled, staged house fire off in the distance, they did not need to ignite a blaze at the ballpark to warm the crowd. The observers' impervious attitude toward the cold was due to another round being performed in the premier National League pitching matchup of the era, as Bob Gibson and Ferguson Jenkins issued their own "heat." It was the seventh-consecutive season opener for Gibson, who had logged a pair of wins and no losses in those games (which included having been battered by the Cubs at his very first opener at Wrigley back in 1965 in a no-decision). Conspicuously absent from the Cubs lineup he would face in the first game of 1971 was another future Hall of Famer, Banks, whose arthritic knees had not improved over the final days of spring training despite his having hit .407 in Arizona. For "Mr. Cub," it was the first time in seventeen years that Ernie would not be in the batting order on opening day. "I don't want to embarrass the team, making it look as if the Cubs were playing someone who is hurt," Banks said in reference to, in his mind, the relative unimportance of his personal seventeen-year opening-day string ending. Banks had long jostled with Durocher in fending off being moved from first base, as the manager had wanted to make room for the next "can't-miss" prospect at the position each year in Chicago. Over the past several seasons, Durocher had tried out such men such as Dick Nen, John Boccabella, and others to claim the spot. Then, in mid-1970, the Cubs had acquired the excitable Joe Pepitone after the career Yankee had spent a half season in Houston with the Astros. Back in the 1964 World Series while playing for New York against the Cardinals, Pepitone claimed that he had been hit by a Gibson pitch, only to have his plea to the home plate umpire fall on deaf ears; he then proceeded to drop his pants in the locker room to show the writers and photographers the red mark on his upper leg. Now, in Chicago, he tried to keep his purpose as simple as possible. "If I'm not happy, I can't play. Here, with the Cubs, I'm happy. I do what I want to do, as long as I don't hurt anybody doing it. That's my bag."

Durocher had hoped that Pepitone would claim the everyday role in center field. But while Pepitone told the press that he preferred playing the outfield, he had also won three Gold Gloves at first base—which, if he made the switch for the Cubs and took over at first, would perhaps open more room in center for a much-hailed youngster, the fleet-footed Jose Ortiz (as it would turn out, Ortiz would play in only thirty-six games in this, his final season in the big leagues). And it would take Banks a long time to round himself into playing shape anyway, as he would be stuck on the disabled list until April 21.

Throughout the frigid opening afternoon, Torre's seventh-inning homer would be the Cards' only run—and he was actually the only Cardinal runner whom Jenkins permitted to advance past first base. Despite the grand matchup on the pitching mound, the fans were nonetheless grateful that the two combatants ran through the opponents' batting orders in quick regularity. For even as the game headed into extra innings at a 1–1 score, the contest was, in the typical Gibson-Jenkins fashion, just over an hour and a half old; in fact, it was still under two hours when the deciding blow was finally struck. In the bottom of the tenth with the game still knotted, the Cubs' Beckert—who later claimed that it looked like the dominant Gibson was throwing "from 30 feet"—grounded out before Gibby's personal tormentor, Billy Williams, stepped into the batter's box. Of what happened next, Williams would later say that "I normally don't see him make a pitch like that to me—a fastball down the middle." Billy took hold of the opportunity and sliced the ball through the icy gale, landing it in the midst of his allies in the bleachers and sending the Chicagoans home with a happy 2–1 win, the fifth time in seven decisions that Jenkins had gotten the better of Gibson. The Williams homer was the only hard-hit ball off the Cardinals right-hander the entire day, save for a moderate drive from Ken Rudolph into the gap that Brock was able to flag down in deep left field. When hearing of Williams's evaluation of the events, Gibson respectfully disagreed on the location. "It was not down the middle," he claimed. Added his catcher, Simmons, "The ball Williams hit was on the outside corner around the knees. He just golfed it."

By the time he left the Cubs in late 1974, Williams would finish his National League career with ten other homers against Gibson, unable to explain the success that was so unattainable for most other hitters against the great one.

When the Cardinals returned to St. Louis for their first home game of the year, they were happy to greet their old teammate Shannon in the locker room, who with his playing days behind him was able to devote his full attention to his family, his new front-office job, and battling his disease. He told them how, in recovery, he was so heavily medicated back in November and December that he had slept nearly twenty hours a day, with his weight ballooning up near 250 pounds at the time. He had last seen his comrades back in St. Petersburg, having been able to get down to Florida and see a few spring training games. Since getting heavier from the sedentary recovery back in the fall, he had gotten back down to 220 pounds, looking toward his goal of returning to his playing weight of 205, regardless of whether he ever returned to the field. Shannon was enjoying parts of his role in the promotions and sales department with the ball club, although he did not entirely rule out a return to playing in 1972.

As Shannon chatted with his friends in the locker room, he noticed that they were getting into a different-style uniform. In 1971 the Cardinals had, for the first time in the modern era, opted for pullover jerseys, a fashion believed to have been introduced by the Pittsburgh Pirates in the previous season. In addition, the new outfit would display red and white stripes around the sleeves, collar, and the outer seam of the pants, features previously absent. Of course, the traditional "Birds on the Bat" logo remained unmoved on the jersey—although the new top would now have the two redbirds outlined in blue. In a January article in the *Columbia Missourian* titled "Cards Try Pajamas after Sleepy Season," unimpressed writer Paul Stillwell described the strange new uniforms as "the kind with no buttons, no zippers, no flies, and no visible means of support." Added Broeg in another view, "They're lighter and more comfortable than the old models . . . [but] the only problem with the close-fitting, beltless double-knits is that they put a premium on a trim profile. Joe Torre said he was glad he'd taken off 25 pounds." Nonetheless, Torre did not wish to lose any of his long-ball strength. He was well aware of the power vacuum he needed to fill—in the absence of not only Shannon but the other departed slugger as well. "With Richie Allen gone," Torre had said late in spring training, "we're going to need the RBIs. And with quality hitters like Matty Alou, Ted Sizemore, and Lou Brock, I'm always going to have a fast man on base ahead of me. I know what's going to be expected of me—to fetch 'em home and often."

Having arrived in spring training *in* shape (as opposed to using March for *getting* in shape, as had typically been the case for him), Torre reaped the rewards in having batted .333 in exhibition play—one of the best preseason marks of his career, and a hopeful sign for great things to come. "I've never enjoyed a spring more. In fact, I've never enjoyed *baseball* more than these last two years."

And in the Cardinals' home opener on April 13, he delivered the first truckload of what would be a season full of production. He drove in three runs with a homer and a single, which was still not enough to rescue Reuss, who suffered a 6–4 loss to San Francisco. By the time the Cardinals finished a ten-game road trip on April 21 in meeting the Giants back in the Bay Area, Torre would have batted .419 during the voyage, destroying all pitchers in his path. He would also bat safely in every Cardinals game to start the season up until the twenty-eighth, a string of twenty-two straight games.

After the Pacific journey, Torre and the Cards returned home to St. Louis. Their final opponent on the road trip, the Giants, was then leaving town themselves for their own stretch of away games. In the Giants' absence, a sprawling public event would take over the local headlines in San Francisco, a place considered one of the epicenters of civil unrest during the turbulent years of the recent past. Young people were still commanding a voice in American society, formalized in part the following July as President Nixon would sign a bill lowering the voting age from twenty-one to eighteen. On April 24 an estimated crowd of 125,000—mostly students—gathered on the downtown streets to protest the war on the other side of the globe, a conflict while associated with the 1960s still unrelenting sixteen months into the new decade (by the end of October 1971, however, the number of U.S. troops in Southeast Asia would drop to just over 196,000, the lowest level since 1966; soon after, it would be announced by President Nixon that an additional 45,000 American soldiers would leave Vietnam by the following February). Meanwhile, that same day in Washington, D.C., an additional half-million people staged a similar protest.

Undaunted by the tight-fitting uniform, Torre would even improve upon his hot hitting into May, following his .355 average in April with a .366 mark for the next month (and then bettered by a blistering season's-best .392 in June). The rest of the Cardinals would follow suit, with the club surging to a 19–6 record for May that nudged them slightly ahead of the Pirates and Mets by Memorial Day (and saw the team's first-ever series at the new Veterans Stadium in Philadelphia, at the time the largest stadium in the National League). Even Javier, fighting for his professional life, was at .325 near the end of May (and Alou had nearly matched him at .323 after his own poor start). "Javier's been swinging the bat better than he ever did," Schoendienst claimed after a two-for-three effort by the old second baseman that led to a 6–1 win over San Diego on May 23. It was also a day that marked a complete-game win for first-year starting pitcher Reggie Cleveland on his twenty-third birthday, who was now victorious in four of his first six decisions. Javier would sail up to .337 three days later, as the team would take over first place in the Eastern Division with a 1–0 shutout pitched by Chris Zachary, like Cleveland another virtual unknown on the pitching staff until now, having been acquired in a trade the previous July. "I feel that I finally know how to pitch—after nine years," the twenty-seven-year-old Zachary said, who had previously toiled for the Astros and the Royals. He had a career record of 7-18 in the Major Leagues when he was recently summoned to St. Louis from the Cardinals' farm system. "I was just a thrower when I was with Houston. I'm just glad I got a second and third chance. Some guys don't get those extra chances."

It was more than just performance on the field; it was a team that was also coming together in a personal sense, in the most positive way Schoendienst had seen since the "El Birdos" teams of the late 1960s. They had discarded many of the antics of 1970, with some of them going to church together; others, like Torre, Simmons, Javier, and Leron Lee, played cards in the clubhouse before games; and some others were conducting friendly wagers on the outcome of the hotly contested Stanley Cup hockey playoff series going on between Chicago and Montreal or discussing the unlikely run of tiny Macon, Illinois, to the state high school baseball state championship game. Regardless of the actual activities, all were seeming to form a cohesive bond rarely seen in the St. Louis locker room over the past two seasons. "That whole group of Cardinals [in the early 1970s] was pretty close," confirmed pitcher Rich Folkers, who would join the club after the season in an October trade with the Mets. "We did a lot of things together. Going out to a pizza place, we might have twelve guys." Inspired by the newfound fraternity was Sizemore as well, who in his initial days with the Cards had struggled with an average in the low .200s—and worse—before a late-May burst of his own that shot him up near .300. By September, Sizemore would philosophically look back upon those early-season struggles that ultimately pushed him to excel. "I felt as if I were a rookie, and had to prove myself all over again." Sizemore had been put at ease by the numerous pranksters who now dotted the Cardinals roster, ready to spring a practical joke at any moment—and no one, not even Schoendienst, was spared (Sizemore recalled only Len Gabrielson and Tom Haller having a reasonable sense of humor in his time with the Dodgers). And Reggie Cleveland—though only a rookie— was among those whom one needed to watch the closest for a potential "hot foot" or dead snake in one's locker

The snug material being used with the new jerseys and pants made it, perhaps, poor timing for the stocky Cleveland to have a regular stay in the Major Leagues—if such a concept is possible. In actuality, however, his timing was perfect. Nicknamed "Double Cheeseburger" by his teammates, the weighty Canadian had been hit hard in two brief call-ups to the Cardinals in 1969 and 1970, but proceeded to be successful in winter ball after each season was completed and attempted to build on his dominant 15-6 campaign at Little Rock in 1969. "I can really push down the food," Cleveland had no problem admitting. "I'd like to stay between 200 and 205 [pounds]. The club would like me about 198, but I don't think I'll make it. I can't stay away from food." Accustomed to long hibernations in his native Saskatchewan (the likes of which Shannon had just experienced in a hospital bed in St. Louis), Cleveland's high school did not have baseball due to poor weather conditions and lack of interest, but he managed to cultivate his love for the game through different outlets as a young man. He was playing semipro ball in Moose Jaw when he was discovered by a Cardinals scout in 1965 and was quickly signed. Now, with no young starter (with the exception of Reuss and, to a lesser degree, Zachary) making a concerted claim for a permanent spot in the starting rotation, Cleveland sensed his chance. After dropping his first two starts, he would win five straight through the twenty-eighth of May, with four complete games that included a shutout of the normally troublesome Braves lineup that night in Busch Stadium. It was part of a four-game sweep of Atlanta and a seven-game winning stretch altogether, the team's longest since the last pennant year of 1968. Their 12-2 home stand to finish the month, additionally, was the best run at Busch since the new park opened. Brock, while seeing a twenty-six-game hitting streak end at the hands of the Braves' George Stone, was leading the National League with a .372 average (including a .406 mark over the month of May). Brock, Torre, and Sizemore, in fact, had all batted over .400 over the course of the tremendous run at home.

But unfortunately, another free fall was in store for the team, as like in 1967, it was once again forced to endure a stint in the calendar with its best pitcher laid up with an injury.

Gibson, personally off to a poor 4-5 start to the year (and the worst beginning to a season he could recall in his professional career), was shelled on May 29 by the same Atlanta lineup dismantled the previous evening by Cleveland (although Moe Drabowsky would gain the victory in relief for the Cardinals to keep the winning streak alive). He gave up five runs over three innings in a game that the Cards rallied to win with three runs in the ninth, 8–7. Despite allowing Atlanta to jump out to a 5–0 advantage, Gibson was not removed by Schoendienst as he was permitted to bat for himself in the bottom of the third inning and responded to the challenge by lining a single after Dick Schofield led off with a walk. (Gibson typically pulled no punches in discussing team-mates that did not sit well with him, and the reserve infielder Schofield hap-pened to be one of them. "Schofield was one of the great 'red-asses' of all time," Gibson once reflected. "That being the baseball term for someone who's always bitching about something or other.") One pitch earlier in the at-bat, Gibson had strained his right thigh muscle in jerking away from an inside pitch from Atlanta's Jim Nash. After driving the ball into the outfield and rounding first, Gibson thought he saw Schofield break for third, but then suddenly stop. Gib-son, in turn, threw on the brakes as well. And when tried to accelerate back toward the bag at first, he further aggravated the injury. He would be out for nearly a month, and the pain from the incident would resurface for the remain-der of his career. Zachary was sent in to run for him, as Gibson limped in great frustration off the field to the Cards' dugout.

As if more of a psychological blow to the team than a strategic one, the im-pact was deep and immediate. As quickly as they had ascended the standings with the best month of May in the history of the franchise, they just as rapidly fell. Gibson was placed on the twenty-one-day disabled list, and Devine knew that, just as in July 1967 when a line drive off the bat of Roberto Clemente broke his leg (the same leg that had been fractured in 1962 when he got a spike caught in the batting cage), it would take a lot of persuasion to get the competi-tive pitcher to rest and heal and not return to the lineup too quickly. "I knew that [team physician] Stan [London] would need ten days or so to rest the leg, but I also knew Gibson was a great competitor. So I flatly told him that I didn't want to see him risk permanently hurting his career the way Dizzy Dean did." Dean had broken his toe from a line drive off Earl Averill's bat in the 1937 All-Star Game and, in rushing back from the injury too soon, was forced to alter his arm motion, which put too much strain on his elbow. The result was a dead arm, which Dean would carry with him when sold to the Cubs the next year.

The truth was that Gibson, now in his thirteenth Major League season, was physically wearing down anyway—just as Dizzy's younger brother, fellow Cards pitcher Paul Dean, had claimed about Diz even before the Averill incident. Dean and Gibson, in a public St. Louis poll in 1969, had been named the two greatest Cardinal pitchers of all time, and Gibson, in many regards, was in much the same worn condition as Dean had been, having been relied upon as the workhorse of the pitching staff for an entire decade (in Gibson's case even longer, as Dean was at full capacity for the Cardinals for only five seasons from 1932 to 1936). Every day for the next six weeks, Gibson would faithfully meet with team trainer Gene Gieselmann for treatment on the leg (as well as for fluid in his knee, which had bothered him for two years as well), whether the Cardinals were at home or on the road. Earlier in the year, some teammate overheard him complaining of more arm stiffness and pain than he ever had before; in fact, once as he sat in front of his locker in Montreal's Jarry Park, he was actually relieved that his starting assignment had been canceled that night. "One thing about the rainout," Gibson smirked with a line he figured no one would remember him uttering, "at least I don't feel as sore as I would have if I had pitched."

In order to counterbalance the sudden youthfulness of the starting staff with Gibson down, a veteran presence was added to the bull pen in Drabowsky and Daryl Patterson, the latter formerly of the Detroit Tigers who had pitched in two games in the 1968 World Series against the Cardinals. The thirty-six-year-old Drabowsky, originally from Ozanna, Poland, was a veteran of sixteen Major League seasons but had not lost his own frivolity of youth. He fitted in nicely with this new Cardinal team of jokesters, exemplified by the fact that he liked to set off firecrackers in the locker room—which Schoendienst naturally denounced, afraid that someone was going to get hurt. After the latest "boom" went off in the dressing area, Red sprinted in and hollered that the whole team would be fined the next time one went off. The practice quickly ceased.

Everyone was confident, of course, that Gibson would ultimately return, and Carlton had already righted himself from his disastrous 1970 season, winning five of his first six decisions (and going to win five of the next six as well, thus sporting a 10-2 record by early June). Thus, on June 11, the Cards rid themselves of left-handed pitcher Freddie Norman by dealing him to San Diego, a hurler who had made only five relief appearances for the team over the past two seasons. Originally signing for a large bonus with the Kansas City Athletics in 1961, Norman had once struck out Carlton in facing him in a Miami high school game. He had gained notoriety as a youngster by dunking a basketball by jumping off a trampoline and having the act captured in a photo shoot by *Life* magazine (Norman needed the trampoline as he was only five feet, eight inches tall). Next, on June 15, the Cards more surprisingly gave up on Mike Torrez as well, sending him to Montreal and purging themselves of one-half of the dynamic combination he and Reuss had been expected to become (while Hague, another youngster at first base, had also disappointed; in the game in which Gibson had been injured, Hague had one of his few strong performances in going three for three, raising his average to .252 after having been in the .100s for much of April and May). Torrez, who in recent weeks had been banished to the bull pen in favor of Zachary, would have several ups and downs with other clubs over the remainder of his long Major League career. Norman, meanwhile, would have a hand in the fortunes of the "Big Red Machine" championship teams in Cincinnati by the middle of the decade.

Yet the trading of Norman and Torrez was nothing compared to the magnitude of young pitching talent that would be dismissed the following spring, roster moves that would call the competence of the club's executives into question.

For the time being, the issue debated by local sportswriters in early June was the failure by the local hockey team, the Blues, to not re-sign their successful coach, Bowman. He was quickly plucked by the Montreal Canadiens to lead the legendary organization, and the result was five Stanley Cup victories for Montreal in the next ten years. "It wasn't difficult for me to accept the job," a grateful Bowman said in being introduced by the Canadiens' officials to the press. "I was born in Montreal and played junior hockey here." Bowman was replacing Al MacNeil, who despite leading the Canadiens to an upset victory over the Chicago Blackhawks for the Stanley Cup in recent weeks was fired due to his unpopularity among the players.

June 1971 would be a horrific mirror image of the Cardinals' July of the previous year, as the team sank to another 8-21 record over the four-week segment—the same as the previous July—to plummet them into fourth place and back near the .500 mark as the season approached its halfway point. On the seventeenth, they were downed by rookie pitcher Burt Hooton of the Cubs and his unique knuckle-curveball in Wrigley Field, making his much-heralded Major League debut fresh off a legendary career on the campus of the University of Texas (where he authored two no-hitters) as he struck out Brock to open his career. Don Kessinger pounded out six hits in as many at-bats—the first Cub to do so in thirty-four years—and plated the winning run off Santo's single as Zachary lost in ten innings, 7–6, a game emblematic of the tough month for the Redbirds as the pitching staff's ERA would sink to the bottom of the National League by June's end.

It was, however, a good month for at least one other local baseball team in the St. Louis region. That day in Gibson's hometown of Omaha, the boys of coach Richard "Itchy" Jones from Southern Illinois University fought through several clubs to the championship game of the College World Series. They would ultimately fall to Coach Rod Dedeaux and his mighty Trojans of Southern California in the final by a 7–2 score; earlier in the opening round of the double-elimination tournament, SIU had beaten USC 8–3 behind the play of future Major League outfielder and St. Louis native Joe Wallis. With a majority of starters returning for both teams, USC and SIU eyed a possible rematch for the national title in 1972.

Four days after the collegiate icon Hooton had disposed of the Cardinals, Gibson returned after being out for nearly a month but was also bested by yet another pitcher making his first Major League start. In the warm winds of Los Angeles, Gibson figured it was a good time to come out of the infirmary and test his thigh injury. Instead, it would be the performance of a lifetime for Bobby O'Brien of the Dodgers, who shut out St. Louis 4–0 in what would be one of only five starts in his only season in the big leagues. Torre had half of the team's six ineffective hits, as O'Brien dominated even those who had dominated *him* previously. "That Beauchamp wore me out in the Winter League," the rookie hurler said of the Cardinal sub getting a rare start at first base on the evening, as Schoendienst had received the tip from Boyer on the history between the two. "I think he got ten hits off me out of the first twelve times I faced him." After Gibson dropped his next start as well to Ken Holtzman and the Cubs in Busch Stadium on the twenty-sixth, his record fell to 4-7 as the Cards faded further down the standings.

Hague and Cardenal struggled much more than the club had imagined; of particular concern was Cardenal, who possessed substantial big league experience with the junior circuit before coming to St. Louis. He had shown flashes of physical brilliance, including his throwing out of pitcher Don Sutton at first base from his right-field position on May 18. Yet over the course of the season, Cardenal's batting continued to suffer. As he just narrowly escaped above the "Mendoza Line" by the end of May (the .200 level attributed to the light-hitting Pirates shortstop of that name), Alou was moved to first base on almost an everyday basis on July 20, at which point Hague had been hitting .215. While Schoendienst did not relish the thought of having to remove Hague and take Alou out of the outfield, the move did free up more time in center and right fields for Cruz and Melendez to get some more experience. The manager thus considered sending Hague back to exclusively a pinch-hitting role for a while, a job at which he had excelled in 1970 (batting .412). Hague had not met expectations, pulling off the ball at the plate and not making the necessary adjustments. Hague had also allowed his weight to balloon back up (while Torre, across the diamond from him at third base, continued to lose pounds while having the best year of his career—from which the rookie apparently took no example). "It's hard to believe that Hague," wrote Broeg, "would attack the candy bars and soft drinks to the point where his weight could be part of his problem." Hague had even been passed on the batting statistics sheet by Maxvill, as the shortstop—now getting a chance to rejoin the starting lineup—had improved his batting mark by eighty points in June by going from .136 to .216.

Cardenal had tried everything to shake his yearlong slump, which had his average as low as .180 at one point. He shaved off his Afro haircut (which would resurface later in his career) and went with a flat-top look, in the hopes that it would lead to new base hits. While the team was in Philadelphia, Cardenal took a cab ride to a local church for Catholic mass to also add some prayers into the mix; the result was four hits over the next two games. As a faithful old Catholic himself from southern Illinois, Schoendienst then offered to pay for a cab ride to mass for Cardenal each time the team traveled to another city. Nonetheless, Cardenal's frustrations would continue to mount, culminating in his being fined three hundred dollars for being ejected by home plate umpire Ed Vargo in arguing balls and strikes in a July 9 game against the Astros at Busch Stadium. "The National League rules say it's $100 every time you throw something," Vargo explained in the wake of Cardenal's firing his bat, helmet, and ball cap (underneath his helmet) in disgust after a third-strike call. Sadly, it would be one of the final notable moments for Cardenal in a St. Louis uniform.

A temporary surge led to a four-game sweep of the Astros before the Cardinals headed into the All-Star break, their first series victory since the month of May. While the home games were not shown locally on television in St. Louis (as was typical of the era), the medium was seeing a continued explosion nationwide. Televised sports—and its accompanying endless flow of dollars—was certainly expanding into 1971. *The Ed Sullivan Show* would go off the air on March 28, but viewers would see the debut of the popular program *All in the Family* the same January. Baseball viewership would grow in kind as well, marked by the noteworthy 1971 All-Star Game in Detroit on July 13, considered one of the greatest versions ever. It was a refreshing breath of baseball life for the city, which had seen its great 1968 team fall apart due to age and other attrition, exemplified no more poignantly than by the demise of McLain. McLain, while no longer All-Star caliber, would be considered good enough for the Senators in 1971 to be permitted thirty-two starts; nonetheless, he was a shadow of the pitcher he had once been, as he would also post a league-high twenty-two losses, a career high for the pitcher as well. After brief stints in Oakland and Atlanta in 1972 and a Minor League try with the Chicago White Sox the following year, McLain would be out of baseball at the age of twenty-nine.

And just as McLain had officially fizzled out as the city hero in Detroit, a new one was developing—albeit starting in the most unlikely of places. Down Interstate 94 west of Detroit in Jackson State Prison sat inmate Ron LeFlore, serving a sentence of five to fifteen years for his role in an armed robbery of a Detroit bar. While incarcerated, the athletic exploits of LeFlore became famous throughout the prison, and then beyond its walls. He not only excelled in baseball prison games—a sport he had never formally played as a youngster—but also as a football player, as the prison team would occasionally play exhibition contests against local schools such as Hillsdale College. As a special privilege on July 13, 1971, LeFlore and some other inmates had been excused from their cells for an evening and escorted down to the commons area in the lockup, where they were permitted to watch the All-Star Game taking place down the road at Tiger Stadium, along with millions of others tuning in on television. It would turn out to be one of the storied such contests of all time, with a total of eleven future Hall of Famers taking part. The game was highlighted by Reggie Jackson's momentous home run deep into the Michigan night, as the ball cleared the roof of the right-field grandstand, en route to a 6–4 win for the American League ("The longest I ever hit," Jackson said at the time). As part of an attempt at a National League rally, Clemente would take his final All-Star cut in the eighth inning and drive a home run himself off Detroit's own Lolich, the unexpected pitching hero for the Tigers against the Cardinals in the World Series three years earlier. Aaron, Bench, Harmon Killebrew, and Frank Robinson would also homer, adding to the immense artillery on display. Torre, Brock, and Carlton had been on hand to represent St. Louis as Torre, continuing to lead the league in hitting at .359 at the break, went zero for three, which further dropped his career batting average of .067 in All-Star play. And as for maintaining his lead in the batting race over the second half of the season, it was Clemente whom Torre watched the closest. "He's the one I have to fear the most. He gets a lot of hits with those high choppers, especially now that Pittsburgh has artificial turf. Glenn Beckert has a great chance, too, and it would be even greater if he had Astroturf in Chicago. He likes to beat out those choppers, too."

Many on the Cardinals—including Gibson—were surprised that Sparky Anderson did not name a third catcher to the National League roster and that it should have been Simmons. In his first full year as the starter, Simmons was batting .292 with forty RBIs heading into the break. In addition, being passed over was even more disappointing for Simmons in that the game had been held in Detroit, near his hometown. As it turned out, not even the second catcher, Pittsburgh's Manny Sanguillen, would make an appearance—Anderson's own Bench, even with an injured left wrist, would catch the entire game. As for Gibson, his absence from the game had snapped a string of six straight All-Star appearances in the game for him, while his victory in San Francisco on July 2 was his first win in forty-nine days. "I'm not mad about not being picked this year, because I'm not doing good," the pitcher explained simply.

LeFlore, who was attracting the interest of Tigers general manager Jim Campbell, watched the events unfold on television and bragged to his skeptical fellow inmates that he would one day be in the All-Star Game himself. Five years later, he would be the top vote getter and the starting center fielder for the American League, a representative of the Tigers for the 1976 midsummer classic in Philadelphia.

In the interim, LeFlore had been visited at Jackson by Campbell and Billy Martin, who arranged a tryout for him at Tiger Stadium. LeFlore proceeded to pound several balls into the upper deck at batting practice and impressed Mickey Stanley, the regular Detroit center fielder, with his throws from the outfield to third base. He was signed to a contract, and LeFlore ultimately became the MVP of the Florida State League in 1974 before becoming his hometown's starting center fielder in 1974. In 1976, he overcame the shooting death of his brother on the tough Detroit streets to post a thirty-game hitting streak. That season, he paired with colorful rookie Tigers pitcher Mark Fidrych, the starter on the mound for the American League in the '76 All-Star Game, to inject new life into the franchise, which had lain mostly dormant after the wondrous year of 1968, save for one more playoff appearance in 1972.

But for now, in 1971, it was the Cardinals' turn to have a rookie pitcher quickly rise to the top of his craft. "If there were any doubts that [Reggie] Cleveland is fast qualifying as an established major league pitcher," Neal Russo wrote in the wake of his performance on July 16, "Reggie dispelled many of them last night at Busch Stadium."

Cleveland had spun his second rookie-year shutout, this time victimizing the flagship club of his home country, the Montreal Expos, by a 6–0 score—the first blanking of an opponent by any St. Louis pitcher since the end of May. It only evened his individual record at 8-8 for the year, but nonetheless suggested to Devine that he had made the right decision in instead parting with Torrez and Norman back in June. The success of the young right-hander must have been expected by clubhouse manager Yatkeman, for the evening saw one of the few times in Butch's thirty-seven-year history with the team in which he fell asleep on the dugout bench next to an amused Gibson during the game. "With all my chatter [in support of Cleveland], I still couldn't wake up Butch." Yatkeman would have another chance to catch Reggie in action five nights later against Philadelphia, as he crafted yet another complete-game win in front of the home crowd in a 6–1 decision, using only seventy-eight pitches through the first eight innings with the lone tally being a home run pitch to Oscar Gamble in the fourth. The Cards got their final runs in the eighth inning off Bunning, who arrived out of the bull pen at that point for one of his last appearances in the big leagues.

The unanticipated emergence of Cleveland was helping to keep the Cards at least within vision of the Pirates as August approached, as the Pittsburgh club was threatening to open up a double-digit lead in the Eastern Division behind the blistering first-half performance of odd-ball pitcher Dock Ellis and his 14-3 record at the break. A pessimistic Russo estimated they would have to win at least two-thirds of their games through September to have a shot at catching the Pirates. The Pittsburgh team was a fun-loving collection with representatives from every corner of the globe—or so it seemed. One Cardinal player recalled arriving at Three Rivers Stadium early before a game one day and hearing a *ping-ping-ping* sound, followed by a bunch of laughter. Looking out onto the field, he saw that the Pirates were taking hitting practice with aluminum bats, seeing just how many homers they could hit with the different weapon.

The Cards inched forward by taking three out of four from the Mets in New York (led by the unrelenting Torre, even though the native Brooklynite temporarily fell off his weight-shedding wagon by indulging in an "Italian smorgasbord," as he put it, at his mother's house while on the trip; more than half of Torre's fan mail, he claimed, now consisted of requests for copies of his diet). He was aided by the continuing development at the plate by Sizemore, who ditched his thirty-four-ounce bat for a lighter thirty-one-ounce variety due to ongoing pain in his injured hand and playing in the draining heat and humidity of St. Louis on a regular basis for the first time. The result: an average that had peaked at .305 with a four-for-four effort against the Pirates on June 13 in Busch Stadium after being in the low .200s for most of April and May (Sizemore was also learning that, despite the hot conditions in St. Louis, Yatkeman would issue each player only one cap for the *entire season*—no matter how sweat soaked the cap would become).

The outfield, however, remained a bit of a question mark, as Cardenal saw his last action in a Cards uniform on July 26. On the twenty-ninth, he was sent with Schofield to Milwaukee for infielder Ted Kubiak. Apparently, there was not even room for Cardenal on the St. Louis bench, as he had been batting .500 as a pinch hitter—the same rate at which he had done the same role for the Cardinals in 1970 (eight for sixteen). For now, it was decided that Cruz and Melendez would bode better for the future in the outfield alongside Brock.

The Cardenal deal—despite the player's easygoing disposition—nearly turned into a mini replication of Flood's reaction to his own trade to Philadelphia. Upon learning the news from Devine, Cardenal got in touch with his attorney, Martha Hickman, who advised him to "publicly protest" the trade. "Jose has nothing against Milwaukee," the lawyer was quick to point out. "In fact, he's heard some good things about Milwaukee. He's just protesting the fact that he's being treated like a piece of luggage. He was upset. We talked and he said he was thinking of quitting . . . but then I told him the only way professional athletes can ever hope to avoid being treated this way is to have it publicized." Cardenal claimed that he had learned of the trade through a teammate—not Devine. Schoendienst, in coming to the general manager's defense, explained that the team was in the process of getting ready to travel from New York to Philadelphia at the time of the deal. Before boarding the team bus for the trip to the airport in New York, Schoendienst had searched for the outfielder the entire day. When it came time to load the plane, club officials did not want Cardenal's baggage sent on to Philadelphia, so it was removed. When a player saw the bags being taken away—it was later reported to have been Javier—Cardenal was informed. Hickman implied that Cardenal would honor his contract and report to Milwaukee, but some in the Cardinals' front office were fearing a replay of the Flood situation all over again.

Just as the Cardenal trade had developed, Melendez went down with a torn hamstring injury in his left leg, leaving the once-deep Cardinal outfield in a state of weakness. Thus, Alou—who had been playing first base for the past month to relieve Hague and make room for Cruz in center, who had been tearing it up at Tulsa—was moved to right as Hague (and his .218 average) had to take over at first base, with Bob Burda the only remaining reserve outfielder on the roster with any Major League experience.

The road trip then carried on to Veterans Stadium in Philly without Cardenal, where the team lodged a successful protest of its August 1 game against the Phillies that was then ordered to be replayed on September 7. The Cardinals had scored three times in the top of the twelfth after taking the Phillies into extra innings. When a second rain delay hit the contest, however, the Phillies claimed that they had been unable to get the stadium's Zamboni to work, a tanklike vehicle that pushed the sitting water off the Astroturf (and a device normally seen smoothing the ice surface at hockey games). Unable to wait any longer, the umpires declared the game "called" and reverted the score back to what it was in the eleventh inning, which officially left the game a 3–3 tie.

In the later summer of 1971 Gibson was once again being called "finished" because of a mediocre 10-10 record. It was at this very time that he achieved an unprecedented—and, even to him, unexpected—personal pinnacle of his career.

As construction began on the spectacular Louisiana Superdome in New Orleans on August 9, Gibson was being shelled for fourteen hits in seven innings of work in Busch Stadium against the Dodgers. It had certainly been a roller-coaster year for the veteran, as in his previous start he had become just the sixty-sixth pitcher to notch two hundred wins in downing the Giants at Busch Stadium on the fourth (he had celebrated the milestone with a glass of champagne in the locker room—as compared to, as Gibson recalled, the bottle of orange soda with which he toasted his first big league win back on a July day in Cincinnati in 1959). Now, with the recent assault from the Dodgers, it was feared that he was entering another downward spin, with having to face the awesome bats of the Pirates in his next assignment on the road on the fourteenth.

In a statement many had found particularly interesting, Gibson had once said he did not think he would ever throw a no-hitter. His reasoning was that, although he always attempted to own the corners of the plate, he nonetheless knew that he challenged batters more often than most pitchers; the result was more pitches *over* the plate, and thus a greater likelihood, as he put it, to make at least one mistake to one batter or another over the course of a game. However, on August 14, 1971, in looking up at the scoreboard in the vast Three Rivers Stadium, he noticed during the evening that he was on his way toward the only hitless game of his career against the great Pittsburgh batters. As Gibson refocused his attention on his work, Dave Cash of the Pirates stepped to the plate in the eighth inning and hit a high chopper that Torre nearly misplayed at third, as he momentarily lost it in the lights but was able to recover and nip the speedy Cash at first to keep Gibson's masterpiece in check for the time being.

Back in St. Louis at that very moment, the football Cardinals were having a preseason game at Busch Stadium, in which they were showing off their impressive rookie lineman from Michigan, Dan Dierdorf, to the home crowd for the first time. More attention was being paid to the scoreboard, however, as the cheers grew louder with reports of Gibson's progress in Pittsburgh. Broeg, who was home covering the football contest, said that many of the forty thousand in attendance were "armed with transistor radios."

By the time Gibson was one out away in the ninth, he would have to face the intimidating Stargell, a man whom Gibby had already struck out three times on the evening. Stargell had been off to a magnificent start in 1971, on his way to perhaps the best year of his career. He had belted eleven home runs in April (which broke the big league record for that month at the time), a far cry from the .063 one-homer start he had endured in 1970. And Stargell—who had gained more than 75 pounds since entering pro ball as a 150-pound Minor League rookie in 1958—would go on to match his April total in June as well, while en route to a majors-leading forty-eight home runs by the end of the '71 season, which wound up edging Aaron by one. The lovable, personable Stargell, who had recently opened a restaurant in Pittsburgh called "All-Pro Chicken," offered a free meal to a customer each time he belted a long one.

Gibson built a two-strike count on the elbow-pumping beast, looking for an edge in an ultimate power-versus-power matchup. He then reached back a third time and sneaked a slider over the outside corner on Stargell as umpire Harry Wendlestedt rang him up. In a scene perhaps similar to Kevin Costner's character Billy Chapel in the movie *For Love of the Game,* the salty old veteran pitcher had finally claimed the one individual achievement that had long eluded him as thirty-one thousand Pittsburgh fans stood and saluted. Not only was it his first (and only) no-hitter, but Gibson had also logged an important 11–0 win for his team against the division leaders they were chasing and aided the offensive cause with three RBIs himself at the plate.

The act of watching Gibson reach the one milestone he had yet to accomplish caused Jack Buck, as he would later admit, to slightly weep on the air for the first time in his career, and when he did, the station engineer for KMOX, John Toler, was also overcome by the moment and started crying as well. There had never been another no-hitter in Pittsburgh to date, and except for Ray Washburn's in 1968, it had been the only Cards no-hitter in the past three decades. "I was throwing hard," Gibson said in the locker room. "I think I threw harder in that one-hitter in San Diego last year [June 17, 1970], but I had better control of my breaking pitches this time. . . . I had a no-hitter going for six innings in college, but then the manager took me out. I don't know why. He just took me out and put me in center field." Unbeknownst to Gibson was that very evening back in Omaha, a fellow student of Creighton University was doing the same thing. Creighton hurler Wayne Piper—pitching for his hometown of Garland, Nebraska, in the National Baseball Congress tournament, an annual amateur baseball competition in the heartland city—pitched his own no-hitter, a 16–0 whitewash of the team from Lawton, Oklahoma.

Over at Simmons's locker, the young catcher (who had four hits on the night) called the game "the greatest thrill of my life." Nearly twenty-five years later in his autobiography, Gibson confirmed what he had said to Neal Russo about his velocity that evening in 1971. "[The no-hitter was] not the hardest I'd ever thrown, but close." Contrary to the myth of pitchers not recognizing such things until late in the contest, Gibson admitted that he was aware of the potential for the no-hitter from the early innings of the game.

Whatever the actual speed of Gibson's pitches that night, Pittsburgh outfielder Al Oliver, who at least (unlike Stargell) was able to put the ball in play all four times up, said it was the first time in his career that he felt completely overpowered by a pitcher—and the first time in his career he was not mad at himself for going zero for four, for he knew he had done all he could. "All those people who said Gibson was washed up," Stargell warned in a similar way Sparky Anderson had done earlier in the season, "should have had to bat against him tonight." With Gibson's cap and the game ball already on their way to the National Baseball Hall of Fame in Cooperstown, New York, the next day Stargell would pound his fortieth homer of the season off Reggie Cleveland, but it was not enough to prevent another win for the Cards and a four-game sweep of the Bucs from August 12 to 15, drawing them to within a mere four games of the lead in the National League East.

After meeting with reporters, Gibson called home, wishing to share the good news with his family, but nobody answered the phone at his house for several hours. After quietly celebrating the feat with a glass of wine with Sizemore, Brock, and former Cardinals pitcher Brooks Lawrence, Gibson's teammates later gave him a diamond ring with the number 45 engraved into it as a prize for the effort, as well as a bottle of champagne from the rest of the pitching staff. Instead of a monetary bonus, Devine and the rest of the front office instead planned to hold a large party for the pitcher at some point when the team returned home from the current road trip, a two-week affair in which Atlanta, Houston, and Cincinnati still needed to be visited (and a trip on which Torre would bat .412, further opening his lead in the National League batting race; in addition, Torre would notch 111 RBIs by the trip's end on August 25—18 of which had been game winners—10 more RBIs than Dick Allen had achieved in all of 1970 and equaling Orlando Cepeda's total in his much-celebrated MVP season of 1967). Gibson was also personally congratulated at the team hotel by Musial, who had been fortunate as a Pittsburgh tourist as well—for the Pennsylvania native had won an automobile on the team's previous trip to the city, thanks to his purchase of ten dollars' worth of raffle tickets to the Pittsburgh Civic Opera House's fund-raiser and the draw of his name from the hamper.

The day after Gibson's feat, young Vida Blue advanced his record to 22-4 for the Oakland A's with a 6–4 win over the Yankees in New York, having long progressed from his season-opening loss to Flood and the Senators. However, the toll of being mentioned as not only a potential thirty-game winner in his first full season but also, in the minds of some, the heir apparent to Gibson as the dominant African American pitcher in the game was starting to show. "Physically, I'm all right," he told the mob of New York reporters that had formed a suffocating ring around his locker in the visitors' clubhouse in Yankee Stadium. "But I feel like I'm about to crack up mentally. I feel the tension every day. I'm always surrounded by people like you. Sometimes I wish you would just pass me by and give me a couple days off."

August was also the traditional time of year on the baseball calendar for the Little League World Series in Williamsport, Pennsylvania. The 1971 version, as usual, held intense drama in the championship game. Taiwanese pitcher Hsu Chin-mu was ordered by his coach to intentionally walk Lloyd McClendon of the Gary, Indiana, team every time he came to the plate. The crowd of twenty-five thousand booed, but Taiwan wound up winning the game 12–3—despite the fact that McClendon was able to reach out on one of the pitches in the first inning and hit a home run, his fifth homer in the past three games of the round-robin tournament.

The four-game sweep in Pittsburgh helped spark the Cards to a second-consecutive eighteen-win month in August, continuing a streak that sent them to fifteen games above .500 (78-63) by Labor Day. Gibson's triumphant return to the Busch Stadium mound on the twenty-eighth was a thirteen-strikeout blanking of the Reds, 4–0 (as well as the official home celebration of his Pittsburgh no-hitter on September 4, in which he was greeted at Busch by other Cardinal pitchers who had accomplished the feat, including Paul Dean, Lon Warneke, Jesse Haines, and Gibson's old teammate in Washburn). Yet by the holiday, they had actually lost ground to the juggernaut Pirates since their sweep in the Steel City, now trailing by seven. As was typical, the rosters were expanded for the season's final month, with prospects Stinson, Roque, and others being added to the cause for the stretch run (in addition to veteran relief pitcher Stan Williams, who was purchased from the Minnesota Twins) as the team hit the road east once again, this time to Philadelphia.

Labor Day in America has always been a time to take measure of one's accomplishments over the summer, and in the first game of a doubleheader on the workman's siesta in Philly, the Cardinals showed that they were willing to keep fighting for that which they had battled since April—even against old friends.

Leading off the Cardinal third, Brock singled and easily stole second on his former teammate, McCarver, who was clearly having trouble with his throwing arm. After Sizemore walked, Alou stepped to the plate and lofted a high, foul fly near the Cardinals' dugout that he misplayed and dropped, much to the delight of the visitors. A few moments later when Torre had gotten on second base himself, the razzers really got on McCarver during another pop fly, yelling, "He's going! He's going!"—to suggest that the slow-footed Torre was going to tag up and go to third base on the play. McCarver and the Cardinals' bench continued to go back and forth verbally over the next inning.

When Brock returned to the plate to lead things off once again in the fourth, a culmination of years of frustration boiled over with McCarver. Several of the Cardinals of the 1960s—among them Gibson and McCarver—felt that Brock sometime went for stolen bases when it was unnecessary, such as when the team was far ahead or far behind in a game, with no other purpose than to "pad" his own statistics. On the mound for the Phillies was pitcher Manny Muniz, making one of only five big league appearances he would have in his one-year career. His first pitch came near Brock's head; the second was not even retrievable by McCarver, going all the way to the backstop. At that point, Brock turned and said something to McCarver. The catcher sprang up from his squatting position, removed his mask, and punched Brock in the head, sending the Cardinal player sprawling to the ground. Umpire Al Barlick immediately got between the two men and ejected McCarver from the game. Many on the Cardinals' bench, including Kissell, were surprised at McCarver's reaction. "It was a sucker punch. I've known McCarver since he was a kid, but I lost a lot of respect for him tonight. He shouldn't let his emotions take over like that." Added Benson, "Tim lost his cool, all right. And I'll bet if the truth were known he really feels embarrassed about what he did out there." Shortly, McCarver indeed expressed regret about the incident from the moment his fist began to fly. "I was agitated and apparently misunderstood something that Lou had said," he explained the following week. "I like to think that out of this unfortunate flare-up, we're better friends than before. I hope so." While McCarver denied that the fight had anything to do with Brock's trying to steal bases with his team far ahead (as Brock had four stolen bases in the game), the issue was raised once again in the wake of the altercation; when Brock had stolen his last base of the evening, Larry Bowa, the Phillies' fiery second-year shortstop who was on his way in 1971 to Major League records at the position for fielding percentage (.987) and fewest errors (eleven), had also been jawing at him.

Despite his old respect for McCarver, Gibson would understandably—and as expected—launch his own salvo in the bottom of the fourth inning to protect his teammates. The unlucky recipient was Mike Ryan, McCarver's replacement who was greeted with a pitch behind his head to lead off the inning as Gibson received a "warning" from Barlick. Jack Buck, once again steaming with strong emotion on the radio for the second time in three weeks, was disturbed with what was happening. Buck had witnessed so much friendship and closeness among the group of men just a few years earlier, and it troubled him. He wrote that "it tore my heart out" to watch the ugly scene unfold on the field. For his part, McCarver claimed that the incident was his first fistfight since he was twelve years old.

Another on-field encounter between Brock and McCarver a week later in St. Louis suggested that while the hatchet might not yet be buried, it would ultimately be resolved in a peaceful manner. As fate would have it, the two were once again forced to physically confront each other due to the nuances of baseball. With Brock on third base, Torre sent a fly ball to shallow right field in the direction of Willie Montanez—the very same man who had earlier been sent to the Phillies from the Cardinals as compensation for Flood's failure to report. Despite Brock's speed, the proximity of the fly to home plate made it an easy play for Montanez, and he flung his throw toward the catcher. With McCarver already holding the ball and waiting for Brock's arrival, all watching the play were already imagining another melee breaking out in those momentary seconds before the imminent collision. With no chance to slide around the catcher, Brock was forced to knock over McCarver in an attempt to jar the ball loose—as any runner would do in such a situation. Observers held their breath as the clash took place. But when it was over a second later, the result was Brock returning the favor of the previous week; he knocked McCarver to the ground, who held onto the ball for the putout. Showing no hard feelings, Brock even retrieved McCarver's helmet and mask for him, and they tapped each other on the backside as a display of forgiving and forgetting. But even worse for the Cardinals, Montanez's play ended the game in the ninth, a 5–4 win for the Phillies that was a key loss in their pennant hopes. Montanez was truly casting his revenge on the organization that gave him away, for twenty-four hours earlier, his extra-inning homer—his second of the night—beat the Cardinals 6–5 on that evening as well, two important defeats for St. Louis in their pursuit of Pittsburgh.

It had certainly been a few weeks full of fireworks associated with Philadelphia baseball—some of which, a few had believed, may have been caused by forces "beyond the grave." Back on August 19, the Phillies had uprooted a statue of city baseball legend Connie Mack—the longtime owner and manager of the A's when they resided in town—from the stadium that bore his name on the north side of the city where the Phillies and A's both had played. The statue was transported to the recently opened Veterans Stadium at the new, expansive sports complex at the south end of town next door to the Spectrum, the four-year-old indoor arena that was home to the city's professional hockey and basketball franchises. As the team dedicated Mack's statue at its new location, the old man was perhaps issuing a statement on his feelings about the club abandoning his old park, for within minutes of the ceremony's beginning, a fire broke out back north at Connie Mack Stadium, a five-alarm blaze that summoned more than one hundred firefighters and thirty trucks to the scene whose effectiveness was lessened by the unexpected low water pressure from local hydrants. The flames engulfed and downed the entire left-field grandstand as well as other parts of the park, as residents from the blighted ghettos surrounding the old yard—a major reason for the Phillies' wanting to move across town—were evacuated for their safety. It was wondered if Mack had placed a hex on his Keystone rivals the Pirates as well, for in the same few weeks, Pittsburgh had gone 7-17 and squandered much of its large lead in the National League East.

But while Reggie's Cleveland's victory over Pittsburgh the day after Gibson's no-hitter got the Cards within four of the Pirates in the standings, that was as close as they would get. The "Montanez losses" to the Phillies, followed by a two-game sweep at the hands of the Pirates, effectively ended the divisional chase in putting the "magic number" for Pittsburgh at three with two weeks to go. Even so, Pirates assistant Virdon—himself a former star center fielder for St. Louis, and still residing in his original home area of Springfield, Missouri— was confident that the Redbirds would be a team to be reckoned with in the future. "The Cardinals ought to have a good club for the next four or five years. They've got speed, solid veterans, good young talent like Ted Simmons, Jose Cruz and Luis Melendez, and they can score runs." Added to the mix were Roque, the forgotten one of the young outfielders who went three for four in his first major start in the Cards' final home game of the season on September 26, and the potential emergence of another young pitcher in Santiago Guzman. Guzman began his career with a 16-3 record as a seventeen-year-old with the Cards' Minor League team in St. Petersburg in 1967, and now would close 1971 with two innings of scoreless relief against the Pirates (including an overpowering strikeout of Stargell—who had tied Aaron for the league lead with his forty-sixth homer against Cleveland earlier in the game) and an eight-inning, ten-strikeout start against the Mets on September 27. Suddenly, despite the earlier dismissal of Torrez and Norman, it appeared as if the Cardinals had more starting pitching options than ever before.

Yet it was clear that the National League Eastern Division was still undoubtedly in the clutches of the Pittsburgh Pirates. A week later at Busch Stadium, the visitors' clubhouse was awash in champagne as the Bucs finally clinched. Among the celebrants were many former Cardinals—including Briles and Davalillo (picked up by Pittsburgh in the Alou trade the previous off-season), pitchers Bob Miller and Carl Taylor, as well as another in Dave Giusti. Giusti, discarded by St. Louis after only a brief trial, was capping his second season as a dominant relief pitcher for the Pirates and had held the Cards scoreless in the final three innings of the clinching 5–1 win. The team had also been aided by the emergence of infielder Rennie Stennett, who filled in at second base when Cash undertook military duty on August 21. Stennett responded with twenty-two hits in his first eight games afterward. Despite his performance, Stennett would be left off the playoff roster with the return of veteran utility man Jose Pagan, who had been on the injured list since August 6. "Last spring, everybody said we didn't have enough pitching," manager Danny Murtaugh scoffed. Murtaugh would vacate the manager's post for a second time in 1972 but return to lead the Pirates once again the following year. "But where are we now? And how do you explain that?" Their fortunes would continue with an upset victory over the heavily favored and defending-champion Baltimore Orioles in the World Series, as many writers—including Wilks—scoffed at the idea of any National League club having a chance against Earl Weaver's team. "[Who] will follow the Cincinnati Reds [losers in the 1970 series to the Orioles] into oblivion as the National League's sacrifice to World Series continuity?" he wrote. Added Red Smith's headline to his article in the *New York Times,* "Pirates Are Murdered: Can Baseball Survive?" after Baltimore had won the first two games of the series by an aggregate score of 16–8. "Postal regulations," he continues, "do not permit an unexpurgated report of everything that went on." The Pittsburgh resurgence in the series would be fueled in part by Briles, a man written off by the Cardinals after helping them to pennants in the late 1960s. Briles notched a key Game 5 win in advance of Murtaugh's troops taking the title in seven.

Meanwhile, on September 18, a pitcher in Philadelphia named Rick Wise neared a Major League record by retiring thirty-two Chicago Cubs in succession, waiting until the twelfth inning to drive in the winning run himself with a single, his third hit on the day. Wise did not permit a Chicago base runner between the second and the eleventh frames, when Santo singled to leave Wise six batters short of Harvey Haddix's big league mark. In a matter of months, Wise would become a prominent name around St. Louis.

In finishing with ninety wins—achieved by virtue of Carlton's twentieth personal victory on the second-to-last day of the season—the Cards had at least issued a fourteen-game improvement over their performance in 1970, having clinched second place in the Eastern Division a week before the season ended with a win over Montreal on September 25. Expos manager Gene Mauch summed up how many felt and how impressed he was with the St. Louis team. "I thought Red [Schoendienst] did his best job this time—even better than in 1967 or 1968." Had the Cardinals been placed in the Western Division when divisional realignment occurred in 1969, their record would have tied the Giants for the Western crown; despite the improved win total, Busch Stadium would see a decline in attendance for the third straight season.

The riveting victory for the Cubs' Ferguson Jenkins over Gibson on opening day helped launch him into his own Cy Young Award season in 1971, taking the National League honors away from the Cardinal ace in winning twenty games or more for the fifth consecutive season. Meanwhile, the prodigy Vida Blue rebounded from his late-summer mental stress to continue to overwhelm the junior circuit, taking home the MVP as well as the Cy Young as he planned a celebratory trip to Walt Disney's new theme park, "Disney World," which had just opened outside Orlando on October 1. And with his accolades, Blue would become the answer to an astute trivia question—the last switch-hitting MVP in the American League (as it was yet two years before the league would adopt the designated-hitter rule, ending the batting role of pitchers).

On the positive side for the Redbirds, it appeared as if Gibson finally had, once again, the support of a deeper pitching staff. Carlton's first twenty-win season was a fine rebound from his horrid 1970, Cleveland was named the National League Rookie Pitcher of the Year in a poll of the league's players, and Reuss had further developed in winning fourteen games and joining the other three starters in striking out more than a hundred batters each. The rapid defensive development of Simmons behind the plate cannot be ignored in looking at the success of the staff, a player whose hitting was never in question but had been wrongly imagined to still be a few years away from Major League material at the catcher's position.

Willing to share the glory in deference to Jenkins's great year for the Cy Young, Gibson also said that Torre's 1971 season at the plate was the most amazing he had ever seen by a player, as the third baseman beat out Jenkins, Stargell, Aaron, and others to claim the MVP honors on the National League side. He was the tenth Cardinal to win the award, and the fourth in the last eight years, joining Boyer, Cepeda, and Gibson as the most recent recipients. "Torre was anything but a speed merchant, and for him to win the batting title at .363 [the highest average for a Cardinal in twenty-three years] meant that he was putting dents in the ball," Gibson said of the 230 hits that Torre scattered in ballparks over the course of the season. In addition to being the first Cardinal to win a batting title since Musial in 1957, Torre fulfilled his promise to replace Allen's run production in the lineup as well, for he also took home the National League RBI crown with 137, a figure that easily broke Boyer's team record for a third baseman (the ball Torre struck to set the record back in Philadelphia on September 6, ironically, had been saved in the pocket of Boyer during the inning, as he was taking a turn as the Cardinals' first base coach). His closest challenge in that category came from Stargell, who was slowed in the season's final weeks with a knee injury suffered from running into the outfield wall at Chicago's Wrigley Field. Stargell, however, would enjoy many more memorable moments in Pittsburgh—not the least of which was the Pirates' 1979 run to the world championship behind his famed enthusiasm. And when Pittsburgh said hello to the new ballpark that would replace Three Rivers Stadium on April 9, 2001, they would say good-bye to the man known as "Pops." Willie Stargell passed away the same day, dampening the excitement for the city on that day as he had been suffering from kidney disease and a recent stroke.

After beginning the season with a twenty-two-game hitting streak, Torre's batting average was never below .282 all year; he had posted 118 hits and 60 RBIs by the All-Star break and, perhaps most astonishingly, never went more than ten straight at-bats without a hit all season long. At only one point—in the latter part of the summer on August 8—did he relinquish the batting lead, and that was for one day and by one point to Glenn Beckert of the Cubs, .357 to .356. Beckert, with the exception of a late charge from Stargell's teammate in Clemente, was the lone true batting-title threat to Torre for the majority of the season. Nonetheless, Beckert would see his pursuit of St. Louis slugger end prematurely. He was knocked out for the season in a game at Busch Stadium on September 3, damaging ligaments on the thumb of his throwing hand while diving at his second base position for a hit off the bat of Simmons in the first inning. Even if the Cub player could have stayed healthy, however, it was unlikely that anyone would have matched Torre's numbers during the 1971 schedule. "For the first two months of the season, Torre was as good a hitter as anyone I've watched," said Boyer. It was also the first time in nearly sixty years that a third baseman won the National League batting title. "After July, I began to hold onto the wall after leaving the shower," Torre would later reflect. "I thought this was the kind of year you have once in your life, and I didn't want to slip and ruin it." His contribution was the most significant to the Cardinals' lofty team batting average of .275 for 1971, their highest mark since World War II. Torre had indeed supplied run production in the absence of Dick Allen, the one-year wonder for the Cards whom St. Louisans had already seemed to forget. The main beneficiary was Brock, who led the National League for the second time in runs scored with 126, a career high, while also claiming his fifth league stolen-base title with 64 (Torre himself scored 97 runs).

Other performances for the Cardinals boded well for the future as well. Alou's 74 RBIs was the highest of his career at any level of pro ball, and 22 more than he would post in any of his Major League seasons, and fellow outfielder Brock notched his 200th hit on the season's final day in New York against Seaver and the Mets, as the ace fanned thirteen Redbirds on the day in matching Carlton's twenty wins for the year, which the Cardinals' lefty achieved in Shea Stadium twenty-four hours earlier.

When Dick Allen ran into Devine in a hotel lobby late in the 1971 season, the player told his former general manager that the Dodgers were *also* now looking to trade him, less than a year after Devine and the Cardinals had done so. Allen looked at Devine with a perplexed expression, then wondered aloud why he was being dealt so often. Devine then told him, "You might take a look at what *you're* doing to make people feel that way." The 1972 campaign would see Allen land on the South Side of Chicago with the White Sox, his fourth team in as many years. That season, Dick's little brother, Ron, would appear in seven games for the Cardinals in 1972 between August 11 and 21.

The addition of Alou and the elevation of Torre's play made the absence of Allen's power bat more tolerable. However, just as the starting pitching staff seemed to be emerging as a dominant force, as it had been in the 1960s, it would experience a shocking overhaul before the 1972 season.

6   Loss of the Lefties

[Rick] Wise was a reliable pitcher. But Carlton was obviously a great one, and delivering him to Philadelphia was a matter of depositing another two hundred–something wins into the account of one of our division rivals.

—Bob Gibson

Capped by his twenty-win season in 1971, Steve Carlton was indeed riding high by early 1972. He had invested ten years in the Cardinals' organization, signing as a nineteen-year-old in 1963 and working for the last five full seasons (and parts of seven overall) in the Major Leagues. It was unmistakable that he was finally harnessing his immense physical talent, and with Gibson aging, he was asserting himself as a potential number-one starter on the pitching staff. The club was also fully aware that he could be a nuisance when it came to contract negotiations, and Devine did not relish having to now deal with him in the wake of his best year as a professional. Only two years earlier, he had demanded more than twice his 1969 salary for 1970; while not meeting his desired figure, the team nonetheless agreed to a hefty raise, and the result was Carlton posting a nineteen-loss season. As the winter snow continued to pile up in the Midwest, Carlton and the brewery were more than ten thousand dollars apart in salary figures by February 1972. Now, with Carlton hinting at staging a spring training holdout once again, Gussie Busch and his henchmen would have to further extend their creativity to have the pitcher ink his contract and arrive in Florida on time. An idea to this end would spring forth, strangely enough, from the current year's U.S. presidential election.

The following November, Nixon would be reelected in a landslide victory over Senator George McGovern despite the lowest voter turnout in almost twenty-five years, with only 55 percent of those eligible casting a ballot. In an effort to stem runaway inflation in the early 1970s, Nixon urged private businesses to place a 5.5 percent cap on employee raises for the coming year as part of his campaign proclamations. Still a sharp businessman with financial acumen, Busch seized the moment and utilized this point in his negotiations with Carlton and a few other Cardinals seeking substantial raises. Carlton, however, ignored the federal guidelines and was seeking an amount in the neighborhood of seventy-five thousand dollars, which was around 20 percent more than the sixty-two thousand Busch was prepared to offer him. Years later in reflection, Devine could not believe how inane the situation would become. "He [Carlton] was being very difficult to sign for the ridiculous amount of $10,000 between what he wanted and what we'd give him. . . . [F]requently, Mr. Busch and I would have conversations where he'd say, 'Have you got Carlton signed yet? If you haven't got him signed, figure out what you're going to do with him.'" Although often difficult to deal with when it came to contracts, Carlton had never been more stubborn, and never at a worse time; Gussie's view of the "modern player" had certainly not improved since the Flood situation, and because of this, he was about to ignite a near-complete explosion of the pitching roster.

At this same time, wanting nearly as much money from the Phillies was Wise, who had performed admirably for his team in 1971 in winning seventeen games (but with as many losses as well) for the last-place club.

So, on February 25—just as Nixon was in the middle of his historic eight-day meeting with Mao Tse-tung, the first-ever trip for a president to the People's Republic of China—the Cardinals began their own "Cultural Revolution" of the pitching staff. Carlton and Wise were exchanged in a trade, in effect relieving both organizations of their prime hassles in salary negotiations.

"Wise was a reliable pitcher," assessed Gibson many years later, "but Carlton was obviously a great one, and delivering him to Philadelphia was a matter of depositing another two hundred–something wins into the account of one of our [at the time] division rivals." In continuing his reflection, Gibson then referred to another deal involving another young Cardinals pitcher that was still to come in early 1972. "In the course of a year, the organization managed to rid itself of a grand total of 671 future victories, replacing them with pitchers who would win 140 for St. Louis." Devine, in his own recollection of the event, knew this momentous twist of baseball fate could have, at the time, so easily gone in the other direction. "Mr. Busch sometimes would take a very strong stance when he thought he was being taken advantage of. . . . [E]ven though we were very close in money with what Carlton wanted, Mr. Busch felt Carlton would be difficult to have around down the line."

And as Gibson had implied, soon another prominent pitcher for the Cardinals would be shown the door as well. Wise, like Dick Allen, had been a rookie on the ill-fated 1964 Phillies team that lost out to the Cardinals in the stretch run of the pennant drive. After signing with the Philadelphia organization out of high school for twelve thousand dollars, he had pitched in twenty-one big league games before his nineteenth birthday that year, having to stick on the big league roster due to the bonus rules of the time. The precocious Wise had always shown talent, having at age twelve led his team from Portland, Oregon, to the Little League World Series in 1958, four years after Colton, California (with its own future Major Leaguer in Ken Hubbs), would be the first West Coast team to make the cross-country trek to Pennsylvania to appear in the finals. Like Carlton, Wise had only recently grown into his potential at the big league level, for in addition to his recent epic thirty-two-out string in the game against the Cubs in late-September 1971, he had also thrown a no-hitter on June 23 as well as hitting two home runs himself in that same game against the Reds. Ironically, earlier in the season, a disgusted Wise complained that "to win on this club, you have to pitch a shutout and hit a homer." (Wise would also have a second two-homer game as a batter in 1971 as well.)

The no-hit victory, however, made Wise only a .500 pitcher for his career, with a record of 61-61 at the time. As with most players arriving to St. Louis in a trade, Wise was excited to take the mound with a talented cast behind him. "Here I know, for one thing, I'm going to get more support in the field, and I know the Cardinals are going to score runs," Wise said after the deal was made. "Darn it, I don't feel like I'm a .500 pitcher. I'm glad that now I've got a chance to try to show it." Seeking a refreshing start to all aspects of his life, Wise dropped a cigarette-smoking habit in coming to St. Louis—and went to cigars instead.

The Wise-Carlton transaction precluded another one the Cards *could* have made, which also could have altered their fortunes in the future. Back in November when the 1971 season had concluded, the Astros and Reds had completed a blockbuster trade in which Joe Morgan, Jack Billingham, Cesar Geronimo, and Ed Armbrister went to Cincinnati. Morgan and Geronimo—along with the emergence of young outfielder Ken Griffey Sr. in 1973—would add an extra dimension of speed to the previously lumbering offensive power show of the "Big Red Machine." It was a deal on which Schoendienst had privately felt the Cards had missed out, as Red had been hoping that the Cardinals would beat the Reds in getting to Morgan and acquire the star second baseman from Houston beforehand. "If we had kept Carlton and made the trade for Morgan, there's no telling how many pennants we could have won in the 1970s," he would later mourn.

Although being one contractual headache gone, the dismissal of Carlton had hardly relieved Busch and Devine of their difficulties. Simmons and Reuss were pursuing a doubling of their salaries to $35,000 each—proportionally larger increases than even Carlton had sought. While Simmons had batted over .300 and performed better defensively than expected in his first year, Reuss, while solid, had done little to warrant such an increase after his own initial full-time season in the big leagues. The left-hander had an even 14-14 record but, more significantly, permitted a bloated ERA near five. When the $35,000 was not approved for either man, Simmons decided he would play the season without a signed contract; however, by early March, the Cardinals invoked the "renewal clause" on both players, a codicil of the reserve clause in which a player unsigned by March 1 must report to camp by March 10 or risk release (at a time when "being released" still meant that a player had no further options with other clubs). After reaching agreements for $25,000 and $20,000, respectively, Simmons and Reuss were at workouts by the second week of March (also under the renewal clause, the club had the right to cut a holdout's salary by up to 20 percent; Devine, however, waived this action on both men, agreeing instead to sign them to the club's last offer on each). Keeping this card up their sleeves during negotiations had evidently long been planned by Devine and Busch, as at the outset the holdouts of Reuss and Simmons went curiously unopposed by the two executives. In the background, some were whispering that the contracts of Reuss and Simmons might be voided by the middle of the summer, as this was the expected time frame of a decision from the United States Supreme Court on the appeal of the Flood case. "Maybe the day has come to alter the reserve clause or the rights of renewal," Broeg considered. "But if baseball is going to exist competitively, someone will have to come up with a reasonable alternative." And whereas Simmons was apparently forgiven, the consequences for Reuss for not signing more quickly would be severe.

Devine was in no mood to celebrate his fifty-sixth birthday on March 1, for also seeking hefty new contracts were Alou and the reigning National League MVP and most dominant offensive force in baseball from the previous season, Torre, two men who were also unsigned. Since players had started reporting in late February, Torre had been stopping by the Cardinals' complex in St. Petersburg only to pick up his mail, using his extra free time to travel to New Hampshire and Washington, D.C., to attend events for President Nixon's reelection campaign. Having made $110,000 in 1971, Torre was looking for a large leap in the neighborhood of $150,000, which would match Gibson's current salary and was the highest ever for a Cardinal. The club instead had $130,000 in mind and was ready to exercise the renewal clause on Torre as well (meanwhile, Dick Allen was also trying to extract $150,000 from his new club, the Chicago White

Sox, and its general manager, Stu Holcomb; the Sox were offering $120,000). While the prospect of the renewal clause frightened Alou into signing the next day on March 2, Torre was not yet ready to commit. He tried to reassure Cardinal fans, however, that he was indeed happy in St. Louis. "I want to finish my career here, but not this year." On the fourth, Torre then declined a two-year contract offer from Devine that would pay him $130,000 in 1972 and in 1973 the $150,000 Torre was currently pursuing—as now the player was looking for a *three*-year deal that the club was unwilling to make. "Obviously, Bing has reached the limit on what he can give me," a frustrated Torre told the writers a day later. "Maybe I should have signed last October when there apparently was more money available." In a hopeful tone, he added that "if the Cardinals invoke the renewal clause in my contract, I'll report because I'm no rebel. But even though there's no animosity, I won't like it."

In the end, the club got Torre to agree to the terms they had last offered. "I realized the difference [in the figures]," he continued, "and it was not worth endangering my relations with the ballclub. Again, I'd like to finish my career with the Cardinals." Even though it was the team's figure to which he agreed, it was far more money than Torre had ever made as a ballplayer. "He raised himself from a journeyman's salary to a superstar's salary by self-discipline," said George Kissell.

For 1972, Torre would share the cocaptaincy of the club with Lou Brock—the first time Brock had ever been formally designated the honor (in another first for Brock, he was also experimenting in right field a bit in spring training, at the behest of Schoendienst as an idea). As was baseball tradition at the time, each man would earn an extra $500 for executing the role of captain. And as soon as Torre checked into camp, he was tracked down by Jim Bouton, who wished to tape a television interview with him. Torre refused. "Bouton has made enough money off ballplayers," he said angrily.

By the Ides of March, the Cardinals were 0-5 in their exhibition games and had not scored in their last twenty-one innings. They had been shut down on the fifteenth by Boston and their impressive young catcher, rookie Carlton Fisk, who embarrassed Melendez by nailing him by fifteen feet in trying to steal second base. "I never saw a catcher throw harder or more accurately than Fisk," Gussie Busch said after seeing him only once at the day's game, even though Busch had viewed the exploits of Johnny Bench for the past four years.

It was while sitting in the stands that Busch, for the first time publicly, became engaged in a discussion about the possibility of a players' strike at the opening of the season. The owners' current agreement with the Players' Association was set to expire on March 31, and the union was threatening to walk out if improvements were not made to their health insurance and pension funds—specifically, to the tune of nearly $1 million annually and indefinitely—among other conditions they sought. The owners, meanwhile, had offered a $400,000 payment per annum. "I can't speak for other clubs," the Cardinals' CEO gruffly concluded, evidently more bitter about player greed than he had ever been. "But frankly, I wouldn't give a damn if the players went out. I'd vote to let them take a walk. We've tried to be as fair as we can in providing terrific salaries, a great pension plan and everything while trying not to raise ticket prices. Few American and National League ball clubs really make any money. They [the players] are going to ruin baseball, the way they're going. . . . [I]t's getting impossible to operate reasonably. I'm going to stand up to them."

Dick Meyer stood side by side with his boss. "We've agreed to make certain that their [the players'] medical, dental, and life insurance programs do not suffer, but we're unified in our position that we will not improve an already extremely-generous pension plan," the Cardinals' executive vice president added. Meyer went on to use himself as an example of how ridiculous, he felt, were the demands of the players. "I know of no pension plan that carries with it an escalation based on an increased cost of living. I can't ask Anheuser-Busch to make up for the years when I was making $55 a month."

In the final days of spring training in 1972, as the Cardinals were being visited in camp by a group of baseball ambassadors from Italy, yet another roster bombshell was dropped. Julian Javier, who was a key component to the club throughout the entire decade of the 1960s, had grown in further disfavor of the management with his actions. In March 1972 he was once again late to report for spring training. As a result, Javier was purged from the organization on March 24, traded to the restructuring Reds for pitcher Tony Cloninger as the second baseman joined Flood, McCarver, Carlton, Cepeda, and Shannon as another relic from the glory days of the '60s to leave the team. It was the same day the film *The Godfather* was released to theaters and just over a couple weeks after Javier had finally shown up in St. Petersburg. It had been essentially decided after the 1971 All-Star break that Sizemore was going to be the second baseman of the future (but Sizemore as well, like fellow infielder Torre and so many others, was also seeking a raise; Ted's, however, turned out to be more modest, a $5,000 increase over his 1971 rate of $30,000). The move was not purely a strategic one, for Javier, though an extremely likable person, had also been vocal in his displeasure in being relegated to a reserve role by the manager for the latter part of 1971 and had been viewed by Busch as the actual origin point of the contemporary insubordination of Cardinal players, being the first to complain about his salary at the close of the 1968 World Series loss to Detroit (Javier had even staged a brief holdout *before* the 1968 season as well, once again staking out in the Dominican Republic and telling a frustrated Jim Toomey through his agent to "pay me, or I quit"). With the exception of Gibson, Javier had been arguably as central to the team's success as anyone during the past decade, having played in 1,547 games at second base—more than any other in St. Louis history, including Rogers Hornsby, Frankie Frisch, and Schoendienst himself (who was second on the list with 1,429).

Still, Schoendienst had become so disgusted with Javier that he did not even care to offer reporters an opinion on Cloninger when asked about the man the Cards were getting in the deal. "Javier wasn't in shape, didn't want to play, and scarcely could get the ball from second base to first, yet he wants me to say we didn't use him. I'm tired of people who don't want to play, but say they do." When asked about young Ed Crosby, a potential infield replacement for Javier on the roster, Red continued, "At least he's got a good attitude and really wants to play—not just talk about it." Instead of trading Javier, the Cardinals had reportedly offered him an opportunity to scout for the organization in the Caribbean, but he turned it down. Meanwhile, it took the player more than three days to get in touch with Reds officials after the trade was made, and in doing so, he chose to miss out on three important days of late-March workouts. With the roster move, Sizemore and Maxvill decided to stay out on the practice fields long after their teammates had departed for the showers in St. Petersburg, intent on perfecting their double-play synchronicity around the bag. More thickly built than the normal second baseman, Sizemore looked even stockier in light of the fact he wore the atypical number 41 in playing the position.

Just as Devine was making the final arrangements of the Javier deal on the phone, Busch was in the locker room at Al Lang Field, talking to a roomful of players that still included the lame-duck second baseman. He told the team—while not in the tone of his famous scathing speech of three years prior, but still in no uncertain terms—that the strike that the players' union was considering threatened to "alienate" the fans of baseball, as well as to jeopardize the significant monetary gains already made by the Players' Association in recent years. As examples, he noted to them that a player released from spring training now received thirty days' pay, whereas a player from past decades got only a train ticket home; also, he reminded them that a player got sixty days' pay if released after the regular season started and a full year's salary if dismissed after May 15—again, a far cry from the golden era of the sport. If the players decided to strike, Busch continued, it was their prerogative (even though Devine, sitting nearby, estimated aloud it would cost the organization more than $1.5 million); he said that he would even provide a one-way plane ticket from St. Petersburg to their individual homes anywhere in the United States.

Busch was not alone in giving such speeches to his team this particular March. Edmund Fitzgerald, chief executive of the Milwaukee Brewers, was offering his employees the same deal if a work stoppage surfaced. "All they [the players] would be entitled to is a plane fare home, and I hope they have a nice summer." Added Campbell in discussing the Tigers and those on other teams, "I think the players are damn greedy. This game has been pretty good to those guys, and I think baseball deserves better. They've got a hell of a better pension program and medical coverage than the scouts or other people in baseball who make their jobs possible. I don't know of any benefit program in this world that's any better than the one they've got." Campbell's field manager, Martin, was especially concerned about a lingering strike's impact on his older ball club's ability to stay in shape once the season finally—if ever—got going. With Busch coming off as more subtle than his tirade three years earlier—while at the same time sending Javier packing—it was now evident to all that if established mainstays of the organization could be moved because of having annoyed the boss in some manner, no one was safe.

Even with the now tenuous nature of the roster, the Cardinals apparently felt good enough about their bull pen to release Stan Williams, a Major League veteran of thirteen seasons and former all-star who had won three games in as many decisions as a late-season pickup for St. Louis in 1971. Many questioned the club's decision for putting Williams, a man with considerable postseason experience as well, on waivers. The team figured that two young pitchers acquired in the off-season from the New York Mets—Jim Bibby and Rich Folkers—promised much help for the future. Bibby, the son of a North Carolina tobacco farmer, was, like Gibson, an imposing figure at six foot five and 235 pounds. He was looking forward to pursuing a Major League career after a two-year military stint, a tenure that included a twelve-month deployment in a combat zone in Vietnam. "I was lucky over there," he said about his assigned duty. "I was in transportation. Drove a truck."

By far the most intriguing new face in camp among the pitchers, however, was Jim Maloney, the former fireballing right-hander formerly of the Cincinnati Reds. Signed to a contract back on January 4, Maloney—who despite seemingly having been around forever was still short of his thirty-second birthday—was invited as a nonroster player to spring training. He was battling to return to form after a variety of arm ailments that had plagued him in recent years, as well as a torn Achilles' tendon from 1970. Throughout spring training in 1972, Maloney would regularly complain of shoulder stiffness to Schoendienst, which limited his use in exhibition games. Released by the Reds after making only three starts in 1970, Maloney had just pitched in only thirty ineffective innings in 1971 after being picked up by the California Angels. After being one of the game's top strikeout artists of the 1960s, Maloney would subsequently be released from St. Louis as well by April 9. He gave it one more try with the Giants, but Maloney would not appear in another Major League game and would announce his retirement by June.

Rumors of a strike were becoming more of a reality by the end of March, when on the twenty-fifth Marvin Miller conducted a poll of the players that, according to him, reported that 663 out of 673 were currently in favor of a walkout unless the owners improved their offer. Little sympathy for Miller's cause was found in the press—whose scribes were stating the view that even the typical modern *fan* was complicit in the problem. "Fans shake their heads and cluck over the greediness in professional sports," wrote Milton Richman. "They rarely differentiate between the owners and the players, saying, in effect, a plague on both houses. But these same fans keep paying their money." Added Jeff Meyers in an op-ed piece in the *Post-Dispatch,* "There are actually people still alive today who remember when athletes would come out to the heart of America with thoughts no loftier than getting a chance to wear a big league uniform. In those days, an athlete was an athlete. He was not a college graduate who majored in finance and minored in corporate law and method acting. He was not a businessman who negotiated his contract flanked by a lawyer and a tax consultant." A strike would have far-reaching financial ramifications for the players as well as the owners; for example, of the twenty-five Cardinals on the Major League roster, Jim Toomey estimated that nearly half of them already were in debt to the club, having previously opted to take their paychecks on a twelve-month pay scale instead of within the confines of the "labor time" of the regular season.

Few believed that a work stoppage, something that had never happened in the modern annals of big league baseball, would come to pass. But when the morning of April 1 arrived—the strike deadline—no players were found at their respective Major League parks. The owners made certain to keep the doors to the clubhouses open, so as to illustrate that they were permitting the players the choice to strike or not; otherwise, if the doors had been closed, they would have risked having the scene labeled by the media as a "lockout." Miller showed no signs of relenting on behalf of the players' union, but mentioned that a simple phone call on the part of the owners could end the standoff that had the players now seeking a 17 percent increase to the pension fund. "The fastest way to clear this up," Miller advised, "is for them [the owners] to call the Equitable Insurance people, the people who handle the money in the pension fund, and ask them for their estimate on the amount of surplus money at hand in the fund. That's all it would take." Larry Jackson, the former Cardinals pitcher who was now serving in state government in Idaho, had felt that a strike was inevitable when Miller took hold of the Players' Association six years earlier. Added his fellow former Cardinals hurler Dean from his home in southern Mississippi, "The majority of the players are ready to go out and play ball, but somebody [Miller] is agitating 'em and keeping 'em from playing." And for the first time anyone in St. Louis could remember, rumors circulated that Busch was looking to sell the team due to his deepened disgust.

Bowie Kuhn, meanwhile, was staying completely out of the negotiations, instead turning attention to his personal pursuit of three-division leagues for

1973 when the idea did not materialize for the 1972 season. Kuhn cited a potential conflict of interest for taking part in the labor negotiations, as he was, essentially, placed in the commissioner's office by the owners. Kuhn was also scheduled to testify to a United States Senate subcommittee in the coming month on the topic of Major League expansion. He would tell the senators that the topic was not popular among current owners (with teams having been added just three years earlier), and that any chance of a big league club returning to Washington, D.C., would have to come by way of transfer of an existing franchise.

In a strange coincidence, the doomsday of April 1 also saw Dick Allen finally signing his contract with the White Sox just as the strike was being announced, assuring all that with his fourth team in as many seasons, he would "have a home in Chicago for many years. For the first time in my career, I really feel wanted," Allen mimicked himself in a recycled statement many had heard from him in years past. The following day, on Easter Sunday, April 2, baseball mourned the passing of the man who had brought the New York Mets into prominence—their manager and local icon, Gil Hodges.

Another prominent player in addition to Allen, Vida Blue, was also staging his own personal strike, regardless of the progress of the union's negotiations. The new pitching phenom was demanding $92,000 from A's owner Charles Finley, but Finley had been "standing firm" at his $50,000 offer.

Disbelief ran throughout baseball followers nationwide, with games gradually lopped off the beginning of the schedule as the impasse continued, starting with the traditional opener at Cincinnati on Monday, April 3, between the Reds and the Astros. The anxiety of the players was already compounding a day later, for when Baltimore manager Earl Weaver took a poll of his team, twenty-one of twenty-five were willing to defy the union and play baseball.

The deadlock would last for another twelve days, as the two sides were finally able to come to a compromise. In the midst of the strike, the players' side had originally made clear that there would be no concessions on their part. Some of the owners had suggested that this might include their playing "complimentary games" to make up for those lost, or, at the very least, carrying out a shorter schedule with no pay for the contests missed. The owners figured that this would be a kind gesture to the fans, who had suffered as well. As it turned out, the players would have none of it. "If we play 162 games," Cubs player representative Milt Pappas retorted, "we're entitled to payment for every game." In the end, it was decided there would simply be no makeups, as 86 games were permanently lost on the schedule as both leagues agreed to hold a shortened slate (a couple weeks earlier when there had been no agreement in sight, the National League was originally considering still committing to a 162-game schedule, while the American League was leaning toward picking up where the strike left off—whenever that might have been). In addition, the cities themselves were also losing money from the strike. Such was the case in Atlanta, where the Braves paid the city $500,000 for renting the stadium, which sat empty to the tune of about $25,000 during the silence. As for the St. Louis finances, Gussie Busch figured the Cards would be "lucky as hell" to draw one million fans through the turnstiles for the rest of 1972—meaning, he also figured, that the club would barely turn a profit, if not place itself in the red. He also added that, even though the strike was finished, he would not permit any Cardinals games to take place until the players proved they were in good-enough shape to give the fans a Major League–quality contest. Many of the players had already been working out, with Brock and other St. Louis–area residents from the team throwing batting practice to each other at Florissant Valley Community College, while Maxvill led a contingent on the other side of the river in impromptu practice sessions at Southern Illinois University at Edwardsville. Unimpressed and further resentful, the indignant Busch would not attend a game at the stadium bearing his name until the very end of May.

In fact, speculation was brewing that even the untouchable Gibson might be next in line for the wrath of the owner. As Roger Maris had done, Gibson had discussed the possibility of getting a beer distributorship from Busch, but Gibson would later say that after the strike of 1972, it was never mentioned to him by Gussie again, even though they remained mostly cordial toward one another. Busch was of the mind that he had given Gibson a "second chance" with the team after Gibson's past interview on *The Tonight Show* with Johnny Carson when he suggested a player strike was a possibility in the future. Gibson was now starting to seriously think about life after baseball, as in addition to doing broadcasting back in Omaha, he had also attempted in 1972 to open a bank in one of the black sections of the city. Capital had been provided for the project by Omaha native Warren Buffett—who in 1972 had already been a millionaire for ten years—as "The Community Bank of Nebraska" got set to open its doors in April 1973. Ultimately, however, the venture failed, and its assets were purchased by the Wells Fargo Bank of Nebraska a short time later.

In the end, the Players' Association settled for a $500,000 contribution from the owners to the pension fund—about half of what they had been seeking—and another $490,000 into their health care fund. Final estimates in losses due to the strike hovered around $5 million total for the owners and approximately $1.25 million in salary for the players. Representing another side from Anaheim, California, was another union, the newly formed "United Baseball Fans of America," with the intent to "represent the fans and express their views on rising attendance costs, strikes and possible rule changes to the game." The settlement reached between the players and owners addressed only the short term, as the comprehensive agreement was set to expire on December 31, which forecast even darker clouds for the game down the road, as Kuhn predicted at least some change to the reserve clause at that time.

Kuhn's neutrality during the stalemate was also not well met in the press, as expressed by David Condon of the *Chicago Tribune* when the walkout was finally over. "This [the strike] would never have happened if Judge Landis or Bowie Kuhn were alive," he cracked.

The original calendar showed the Cardinals having a home date with the Montreal Expos April 15, as well as another the following afternoon on Sunday, the sixteenth, so their season would begin there. Afterward, the team would have to immediately embark on a road trip that would carry them all the way into May. Taking off from Lambert Field in St. Louis, they discovered that traveling secretary Leo Ward would have the team flying an Ozark Airlines twin-engine DC-9 as opposed to their usual, more comfortable United 727—a result, the players figured, of the strike. Ward cited the fact that Ozark was based in St. Louis while United was not, which offered lower costs. In addition, the players were now being asked to double up in hotel rooms unless they wished to pay the difference for a single. The lodging move did not sit well with Maxvill, who was paired with Torre—the latter of whom liked to smoke big cigars. "The room looks like Los Angeles in the smog," the shortstop complained. "You need a gas mask." At home in St. Louis, Torre had also taken in a roomie in new pitcher Al Santorini at his north-side apartment. As Ward listened to more groaning from players who were accustomed to being pampered, he further pointed out that the Cardinals up until 1972 had been, to his knowledge, the only Major League team that allowed for a single room for all players.

On the fourteenth—the day prior to the shortened season starting—about three hundred stoic, unenthused people showed up at Busch Stadium for a team practice session that was opened to the public as a gesture of goodwill to the customers. To accelerate their readiness, Schoendienst had requested that the Cardinals be allowed to practice in other teams' ballparks while on the road for the first few weeks of the season, and that the Cards would extend the same courtesy to the other teams at Busch to help shake off the rust.

Not many more—a mere seventy-eight hundred—showed up for opening day twenty-four hours later, which despite being the first game of the season was the third-smallest paying crowd since the park opened in 1966. The threat of rain existed, but the small gathering was mostly attributed to anger at the players (during the traditional first-day introductions, almost all of the Cardinals were booed, but Maxvill got it the loudest as the player representative to the union). Gibson fell short once again in an opening-day assignment, pitching for the first time since March 26 in bowing to the Expos, 3–2. Young first baseman Mike Jorgensen homered off him in the very first inning to put Montreal ahead 2–0; their paths would cross a couple seasons later at a climactic point in Gibson's final days on the mound.

Later in the game, when the Expos' Ken Singleton drove a gapper to the outfield wall for an extra-base hit, Jose Cruz had trouble picking it up. A fan in the bleachers yelled, "Put a dollar sign on it—maybe that will help you!"

While Jack Buck was settling into his third season as the Cardinals' lead announcer in replacing Caray, he needed to get accustomed to another new partner for 1972. As the team was in New York to close out the 1971 season, Jim Woods—who worked alongside Buck in the KMOX radio booth for the past two years—decided to call it quits after a short stint with the St. Louis club. Woods had previously broadcasted games with the Pirates, Giants, and Yankees, but for some reason felt out of place in St. Louis. "The job was more or less misrepresented to me when I took it," Woods complained. "The Cardinals made too many demands on my time in the off season."

The open spot was offered Mike Shannon, who had been looking to get back closer to the action after spending a year working in the promotions department of the ball club. Shannon, however, had no experience whatsoever in working in the media. "I have a poor radio voice," Shannon would modestly tell *Post-Dispatch* writer Jeff Meyers after a month on the job. "I'm not the guy with the golden lungs—nowhere close." At this same juncture, Buck assessed his new partner this way: "I describe [the play] and then push away from the mike. I let him [Shannon] amplify. He's very candid. And we don't agree all the time. He's talking strictly from a player's viewpoint. He uses the jargon of the dugout." Shannon added, "If I was fired tomorrow, I have no doubt I could come back and compete down there," he said in pointing to the playing field from the press box. And Meyers, though impressed with the progress Shannon had made with his radio work in only a short time, figured it would not be a long-term gig. "Shannon gives the impression that he won't be broadcasting by the time his jet-black hair turns silver. He probably will switch his part-time cattle-raising business into a full-time operation." As it turned out, the cattle would have a long time to wait.

While the season was finally being started, Busch and Devine were still at work in attempting to further maneuver the personnel—and another reverberating trade was made just as Gibson was issuing the first pitches of the season.

Despite the fact he was a legendary high school talent in St. Louis, it was nonetheless a surprise to very few that Jerry Reuss was traded on opening day, being sent packing to Houston for fellow young pitchers Scipio Spinks and Lance Clemons. Reuss thought that he knew the very reason—his salary negotiations for the 1972 season. Reuss clarified later misconceptions of what arose from those tumultuous days.

    The Cardinals gave me a $6,000 raise for 1971 (to $17,000) after winning
seven games for Tulsa and seven more for major league club in 1970. Hoping
for at least the same dollar figure raise for 1972, Bing stopped at just a $3,000
raise after winning fourteen games for the Cardinals in 1971. In dealing with
the player development side of the club in the minor leagues, they started low, I
started high and we met somewhere in the middle for that season's salary. I assumed that Bing was following this same pattern so I asked for $32,000 figuring
we would meet somewhere between his figure and mine. It never happened.
For years, I believed the trade was about a difference in salary. It wasn't until a
chance meeting with Bing in 1998 that I discovered the trade was made because
I grew a mustache. To borrow a quote from Dizzy Dean, "Who'da thunk it?"

Reuss made his first spring training appearance on March 21, permitting six
hits in three innings. He followed this performance with a stronger outing
against the Mets on the 29th, shutting them out over nearly seven innings."
    "This was a deal I had to make," said Devine, "because Mr. Busch said, 'Jerry
Reuss is growing facial hair,' and he didn't like facial hair on ballplayers, or executives, either. 'Let's get rid of Reuss,' [Busch said]."
    The other departed pitcher of note, Carlton, had gone to camp with the Phil-
lies in March and encountered pitching coach Ray Rippelmeyer, a native of the
St. Louis area who put the left-hander on a strict workout regimen. The hard
work resulted in Carlton's shedding of fifteen pounds before the start of the
season—a season that would become Carlton's greatest of all.
    Of the two hurlers acquired by the Cardinals in the Reuss deal, Spinks held
the most promise in the eyes of Devine. He had been peaking at the most op-
portune time to optimize his value, as he had enjoyed a dominant spring training camp with Houston just as Gussie Busch was getting incensed at Carlton
and Reuss. His unusual first name was a tradition in his family, as noted by
former Cardinals beat writer Mike Eisenbath. "Spinks was named—as were
generations of first-born Spinks men—for the Roman general who conquered
Hannibal and burned Carthage." A student at St. Rita and Harlan high schools
in Chicago, the talented but erratic Spinks adored Ernie Banks as a youngster
(even though Spinks was being reared on the South Side of the city, which
is White Sox territory) and was disappointed that his hero had retired from
baseball before the two could face each other in game competition. While in
the Minor Leagues, Spinks had thrown a no-hitter in the Kansas City farm
system in 1969—only to lose the game by a 2–1 score as a result of his eight
walks and two wild pitches. Control had been an issue for him in his two
brief Major League auditions for the Astros as well, walking ten men in fifteen
innings of work. Yet there seemed to be magic in his right arm, for in five Minor League seasons through 1970, he had impressively logged more strikeouts
(772) than innings pitched (724). He also possessed the quirky personality of

Minor League legend, as Spinks's antics caused shaken heads and raised eyebrows wherever he went. While being an intelligent man (he was double majoring in German and psychology at the University of Illinois in the off-season), he carried a stuffed gorilla with him in his suitcase on road trips that he named "Mighty Joe Young," as Spinks felt it housed special powers. In feeling fortunate that the Cardinals had given him a new professional life, Spinks even had a spot for Mighty Joe on the dugout bench next to him in Busch Stadium after he arrived in St. Louis. He would talk to the stuffed animal and claimed Mighty Joe would talk back to him. "He talks to Brock sometimes, talks to Torre," Spinks would assert by the middle of the year. "He used to talk to Gibson until Gibson pulled his nose off."

Spinks was one of the more colorful characters to appear on the Cardinals' roster in quite some time. In addition to Mighty Joe Young, he also brought with him a considerable amount of hair, which was common for many ballplayers of the era, along with the various mustaches and beards that were appearing as well. Beards may just have been a point of personal dislike for the owner, for certainly, the trend of long hair clearly had started at least as far back as the "El Birdos" Cardinals of the late 1960s—a club that, just as they had begun winning on a regular basis, began to bring all assortments of hair creams and blow dryers into the locker room.

Soon, Spinks was penciled in as the number-five starter in replacing Chris Zachary, who despite his two-hit shutout of the Cubs back in May had not shown enough over the entirety of the 1971 season and the spring of '72 to remain in the starting rotation.

In addition, the trading of Reuss left the Cardinals' starting catcher as the only player who had not signed a 1972 contract. "The obvious question must be whether, following disposition of discontented Carlton, Bob Burda [traded to Boston on March 20], Julian Javier, and Reuss," wondered Broeg, "the reader can pick up the paper and learn that Ted Simmons has been traded, too." When asked if he thought his own status was in jeopardy, Simmons, who had played the season under the 1971 renewal clause for his contract, responded, "I would hope not. I don't want to leave here—that's for sure."

There was still a core of players who remained faithful to the owner and appreciative of his beneficent hand—and Simmons was considered among them. Also among them, perhaps ironically, was Joe Torre, the Cardinals' player representative to the union in 1972 who in the midst of those very ominous days of spring training had, like Simmons, considered not signing a contract at all. Torre reflected years later that if all the owners were like Busch in their generosity, the players probably would not have gone on strike in the first place.

Traditionally, the second game of the season for any team is one of the worst attended on the year. But in consideration of the nearly unprecedented showing for opening day, it was certainly no surprise when only seventy-one hundred were in the ballpark on Sunday to watch Wise's debut in a St. Louis uniform, another 3–2 loss. The defeats were part of a 1-6 start for the Cards, obviously failing to ready themselves at the quick announcement of the strike's ending. Among the other early losses was a notable clash between Gibson and Carlton in Philadelphia's Veterans Stadium on April 19, the first time the left-hander would face his old mentor and team. Both men went the distance, but Carlton prevailed 1–0—as the Phillies were once again the beneficiaries of the work of the pawn in the Flood saga, Montanez, who tripled off Gibson to lead off the Phillie sixth and was plated by Deron Johnson's single for the game's only run.

Just as the games finally got under way, Alan Eagleson, the director of the National Hockey League Player Association, made a startling announcement. The shifty Eagleson proclaimed that *his* charges, too, would go on strike in June if the hockey owners did not improve contribution to *that* league's pension fund as well. NHL president Clarence Campbell was perhaps most stunned with the idea, as he pointed out that league had a no-strike clause currently in effect with the union. Another menace to the league was the new World Hockey Association, threatening to shave off stars from NHL rosters (just as the World Football League would do to the NFL a couple of years later). By late June the maverick league would shock the hockey establishment by announcing that one of its teams, the Winnipeg Jets, had signed longtime Chicago Blackhawks star Bobby Hull to a $2.5 million multiyear contract. Hull's deal—nothing close to what he could ever get from the tightfisted ownership that had existed in Chicago—included his role as player-coach of the Jets and a subsequent front-office job in the future. At the time of the announcement, the handsome face of hockey from the 1960s smiled in front of the cameras with his family alongside him, as WHA president Gary Davidson presented Hull a large cardboard check.

In time, Eagleson's name would become linked with the players' pension fund in a much more dastardly manner.

With the *Post-Dispatch*'s Neal Russo writing that the team's "June swoon just came a month early this year," an eight-game losing streak in the middle of May sank the Cardinals even further to a 10-20 mark, which included their worst road trip in ten years in being swept in four games at Cincinnati as well as in the following three in Pittsburgh. Gibson—in part thanks to a bull pen whose ERA was soaring near the 6.00 mark—amazingly did not secure his first win of the season until May 25 and was also mired in one of his worst batting slumps ever (.040 for the season, having entered the year as a career .205 hitter). With his frustration beginning to boil over, Gibson began ranting to Russo about his lack of run support; the fed-up Russo, unafraid to confront Gibson, suggested

in his May 18 column that the pitcher "should stop feeling sorry for himself."
While Gibson was still highly respected among his peers, there were those who
felt that Russo's sentiments had needed to be said for a long time, as the veteran had often complained—publicly, to the anger of his teammates—about
the Cardinals' lack of offense when he pitched, while simultaneously trying to
mask it in a jocular manner.

Over in the American League, Gibson's presumed heir in Vida Blue would
still not be found in an A's uniform by the end of April—even after Finley
had twice agreed to the pitcher's demand, and twice Blue inexplicably walked
away from the table with the owner holding out the pen to him over the contract. When Blue had first signed with Oakland as a professional, he was offered
$8,000 in college scholarship money from Finley when his playing career was
finished; now, Blue simply wanted the $8,000 in cash. Finley agreed, but now
Blue was still holding out for more. On May 1, he would sign for $63,000 but
was grossly out of shape and would not enter a game until the twenty-fourth,
throwing an inning of relief against the California Angels, and he would not
post his first win until June 18. Things had certainly changed in a year's time
for Blue, who twelve months earlier had been the darling of baseball. Playing
before packed houses every time he pitched in his magnificent 1971 season,
Blue threw in front of only sixty-three hundred booing fans at the A's home
park as he surrendered eight runs in a 9–4 loss to Milwaukee on July 7, which
would sink his record to 2-5.

In St. Louis, Devine was relatively assuring in claiming that Schoendienst's
job was safe, noting that the only time his administration had ever fired a manager in midseason was Solly Hemus in 1961. "That's the only time in my career
such a thing has happened," the general manager said in a noncommittal tone,
"and I don't expect it to happen again. . . . [T]his has been an unusual year in
many respects." With the troubles of the team and the game in general, the feel-
good story for the Cardinals in the late spring was Spinks, the man acquired
to take the place of the hometown hero in Reuss. On May 9 he posted his second complete-game win, containing his old team in a 2–1 win over the Astros
at Busch Stadium. Two evenings later Reuss undid himself in a return home
against his old mates, as his throwing error in the ninth inning helped permit
the Cardinals to overcome a 3–1 deficit with two outs and beat him behind
Wise, 4–3. Then, on May 19—four days after Alabama governor and presidential candidate George Wallace was shot at a political rally in Maryland—Spinks
snapped the Cards' losing streak in beating the Cubs at Busch. In providing
their usual losing-streak tonic for the Cardinals, the Cubs just three weeks earlier had announced that Pepitone, the colorful but oft-pouting slugger, had decided to quit the team because he had been benched by Durocher (the latter of
whom was in his final days as the Chicago manager). Pepitone placed himself

on the "voluntarily retired" list, which meant he needed to sit out for at least sixty days before he would be eligible to return if he changed his mind. He did so at the end of June, just before Durocher was dismissed.

Spinks's win over the Cubs also celebrated the arrival of talented outfielder Bernie Carbo to the team in a trade with Cincinnati, in which Hague was shipped out. When the Cardinals had lost to the Cubs the day before, Melendez had been sent in by Schoendienst to pinch-hit for Hague with the tying runs on base in the ninth; the trade was completed before Hague reached the clubhouse after being lifted, and he proceeded to throw a fit in the locker room. Hague, whose weight had continued to balloon due to self-admitted indulgence of fatty foods and who never reached the promise he hinted as a ballplayer, had a parting shot for the organization. "The players are giving one hundred percent and getting booed," he spoke of the home fans in Busch Stadium. "That isn't right, and all because of a few quotes that appeared in the newspapers. It isn't the ballplayers' fault. Mr. Busch is more concerned about personalities than he is building a winning ball club." It was not the first time that the underachieving Hague had spoken his mind publicly against the Cardinal organization. Broeg recalled a speech Hague had made in Peoria, Illinois, a couple years prior in which the player criticized teammates Dick Allen and Jose Cardenal and complained about other recent trades the club had made at that time as well. After arriving in Cincinnati, Hague opined a week later that the dismissal of Carlton and Reuss by Busch would doom the Cardinals' pennant chances.

Like with all his other players, Schoendienst tried to be up front with Hague about his playing time. "I learned as a player that the most important thing you want from a manager is communication. You don't want to be left in the dark, wondering why you weren't playing, what role the manager had in mind for you, and things like that." Carbo, a platoon player in Cincinnati who had posted only three hits in twenty-one at-bats for the Reds, was immediately inserted into the starting role in right field as Alou went back to first base.

Spinks's success was able to spark the others on the pitching staff—especially Gibson. After his horrible start, the veteran ripped off eleven wins in his next eleven starts. His victory this day at Busch came with the help of an RBI single from Maxvill, who was batting .063 at the time.

By June the United States would see Nixon travel to Moscow to sign an agreement with Soviet premier Leonid Brezhnev on the first of the Strategic Arms Limitation Talks (the meeting occurred on May 26—the same day that the first break-in associated with the Watergate scandal, the so-called Ameritas Dinner, met with disgrace). Torre, meanwhile, while nearly maintaining the pace he set in 1971, was batting .362 by the beginning of June to once again lead the league. Over in the American League, people were beginning to speak of a potential Triple Crown for the itinerant Dick Allen, who had the league's most RBIs (forty) and was the current runner-up in homers (eleven) and batting average (.327).

On the sixth the Cards met the Giants for the first time on the year for a series in San Francisco. Willie McCovey, having broken his arm on April 18 in a collision with John Jeter of San Diego, had returned to the Giants' lineup only three days earlier (on the same day that McCovey was injured, his former teammate Cepeda announced that he may need to quit baseball due to chronic pain in his knee). With McCovey leaving the team in a couple more years to head down the coast to San Diego, the powerful San Francisco teams of the 1960s, like the Cardinals' juggernaut from the same decade, were also clearly disbanding. Three weeks earlier on May 11, the great Willie Mays was sent back to New York after fourteen years, traded by Giants to the Mets for pitcher Charlie Williams and $50,000 cash. The deal was done with Mays's agreement; the Giants' longtime owner, Horace Stoneham, knew that the legendary player wanted to finish his career in New York. And in return the Mets management had promised to "take care" of Willie when his playing days were over. The forty-one-year-old "Say-Hey Kid" went right to work, helping the Mets win their first four games after his acquisition that included a game-winning homer in the bottom of the eighth against the Phillies on May 21 in front of 57,267—the largest crowd to ever watch a baseball game in Philadelphia. His presence had added extra zip to a 14-1 tear by the Mets through May, surging them into first place in the National League East by six games over the Pirates while the Cardinals stood in last, fourteen games off the Mets' pace (later in July Mays would homer in his first game back in Candlestick Park in San Francisco, beating the Giants 3–1).

San Francisco players had initially been enraged with the news of the Mays trade before learning it had been approved by the outfielder. With Mays back east—as he was in 1972 in the last season of a two-year $165,000 contract—the trade of McCovey at the end of 1973 to the Padres uncovered the financial difficulties Stoneham had been experiencing with the club, as he was looking to dump some of its high-end salaries. But Stoneham—like Busch, one of the old-guard owners in baseball—was believed, like Gussie, to be ever more disgusted with the modern game and looking to get out of the business altogether.

The Cards had played against Mays as a Met for the first time on May 26, shortly before the end of another National League era would arrive on May 31, 1972. This would be the date of the last matchup between Bob Gibson and Ferguson Jenkins, the ninth time the two stoppers had dueled since their first battle on June 3, 1967. Gibson shut out Jenkins and the Cubs on three singles—the fifty-first time he had blanked an opponent in his career—as he faced only three batters over the minimum in Wrigley Field. In a few weeks Jenkins would go public with his sizzling anger about comparisons people insisted on making with him and Gibson, but for today, he said that he was simply "beaten by a better pitcher" on the day. In a bygone era when pitchers did not complain of overuse, did not worry about extended pitch counts, and were not looking to simply attain a "quality start," the complete game by the two stalwarts—who had both played basketball at one point for the Harlem Globetrotters—was the quickest of all their rapid matchups over the years—lasting only an hour and forty-seven minutes. "Two-hour games, or less, were the norm," wrote George Castle and Jim Rygelski. "Jenkins used to run to and from the mound. Gibson pitched, got the ball back, and was ready to go again. No dawdling. There was a minimum of walks and a maximum of 1-and-2 counts." The great misfortune was, however, that only seventy-one hundred people in Wrigley Field had bothered to come to watch. In the final tally of their nine battles, Jenkins would win five, Gibson three, with one no-decision for both.

Spurred by the victory over his archrival from Chicago, a few days later Gibson would throw back-to-back shutouts for the final time of his career. It would also catapult the team into a fantastic June, their best month of the year during which they would win twelve of thirteen in one stretch, the only blemish being the loss of the nightcap of a doubleheader against the Expos in Busch Stadium at the hands of old friend Mike Torrez, who was sporting a 9-3 record for a 28-36 Montreal team. During the game Torre was ejected for the second time in as many weeks for arguing a call, and the St. Louis fans littered the floor of Busch Stadium with debris in protest (many had even flung their shoes onto the field in the direction of the umpires).

And with the Flood saga about to end in the land's highest court, one of the other great Cardinals from the past decade set yet another standard for others to chase. On June 21, Gibson became the winningest pitcher in team history, separating himself from Haines with victory number 211 with a 14–3 win over San Diego in front of the home folks in St. Louis. Adding to the drama, Gibson himself cracked a seventh-inning homer that unraveled the crowd in a hollering frenzy when he crossed the plate. He had pitched most of the game with a pulled hamstring, the leg having been injured once again in a baserunning mishap as he circled the bases in scoring on a Lou Brock triple in the second inning. Thus, after belting the homer, Gibson did not return to the mound for further work as Drabowsky took his place. The crowd, however, insisted on one more appearance, and when the famed right-hander took a few steps out of the home dugout to tip his cap, the roars resumed again. "It's amazing to see him," Schoendienst said in looking back over all the years he had seen Gibson pitch. The manager presented the pitcher with a bottle of champagne in the locker room. "He's thrown hard all his life, and hell, he's still throwing hard. As long as I've been with him, I've never seen him smile on the day he's pitching. . . . [H]e's all business." It was the 389th start in a Cards uniform for Gibson—just three more than Haines had for St. Louis in his own career.

And interestingly, in one of the inexplicable intersections of fate in baseball, the umpire working behind the plate for the game was Stan Landes—the very same arbiter who called the balls and strikes for that very first win for Gibson as a Major Leaguer, recorded at Cincinnati's Crosley Field back on July 30, 1959.

A week before President Nixon announced that no new draftees would be sent to Vietnam, the long, tiring Curt Flood story finally came to a close on June 18, 1972. On Flood's appeal, the United States Supreme Court ruled against him and upheld baseball's antitrust exemption in a 5–3 vote (one justice, Lewis Powell, did not vote for a possible conflict of interest because he held stock in Anheuser-Busch). With no more cards left to play, Flood retreated to Europe for a third time—now, to Barcelona and then the island of Majorca in the Mediterranean, where he purchased an expensive sports car and would run a tavern for the next five years. After a stay in Andorra, he returned to America virtually penniless, as before going abroad, he had cashed out his Major League pension for a lump-sum payment of ten thousand dollars through which he quickly burned.

On June 21 Broeg wrote what sounded like the final words he ever wanted to use on the former outfielder: "It's incredible that a man so sharp could prove so abysmally bad in business. Marital difficulties, unwise financial investments, a free-spending lifestyle and poor judgment did him in." It had indeed been a busy week for the federal justices, for a few days later on June 29, the Supreme Court decided in *Furman v. Georgia* that the death penalty was unconstitutional. Among others incarcerated, the decision would spare the life of Charles Manson, who was sitting on death row in California for being convicted along with followers of his cult for a series of grisly multiple murders in Los Angeles in 1969.

Haines would be in attendance on July 7 for Gibson's 214th win at Busch Stadium, as he was getting ready to participate in an old-timers game two days later at Busch. He watched Gibson shut down the newest Houston superstar, Cesar Cedeno, in an 0-for-4 night. Cedeno was the leader of the upstart Astros, nicknamed by local papers as the "Glass House Gang" for the success they were enjoying in their strange indoor home of the Astrodome. Cedeno was emerging as the club leader in his third big league season, a true "five-tool" talent who had bolted past Torre in leading the National League with a .341 average. "How many men can field like he does, can throw like he does, can run like he does, can hit with power and hit to all fields like he does?" challenged Houston manager Harry Walker. "I'll tell you, there are damn few Hall-of-Famers that had all the talents he has. . . . [H]e's one of the most exciting players I've ever seen." As a sixteen-year-old back in the Dominican Republic, Cedeno in 1967 had been offered one thousand dollars to sign with the Cardinals. He was convinced by his father to instead stay in school and wait for more money, as Cedeno turned down another similar offer from the Mets and then agreed to the three thousand offered by Astros scout Pat Gillick. When a Cardinals scout returned to the Cedeno house the same afternoon that Gillick was present to finalize the contract, Cesar's father—a worker in a local nail factory—told him, "You're 15 minutes too late." Despite playing in the cavernous dome in Houston where many long fly balls merely wound up in outfielders' gloves, Cedeno was helping the Astros amazingly lead the National League in home runs with eighty-nine by mid-July—more than twice what the Cardinals had hit, a team yearning for a power source ever since Dick Allen left town.

The old-timers game in which Haines was participating, a tradition that has since left the Major Leagues for the most part, pitted former Cardinals against former Yankees. The rosters were impressive, including legends such as Musial, DiMaggio, Mantle, Bill Dickey, Tommy Heinrich, Phil Rizzuto, the Deans (both Dizzy and Paul), Enos Slaughter, Walker Cooper, and others. It was the fifty-two-year-old Musial, of course, who stole the show, hammering a pitch from former New York pitcher Allie Reynolds over the right-field wall for a home run. The Yankee Clipper, DiMaggio, also caught the eye of Broeg. "Distinguished and still graceful at 57, DiMaggio loped under a couple of fly balls as if he hadn't missed a day and, thanks in part to the sporting nature of the Dean brothers, plus their inability to throw hard, DiMag drilled a couple of base hits to left field." Dizzy, looking to avoid the Clipper in the first inning, jokingly protested to the umpire that DiMaggio was batting out of turn. Still others from the St. Louis past, Broeg noted, such as "Chick Hafey, Joe Medwick, Johnny Mize, and Terry Moore—sat out the game on the advice of their doctors or the orders of their wives."

With the team climbing back in the pennant race at the beginning of July, the Cardinals were being carried by a streaking Brock (who had hit safely in twenty of twenty-one games) and an improved Maxvill, the latter of whom had gone from a .114 average a month earlier up to .236 (meanwhile, for the Reds Hague had recently gone zero for twenty-one to drop to .226). It was their starting pitching staff, however, that truly shone through June, evidenced by a Major League high of thirty complete games to this point, which only served to cover a bull pen that remained erratic (from late May to early August, in fact, Gibson would fire twelve complete games in thirteen starts, and all but one would be completed in less than two hours). The most recent of the gems produced by the starters came in Philadelphia on June 30 at the hands of the irrepressible Scipio Spinks, now being mentioned as a possible Rookie of the Year candidate. Spinks stopped the Phillies in their home ballpark on five hits in a 4–1 win, and by the time the red-hot rookie pitcher took the mound again on the Fourth of July as the club finished a road trip in Cincinnati against Hague and the Reds, the Cardinals had matched the Mets' earlier 14–1 run in their own last fifteen games and now stood only six and a half games from first. Spinks's confidence was soaring, as despite his mediocre 5-5 record, his 93 strikeouts were third in the league behind mainstays Carlton and Seaver, and his 2.33 ERA rated him fourth (Carlton, enjoying his new surroundings in Philly, was running away from all others in the strikeout column with 166, in addition to several other pitching categories). Spinks also was beginning to act even more strangely on and off the field, still carrying Mighty Joe Young with him on the bench, tailing onto Gibson's backside everywhere the veteran went, and enjoying his status as the talk of the town. As quickly as his star rose, however, it came crashing down on this Independence Day on the Ohio River.

For the Reds, the 1972 season marked an upgrade to their machine dynasty, with Morgan taking over at second base and Geronimo in center field after the landmark trade with Houston in the off-season. What had not changed, however, was the rock they held behind the plate in Johnny Bench, in his fifth full season already being called one of the best ever at the position and on his way to his second National League MVP award that season. And it was against such a stone wall that the rookie Spinks would learn a painful, permanent lesson.

Spinks led off the top of the third for the Cardinals at the plate and laced a single to center field. Always anxious to show off his running speed on the bases, he then took off on a dead sprint when Melendez doubled to the gap in left center. Third base coach Vern Benson clearly held up both arms to signal a stop sign for Spinks at the bag, but Scipio later claimed he had too much momentum to throw on the brakes. When Spinks, Bench, and the ball all converged at home plate, the runner was originally called out by second-year umpire Bruce Froemming—but upon the rough contact that was made between the two players on Spinks's clumsy slide, the ball was jarred out of the cast-iron hands of the Cincinnati catcher, and Scipio had scored. When he tried to raise himself to his feet, however, Spinks crumpled like a marionette whose string had snapped, and he had to be carried from the field. Soon, examinations would reveal torn cartilage in his right knee—the one that had made contact with Bench on the play. He would be lost for the remainder of the season, cutting short what had been a most promising first campaign in the big leagues. "Safe for the day, out for the year," Spinks sighed afterward. Flying immediately home to St. Louis, Spinks had surgery on the knee the very next day, performed by Dr. London at Jewish Hospital.

While chatting with reporters during a one-hour rain delay before the July 4 game had gotten under way, Cincinnati manager Sparky Anderson was ironically mentioning that the Cards' starting rotation of Gibson, Wise, Cleveland, and Spinks had become, in his opinion, the best in the league.

Over the next two weeks, Cleveland (who had lost considerable weight over the previous winter by working on construction jobs in St. Petersburg) would pick up the slack for the missing Spinks and stretch out to an 11-4 record and was miffed when he was left off the National League All-Star roster by Pittsburgh's Murtaugh despite a 1.54 ERA in his last seven starts leading up to the break. The cooling Cards limped into the three off-days with a 45-43 record, ten games behind the Pirates; in 1971 at the break, they were 46-42 and eleven games behind Pittsburgh.

Instead of Cleveland for the Nationals' pitching staff in Atlanta, Gibson was chosen for the All-Star roster for the final time, while Jenkins of the Cubs—coming off perhaps his best season in 1971 and twelve more wins so far in 1972—was, like Cleveland, also left off the team by Murtaugh. By September Jenkins would end his season a week early, complaining of a sore shoulder after having thrown more than 289 innings in each of the past six years. In weighing all their contests over the years and the celebrity that came with them, Gibson still had no feelings for the man. "All Jenkins has done is gripe," the Cardinals pitcher would say at the end of the season when he heard that Jenkins considered himself the elite pitcher in the National League. For Jenkins 1972 would be his sixth and last consecutive twenty-win season; after 1973 he would be traded to the American League. Returning to the Cubs for two final seasons in 1982 and 1983, Jenkins would then retire one season before his long-suffering team would finally make the playoffs. Even though relations between Jenkins and Gibson would warm up in future years, the Cardinal player admitted to not necessarily enjoying the matchups. "The problem was, everyone thought I loved to pitch against Fergie and I liked the competition. Not really. You'd rather pitch against somebody you know you're going to get four or five runs off of. We weren't going to get but one or two runs off him, and that made it tough." Jenkins agreed: "If I gave up two or three runs [against Gibson], I was a loser."

While Broeg was hoping that the Spinks injury story would turn out like that of Gibson's broken leg in 1967 (in which he returned to lead the Cards to the title), he knew that the spot in the starting rotation would have to fall to the little-used Santorini—whom Broeg hoped, in turn, would become the new Nelson Briles, the latter of whom filled in so admirably for Gibson in his absence in '67. Santorini, a former first-round draft pick of the Atlanta Braves, had yet to reach his potential, and the Cardinals were hoping he would now take advantage of a new career opportunity.

Continuing his hot streak in being named the National League Player of the Week heading into the All-Star Game (having posted two complete-game wins including a thirteen-strikeout effort against the Astros), Gibson was named the game's starting pitcher by Murtaugh. Gibson came out and said publicly that he did not want to pitch in the contest, which raised the ire not only of Murtaugh but also of the American League manager, Earl Weaver, a St. Louis native. Gibson said his presence in Atlanta for the contest, however, was proof of his wanting to pitch—just not to start, he tried to make clear. "If I didn't want to pitch," he told Dick Kaegel, "all I'd have to do is come up with a bad back or bad leg and I wouldn't be here. . . . I just want to pitch one inning and get out." He would be joined at Fulton County Stadium by Brock, Simmons, and Torre on the National League squad. They would see Morgan win the game for the National League in the tenth inning with a single, scoring Nate Colbert in front of which was, to date, the largest baseball crowd in Atlanta history (53,107). A sore knee, which he injured while sliding in the last game before the break on Sunday, prevented Clemente from playing. Therefore, the famous 1971 All-Star Game in Detroit would mark his last appearance in the affair for him.

The relieved Simmons had also finally signed his contract in the past week, a two-year deal negotiated with Dick Meyer that was expected to pay him a total of seventy-five thousand dollars with the first half of the first year of the agreement being retroactive for the first portion of the 1972 season. After the agreement was announced, Simmons admitted he had been nervous after Reuss, Carlton, and Burda had been let go for refusing to sign their contracts.

During the break, news was stirring in the National League East off the field as well. Time had finally run out for Leo Durocher in Chicago, as he was replaced by assistant coach Whitey Lockman, who had once played for Durocher in New York. The move was originally supposed to have come the previous autumn, but Cubs owner Phil Wrigley decided to give Leo one more chance. While Lockman was given a temporary manager's tag only, he was also simultaneously promoted to team vice president. It had been a year since Wrigley had taken out a full-length advertisement in the Chicago papers, reaffirming his commitment to Durocher despite public criticism by the fans and the press. Durocher would spend one more year in Houston as a manager in 1973 before calling it quits for good on a Major League career that began as a player with the Yankees nearly fifty years earlier in 1925. Phil Pepe, from his perch in New York, gave his own summary of "Leo the Lip." "His loyalty, it has been said, would make Benedict Arnold look like a super patriot; his language would make Harry Truman blush; his lifestyle has been called a cross between Frank Sinatra's and Henry VIII's. He is a terrible man, vain beyond description, unscrupulous, mean, spiteful. But he has survived in this baseball business through five decades and there has to be a reason. The reason is talent—a talent for controversy unmatched in baseball."

Unfortunately, the injury to Spinks on the Fourth of July seemed to cast an omen on the team's fortunes, as June would be the Cardinals' only winning month of the year. Much of the ineptitude was due to the unsettled situation in the outfield as Cruz and Melendez continued to struggle (Cruz was only starting to improve after batting in the .100s for most of May and June). And as the career of the precocious young pitcher Spinks was being derailed (and another in Santorini being given another chance), a veteran hurler was attempting to resurrect his own a few hours later in another city. In the second contest of a July 4 doubleheader against the Cubs in Atlanta, Denny McLain made his National League debut, keeping the Chicago men scoreless for the first three innings but ultimately permitting three runs that saw the game end in a 3–3 rain-shortened tie. More than fifty thousand fans had turned out to see the last thirty-game winner in the majors and offered McLain a standing ovation when he arrived at the mound for work in the first inning. He had posted a 3-3 record for the Braves' Minor League team at Birmingham before joining Atlanta, and the Fourth of July assignment was his first big league action since pitching for Oakland on May 12 after which he had been traded for Orlando Cepeda. "I've never experienced anything like that, not even in Detroit," McLain said of the thunderous greeting from the southern faithful. "I've got myself in super shape, and I think I could pitch forever." McLain would finally get his first Senior Circuit victory on July 22 against the Cardinals in Atlanta, thanks to a tenth-inning homer by Dusty Baker. By September, however, the irascible, enigmatic McLain would be finished in Major League ball. Released by the Braves in March 1973, he would sign a contract with the Iowa Oaks of the American Association, whose parent club was his hometown White Sox, the team he had loved and followed growing up on Chicago's South Side and the club that had signed him to his first pro deal. The contract gave McLain no guarantees of a Major League call-up, and one would never come.

The Cards' failure to once again launch a concerted attack on the top of the standings led to another round of player dismissals, as Devine would drop several individuals as the team drifted in the standings in August. There was an unmistakable, underlying feeling of "rebuilding" with each stroke of his pen, suggesting that the team was thinking long-term with no pennants likely in the near future. The first big name to be moved was Alou, who had not been under .300 at the plate since April 22 but was dealt to Oakland for two Minor Leaguers on August 27. In acquiring Alou from Pittsburgh, the Cardinals had been forced to undertake some of his salary, which was now being disposed. Three days later Maxvill was sent to the A's as well, and once again, the return prize for St. Louis was two Minor League players. Of those the Cardinals received in the Alou and Maxvill trades—Gene Dusen, Joe Lindsey, Steve Easton, and Bill Voss—Voss would be the only player between both deals who would reach the Major Leagues (and Voss would appear in only eleven games in the final stretch of 1972 and not play in the big leagues again). The St. Louis team, in essence, was simply clearing salary and space for younger prospects to play. Upon getting news of the trade, Maxvill's seven-year-old son, Jeff, advised father Dal to leave for Oakland as soon as possible because the A's were in first place.

Things were quite different in the American League, as Maxvill would soon experience. "The toughest point in adjusting so far," he would comment on being sent to Oakland, "is remembering which uniform to wear." He was speaking of the numerous outfits ordered by the owner, Finley, for the team to show. "We wear white pants every day, but one day we wear green jerseys with a yellow undershirt and the next day yellow jerseys with a green undershirt. Then on Sundays, we wear all white with green undershirts." Indeed, Charles Finley was the forerunner of what would be seen in later years, in which nearly all teams would switch up their uniforms—at least for Sunday games—with the subtle purpose of having another item to sell in the stadium gift shop. One month later on September 29 in Oakland, Maxvill stroked a double in the ninth inning to score Sal Bando as the A's won the American League West for the second straight year.

Now, only Gibson and Brock remained from the 1968 pennant-winning team. It was clear that jobs in the Cardinals infield were now wide open—they were counting on Mick Kelleher and Mike Tyson, both excelling at Tulsa, to take over at short and second, respectively (or at least to have Tyson challenge Sizemore at the position), while third baseman Ken Reitz was on his way up as well. With a late charge at the end of their season, Tulsa nearly edged out Wichita for the American Association title, which according to Tulsa sportswriter Bob Hartsell was due to Tyson and Kelleher, even though the latter had batted only .241 against Minor League pitching. "The defense down the middle, with Reitz at third base and young Bake McBride in center field [gave Tulsa a shot]." In addition, Tulsa catcher Skip Jutze, batting .325, would be brought to St. Louis in September 1972 as well, as Simmons would move to first base for a few games to give Jutze some experience behind the plate. Off the mound for the Cards' top farm team shone Bibby, who was 13-9 with 209 strikeouts in 195 innings. With the team almost twenty games out of first behind the indomitable Pirates by Labor Day, the youngsters were sure to receive a long look from the coaching staff. The first among them to shine was Reitz, who entered the starting lineup on September 5 and would play third base almost every day for the rest of the season (twenty-one games), batting .359, including going seven for ten in a doubleheader at New York on the eighth and going twelve for his first twenty-one overall. Although Reitz made an error in his first game against the Expos on the fifth, he was displaying the skills that suggested he could become one of the premier defensive third basemen in baseball.

Broeg immediately took to Reitz, the son of a San Francisco beer truck driver who raised his family in Daly City, California, in the literal shadows of the Giants' Candlestick Park. The Cardinals' beat writer described Ken as a no-nonsense type who rode rodeo horses in high school, "a 20-year-old throwback to an era when ballplayers came to play nothing but baseball." Reitz's brother, Roy, had been a top prospect in the Giants' system, earning all-star considerations at their single-A club in the California League. When given an initial questionnaire by Cardinals officials before signing a contract, Ken had listed "Baseball is my life" beside a question that read, "What is your ambition outside of baseball?" When the same survey asked him about his "hobbies," he answered, "Hitting line drives. . . . I was born with a baseball glove in one hand and a bat in the other." Finally, when a question was posed about any musical interests the player had, Reitz responded by writing, "I strum the guitar, agitate the piano, and cry the blues." Despite his natural ability at third, the Redbirds had tried Reitz at every position except catcher in the Minor Leagues. Nonetheless, by 1972, his search for a spot in the field appeared over. "The way he gloves a ball at third base," Broeg noticed, "it looks as if he has found a home defensively."

The trend of putting rookies in the lineup continued through September—such as on the seventh, when Schoendienst started seven of them as the Cardinals strangely got a run off Carlton for the year in three games against him. (Yet another first-year player, former Southern Illinois University All-American Bill Stein, led off and played left field in the game, having made his Major League debut the night before. Singling off the mighty Carlton in his first at-bat that night, it was part of his own successful call-up, as he would hit .314.) It was Carlton's hundredth Major League win as he posted 9 strikeouts for a season total of 272 to date, a new Phillies record, surpassing Bunning's 268 set in 1965. It was Lefty's year, as Carlton was dwarfing the achievements of all pitchers in 1972—even those who were throwing no-hitters. The Cubs' Milt Pappas had achieved the feat five days earlier at Wrigley Field against the Padres in a game that, with a slight twist of fate, might have been parlayed into a perfect game. With two out in the ninth, Pappas held a 1-2 count on Larry Stahl, but walked him on three straight sliders that just missed the strike zone. It is often forgotten that the no-hitter would have been ruined earlier by Enzo Hernandez in the fourth, as Hernandez put down a perfect bunt, but Santo let it keep rolling until it ultimately went foul.

Missing a perfect game with one strike to go was a small heartbreak for Chicago fans compared to the one endured two days later. After carrying three times for five yards and two fumbles against the football Cardinals at Busch Stadium, the great Bears running back Gale Sayers announced his retirement from the NFL, unable to keep going on brittle right and left knees that were damaged in 1968 and 1970, respectively.

Carlton had no intentions of relenting in his assault on the National League bats through the final weeks of the season. He faced his old team once again two weeks later, as he beat his trade counterpart, Wise, at Busch Stadium for his twenty-fifth win on Schoendienst's twenty-fifth wedding anniversary. The southpaw had used an extra day's rest before the game because he claimed he had hurt his arm while doing a pitching demonstration on the Mike Douglas television show. On the program Carlton had thrown a Taiwanese baseball, which he claimed was half as light as an American ball, and in the process had strained his arm. In facing the Cardinals, it had been a typical sultry summer night at Busch, and Carlton maintained that he had lost ten pounds in the process. Wise, meanwhile, said he dropped eight pounds himself as he fell to 15-16 on the year, as he lost no fewer than his twelfth one-run decision of the year with the 2–1 score.

The game was a microcosm of the misery and what-could-have-beens for the Cardinals throughout the year. Three days later on the twenty-third—after the Pirates had already clinched the division title—the Cards were swept in a doubleheader by the Cubs in St. Louis by scores of 2–0 and 15–1, committing a near-record eight errors in the second game. Cleveland, the loser in the ugly nightcap, had, like Wise, fallen to a losing record (14-15) and had also fallen out of disfavor with Schoendienst for his lack of personal discipline. "He's too fat to pitch," the manager assessed bluntly. Cleveland had enjoyed a good first half (11-4) in coming off his fine rookie year in '71, but had folded in the latter part of the season, as he was sent to the bull pen when his weight ballooned once again and went 3-11 in the schedule's final months.

A St. Louis public disenchanted with baseball—the likes of which perhaps never seen before or since—would manifest itself in the form of the smallest Busch Stadium crowd ever two days later, a paltry figure of 3,380. The scoreboard at the end of the game read the same as it always did, with the exception of the strange small number on the second line:

Today's Paid Attendance
3,380
The Cardinals and the Mets
Thank You Very Much

When the schedule was completed, the season attendance at Busch would show just under 1.2 million through the gates, yet another dramatic decline for the fourth year in a row.

Despite the Cardinals being far out of the race, the regulars were battling just as hard as the rookies. By season's end, Brock would become the first Major Leaguer to steal at least fifty bases in eight straight seasons. His final total was sixty-three, which allowed him to claim his sixth stolen-base total. Brock had also posted the lowest home run total (three) in his career to date in 1972, illustrative of his willingness to adjust his game further in the direction of his skills. "He's got a body to hit and run until he's 40," San Diego manager Preston Gomez said.

Gibson took his regular turn in the rotation on the last day of the season on October 4, with the team in Pittsburgh. The Pirates had already easily wrapped up another Eastern Division title with an eleven-game lead on the second-place

Cubs. Despite the early clinching, most of Murtaugh's regular players were back in the starting lineup for this game, in order to keep them sharp for the playoffs—men such as Stargell, Oliver, Cash, and others. But not among them was Clemente, who was also missing from the starting lineup that August evening in that same stadium thirteen months earlier when Gibson threw his no-hitter. As a result, all would be winners on this night with the exception of Clemente—Gibson would gain his nineteenth win of the season in downing his former teammate Nelson Briles of the Bucs 4–3, yet also permitting the Pirates batters to tune their sticks for the postseason with thirteen hits.

A month earlier on September 2, with a third-inning double against the Giants in Pittsburgh, Clemente became the franchise's all-time hit leader, passing Honus Wagner at 2,970. In his very next at-bat, he broke his own new team hit record with a three-run homer. Then, on September 30, a few days before the Cardinals came to town, Clemente got his 3,000th hit—the last of his career—the same day that Brock stroked his 2,000th. When Brock was asked the following spring if he thought he himself had a shot at 3,000, he called the possibility "remote."

Clemente—the man who nearly derailed the Cards' charge to the 1967 title with his line drive that broke Gibson's leg in July of that year—had also hardly played the evening before, entering the game against the Cardinals in the bottom of the ninth inning only to play right field for three outs. No one could know that this would be his last regular-season appearance before the Pirates would lose to the Reds in the National League Championship Series.

On New Year's Eve—just eight days after the city of Pittsburgh had celebrated the city's first football playoff appearance since 1947 with its euphoric victory over Oakland—Clemente would be killed in a plane crash off the coast of Puerto Rico, on his way to Nicaragua to deliver relief supplies to victims of an earthquake.

The following March, Clemente would receive nearly a unanimous vote among 424 balloters for a special early entry into the Hall of Fame, as the standard five-year wait had been set aside by the board of directors and the Hall of Fame president, Paul Kerr. Only once before had such an exception been made, back in 1939 when it was learned that Lou Gehrig was dying of amyotrophic lateral sclerosis. "It seemed that Roberto Clemente, a four-time batting champion, belonged only to Pittsburgh," mourned Charley Feeney of the *Sporting News*. "In death, the tributes paid to him proved he belonged to every sports-minded person in the world." Immediately after the crash, the Roberto Clemente Memorial Fund was established with efforts of President Nixon to help the struggling Nicaraguans, with Nixon launching the drive by writing a personal check for $1,000 and handing it to the Nicaraguan ambassador in Washington.

As with Maxvill notching the pennant-winning hit for Oakland in late September, other former Cardinals had flourished with their new teams. The first

American League go-round for Dick Allen would be his best overall season ever, taking home the MVP award in 1972 with circuit-leading stats of 37 home runs and 113 RBIs—and still donning his distinctive batting helmet while playing first base (Allen's performance would lead him to receive a three-year $750,000 deal from the White Sox in February 1973—which made him the highest-paid player in Major League history at the time). Carlton dominated the National League side, winning nearly three-fourths of his decisions for a .730 percentage for Philadelphia (27-10), while the rest of the staff barely won a fourth of their own (.269). Continuing to live in St. Louis for the time being after he was sent to Philadelphia, Carlton's twenty-seven wins led the league, as he also paced the ERA (1.97), innings pitched (346), strikeouts (310), and complete games (30) lists in claiming his first of what would be four Cy Young Awards in Philadelphia. Ironically, Carlton was able to do this despite the absence of his closest co-worker, his "personal catcher," McCarver, who was traded in midseason to the Montreal Expos for fellow catcher John Bateman. The front office of the struggling Phillies had been pressured to make some kind of move, but there had been no takers for the offers that new general manager Paul Owens had been tossing out; with McCarver and Bateman batting .237 and .241, respectively, and with both being nearly the same age, the deal was seen as one simply designed to change some blood on the roster. In 1975 McCarver would be reunited with Carlton for a third and final time. Later, McCarver suggested that the two men should be buried sixty feet and six inches away from each other—the distance from the pitcher's rubber to home plate. It had been a pitiful season for the Phillies, even though manager Frank Lucchesi—after being granted a one-year contract extension in early August 1971 despite a 48-61 record at that point—had earlier announced that there would be "big changes" for 1972 with the team's performance on the field.

While Wise was once again at the .500 mark (near which he had been with the Phillies for the past five seasons) and Gibson showed tremendous fortitude in rebounding from his horrific start to the year, the impact of the Cardinals losing Carlton from the rotation was prominent and immediate. Gibson would later point out that even with twenty-seven wins from Carlton, the difference between Carlton and Wise for the Cardinals would not have been enough to catch the Pirates anyway (Gibson may have forgotten that two other castoffs, Mike Torrez and Nelson Briles, respectively won sixteen games for Montreal and fourteen for Pittsburgh). It is possible that Wise himself (16-16) could have been a twenty-game winner with a better bull pen, considering the Cardinals' poor performance in his one-run decisions and that no one in the bull pen saved any of his wins. Wise certainly was not alone in this regard, for in Gibson's eleven losses on the year, the Cards scored just 20 runs in those games. By the time the season had ended, St. Louis had scored 171 fewer runs—more than 1 per game—than they had in 1971. Power had not been supplied as it had in the past, as the team hit only 70 home runs, their fewest since 1945. Gibson himself had belted 5 of them, leading everyone on the team except Torre and Simmons (Simmons's 16, however—as well as his 96 RBIs—were club records for a catcher). Torre did his best to measure up to the frantic offensive pace he had set for himself in 1971 and was up to .396 by mid-May but fell to the .280s by season's end.

In retrospect of the team's pitching staff in 1972, the absence of a strong left-hander—both in the starting rotation as well as in the bull pen—appeared to be the Cardinals' downfall. The hodgepodge coalition of Drabowsky, Cloninger, Dennis Higgins (who had taken Cloninger's roster spot when he was released on July 26), Diego Segui (signed in midseason from Oakland), Joe Grzenda, and others did little to assist the overworked starting staff, many of whom allowed a large percentage of their runs in the first innings of games but needed to weather each storm because of the lack of depth. Reuss struggled to a certain degree (9-13) in Houston, but would soon emerge as one of the top southpaws in the National League for the Astros (and later Pirates and Dodgers), as had been expected of him.

By not giving in to Carlton's $10,000 and Reuss's unshaven beard, author Peter Golenbock estimated that those moves cost Gussie Busch at least four division championships and millions of dollars at the stadium gate for the brewery.

There would soon be a noticeable absence off the field as well. Leo Ward retired as the Cards' traveling secretary after the 1972 season after thirty-four years on the job, replaced by the team's director of promotions and sales, Jim Bayens. Starting with the team as director of the "Knot Hole Gang" program in 1930 to increase opportunities for children to attend games, Ward would go on to be the longest-tenured traveling secretary in the Major Leagues at the time. In doing so, he would witnesses the many changes in travel accommodations for teams that took place over the decades. His most famous maneuver, perhaps, was once utilizing a boat and a plane to help the team avoid a hurricane in getting from Boston to New York, as rail lines had been damaged by the storm. Ward would be greatly saddened when, the following spring of 1973, one of his greatest friends in baseball passed away in Frankie Frisch. Schoendienst, too, grieved the loss, and remembered some of the advice Frisch gave him about traveling while being the manager, in addition to tips from Ward. "Don't room higher than the second floor on the road, Red," Schoendienst reported Frisch as having told him. "You might want to jump." Schoendienst had certainly endured his share of hotel-related scares over the course of his big league career. Once his room in New York was robbed, during which the thief took a $5.00 alarm clock and a $75.00 bottle of perfume that Red had bought for his wife Mary (this occurred even though the hotel was a reputable establishment; in fact, many of the Cardinal players did not want to pay the exorbitant $1.25

a bottle of beer cost in the hotel bar—so several of them skipped down a few blocks, through some rough streets, to less "pricey" joints).

Heeding the advice of Frisch and others, Schoendienst had always been cautious in hotels, jamming a chair under the doorknob for extra security. The theft in New York had taken place, unfortunately, while he went to another coach's room for just an hour and a half.

"Mom, did they take any of his clothes?" one of his daughters asked Mary when they heard about the incident.

"Nobody would take those clothes that he wears," she responded.

Convinced that Simmons could handle the heavy load at the catcher's position, the team felt comfortable in dealing Jutze to the Astros in November. In return, Devine felt that they had acquired a top-flight shortstop prospect in Ray Busse, who was envisioned to head into spring training 1973 able to challenge Kelleher and Tyson for the starting job. Sizemore also had work to do to keep his spot in the infield plans, as he was merely able to repeat the .264 average he had posted in 1971, although being effective as a protective number-two hitter for Brock.

With this new influx of young talent, Devine was convinced the potential was there for a title charge despite the recent downturn in the standings as the Cards finished in fourth place, back where they had found themselves at the end of 1969 and 1970 as well. "I can't picture myself going to spring training with the club we have," the general manager assessed as he finished his thirteenth overall season in the position over his two tours. "This is a different club, a young club. I think we've got some things to find out, some things to prove."

7   Close to the Top Once Again

I had to face the fact that I wasn't the same pitcher anymore. My ninety-five-mile-an-hour fastball made only rare cameo appearances.

—Bob Gibson, commenting on his 1973 season

By 1973, it had been nearly ten years since the Cardinals had faced the New York Yankees in their tremendous World Series clash, the last hurrah for the proud Yankee teams led by Mantle and Whitey Ford. As the Cardinals continued to build strength and championships through the rest of the '60s, the Yankees fell upon the darkest days the franchise had ever known. The Columbia Broadcasting System had been looking for a buyer for the team; after entertaining several bids, they found a group looking for a bargain.

With the advent of the new year, two new towering figures—the World Trade Center and George Steinbrenner—were about to be open for business in New York.

On January 3, 1973, the Cleveland-based shipping magnate Steinbrenner and his partner, Mike Burke, led ten other individuals in purchasing the Yankees from CBS for $10 million. The price was such a steal that many noticed it was the same amount that the Padres and Expos had to pay to enter the National League in 1969. "Are the fabled Yankees, winners of 29 pennants and 20 world championships, worth no more than a modern expansion club?" scoffed Jack Lang of *Sporting News*. In fact, by the time Steinbrenner and his group took over, New York City had already agreed to pledge more than twice as much—$24 million—to renovate Yankee Stadium during the 1974 and 1975 seasons while the team played in the Mets' home park of Shea Stadium. The value of the franchise had plummeted so much over the 1960s that the $10 million deal that the new owners were getting was also $3.2 million *less* than CBS paid in 1964 to acquire the club. While CBS was shopping for a buyer, it was rumored that another configuration represented by former Giants manager Herman Franks had also submitted a bid, and if it had been successful, it was further reported that Franks was ready to install Willie Mays as the Yankees' manager, which would have made him the first black field boss in the modern history of the Major Leagues.

The forty-two-year-old Steinbrenner, once suitor to buy his hometown Indians, admitted that although he had "always been an Indians fan, [he] could never root against the Yankees." At the time he struck the deal with CBS, he was also part owner of the Chicago Bulls of the NBA, and like Busch, Wrigley, and other owners of the day, he had already made his fortune in another field, as he wished to focus more on wins and losses than the bottom line for the ball club. With Nixon signing the Paris Peace Accords that same January—officially ending American operations in Vietnam—Steinbrenner was getting ready to wage a war on the American League that would continue until his death in late 2010. By 1979 Steinbrenner had bought out all of his partners in the Yankees deal, including John McMullen. "There is nothing in life quite so limited," McMullen said, "as being a limited partner of George Steinbrenner."

And in February Marvin Miller was about to strike his own peace deal with the owners on another new collective bargaining agreement—but one whose expiration in three years in 1976 would lead to yet another cataclysmic event on the business side of baseball, and one in which Flood's name would be evoked many times thereafter.

In the preceding months, the previous ownership had already landed Steinbrenner at least one piece of the team that would lead to further success in the future. Back on November 27, they had secured perhaps the most promising young third baseman in the game from the Indians in Graig Nettles. In the coming weeks, however, Steinbrenner would be immediately confronted with a bizarre off-field situation—the "wife swapping" that occurred between Yankees pitchers Mike Kekich and Fritz Peterson. In a most bizarre idea, the two pitchers had also agreed to *trade children* as well. Kuhn stepped in immediately to voice his disgust, saying that ballplayers must truly recognize the moral impact they have on youth. "It does baseball no good, it does no good for sports in general. I'm appalled by the effect it could have on the many young people who follow our game." On the field what Kuhn was hoping *would* do baseball some good, contrarily, was the installation of the "designated hitter" rule in the American League for 1973, whereby teams in that circuit could place a batter in the lineup in the place of the pitcher for the first time.

With each passing season, it was getting tougher and tougher for Bob Gibson to motivate himself for the start of spring training. Admitting that he was wearing down physically, the thirty-seven-year-old had to drag himself to the 1973 preseason workouts, "knowing damn well that something, if not everything, would soon start to hurt again." In addition to running "poles" (a conditioning tradition for pitchers, whereby they repeatedly jog the length of the warning track in the outfield), Gibson was also know for getting in extra conditioning by fielding ground balls at third base and shortstop in batting practice—but no longer. Once again, he minimized his work in exhibition games, pitching in only twenty innings—the same limited number he had thrown in the spring of '72. On the bright side, he was happy the club reacquired McCarver in November for Jorge Roque after the catcher had spent a half season in Montreal. "It was good just to get back some of the Cardinal spirit from the sixties," Gibson would later write. It was now clearer than ever that Gibby needed help from the rest of the rotation, as he was unable to carry the pitching staff by himself any longer. Less than a year earlier, it seemed that Spinks was on the verge of becoming a new leader, but over the first few weeks of spring training in 1973, he had not proved that he had fully recovered from his July 4 collision with Johnny Bench. Now appearing to zoom past him in the race for a regular job was Santorini, having ended the 1972 season with two shutouts in his final three starts. Reggie Cleveland was a question mark, with his weight becoming a growing problem once again, as he reported to spring training more than ten pounds heavier than when Schoendienst had scolded him on the issue in 1972. With the poor finish Cleveland had to the 1972 season, the coaching staff was disappointed that he did not arrive to St. Petersburg in a more prepared form (despite a promising 10-3 record he had posted over the winter in Venezuela). After showing up at camp in late February, Cleveland was ordered by player personnel director Bob Kennedy to be at 200 pounds by the middle of spring training or face a one-hundred-dollar fine for *every pound* he was found to be above that figure each day of camp. Kennedy was also in charge of enforcing the no-facial-hair policy that was still in effect, although it was a rule that several players were seemingly becoming more compelled to challenge.

Cleveland, however, appeared to be an exception about the fitness of the team, as Schoendienst and Devine were impressed with the readiness with which most of the club came to Florida for 1973. The reacquired McCarver—still only thirty-one years old, despite having spent part or all of the past thirteen seasons in the big leagues—was down to a trim 192, which he claimed to be the first time in eleven years he himself had been under the 200 mark. There was talk of McCarver's being used as an occasional replacement at first base for Torre, the latter of whom had moved there with the emergence of the young

Reitz at third. While admitting he was no longer in Simmons's class as a catcher offensively or defensively, McCarver noted that his hard work enabled him to catch a significant number games for Montreal in the last half of the '72 season. With McCarver returning to the Cardinals, it was envisioned that at least some of the workload could be taken off Simmons, who logged a wearing 135 games behind the plate in 1972 (as well as playing 15 more at first base). Simmons's duties at the dish would increase even more in the coming seasons, as he would catch 153 contests in 1973, 141 in 1974, and 154 in 1975 before finally receiving more extended first base duty himself in 1976. And no matter how often he was catching—even in the doggedly hot days of July and August in St. Louis—his teammates noticed that Simmons never asked the manager for a day off.

Jose Cruz also came to camp in better shape, as the fledgling outfielder sought to rebound from his poor sophomore season and his .235 batting mark. He was also inspired by his brothers Hector and Tommy joining him in spring training as Cardinals prospects (among ten other brothers and sisters they also had back in Arroyo, Puerto Rico). Hector, also known as "Heity," appeared to have the most promise, although the third baseman was in the process of being moved to the outfield with Reitz's emergence. Harry Walker, now working in the player development office for the Cardinals after being fired as Houston's manager, compared Heity's erratic but productive batting style to Joe Medwick's. "You wouldn't take a talent like Hector and make him change his swing," Walker said. All three Cruz brothers would appear together in the same spring training game as outfielders in 1973, as the youthful Hector would also become known as "Caballo Loco" (Crazy Horse) by some around the practice field.

Another reason for hope was the impressive play in exhibition games of Ray Busse. "Is Busse Too Good to Be True?" read the headline of Broeg's column on March 16 after the twenty-four-year-old rookie shortstop flashed a hot glove and bat in yet another spring contest, and would be hitting .341 in exhibition play by the end of March. Busse was exceptionally tall for a shortstop (six foot four), reminding Cards followers of 1940s great Marty Marion. In starting his career it had been a rough few years for Busse, who had endured the suicide of his father, a young marriage that got off to a bad start, and having been seemingly stuck in the Astros' Minor League system for years. But by March 26, Busse would outplay Kelleher and be named the starting shortstop to open the season in St. Louis. And in yet another pleasant surprise, newcomer Alan Foster had also moved ahead of Spinks for a spot in the 1973 starting pitching rotation, giving Schoendienst another option off the mound.

It all added up to a positive enthusiasm in spring training in March 1973, which was reflected in the attitude of the man who had purchased the team twenty years ago that month. "Morale is good, and that gives us a chance," Gussie Busch told the press as he surveyed his troops. Busch, even when he felt jilted by a player or two in the previous season because of contract negotiations or subpar performances, never seemed to go to spring training with a negative attitude. As he spoke with writers at Al Lang Field, he dismissed rumors that he was in negotiations with Don Breckenridge, an owner of local motels around St. Louis, to sell the Cardinals to Breckenridge.

Pitcher Rich Folkers also noticed the spring in his teammates' steps and commented further upon the unusual camaraderie of the Cards in the early 1970s. "During the three years I was with the Cardinals [1972–1974], there wasn't anybody who was disliked. Each had his own disposition but went about doing his own thing his own way. All of them were good guys who worked hard together." Not having started in any of his nine appearances with the Cards in 1972, Folkers was hoped to be the left-handed presence in the bull pen the Cardinals were sorely lacking from the previous year. The Waterloo, Iowa, native had been a four-year veteran of the Mets' farm system and a one-year veteran of the military but had been abandoned by New York when he hurt his back in spring training in 1970. He was then traded to St. Louis, where in 1971 a Cardinals Minor League coach, Fred Koenig, taught him how to throw a screwball that ran away from right-handed hitters and handcuffed the lefties, a move that resuscitated Folkers's career.

The only downer to camp occurred when speedy rookie outfielder Arnold "Bake" McBride, a local product from Fulton, Missouri, tore a muscle in his shoulder while working in the batting cage. McBride had already hit over .300 in three different Minor League levels, and a disappointed Schoendienst had wished to see him in action in a spring training game to witness his famed speed. There had been so much competition in camp that the talented McBride, Al Hrabosky, Hector Cruz, and young pitcher Bob Forsch were all reassigned to the Minor League camp that day (the move of Cruz was most expected, due to his young age). Few seemed to care when Busse's average fell dramatically at the end of spring training, and when Foster became inexplicably wild, for most were convinced that a solid roster was in place for the season. Another interesting development was the possible signing of amateur pitcher Brad Van Pelt, also a star football player for Michigan State University. The Cardinals were in competition with the Giants to secure the rights to Van Pelt, and the teams had until March 19 (the start of Michigan State's baseball season) to sign him, or he would return to the Spartans. The Giants had reportedly bettered the Cards' $100,000 by 50 percent, and were ready to put his name on a contract. In one week, however, Van Pelt would instead sign a $300,000 three-year contract with the New York Giants of the NFL to play linebacker.

With another cadre of new faces in the St. Louis camp, there was no question that another rebuilding job was in progress, particularly in the infield. Furthermore, some players, such as Vern Benson, thought that Carbo should be able to take over in right. "Carbo's got the best right field arm on this club since Mike Shannon," Benson claimed. Whoever would be patrolling the pasture would be dealing with the adjusted fence at Busch Stadium, which would be lowered in 1973 to eight feet (from ten feet, six inches) and moved ten feet closer to home plate between the power alleys (perhaps altered in response to the Cardinals' paltry power showing in 1972). Carbo, like so many other veterans over the past several seasons, expressed his excitement about joining the Cardinals organization as the positive momentum was carrying forward.

Spring training was not nearly so peaceful and productive across Florida in Cocoa Beach, where the Astros were working out with their new manager, Durocher, the man chosen to replace Walker in Houston. It was Leo's last season as a skipper, and he was creating no fewer waves with the league offices that he had in his first managerial job in Brooklyn back in 1939. He had threatened to pull the Astros' representatives out of the collective bargaining discussions, which Marvin Miller said would once again jeopardize the start of the regular season. Durocher had been upset with the numerous meetings being called by Miller, which were interrupting practice sessions. Soon Durocher would be fined $250 by the league office for interfering with an MLBPA meeting, and he said he would quit baseball before paying it.

The Cardinals were anxious to get things going, but hope would appear to be quickly dashed, as the start of the 1973 season in St. Louis would be a disaster like none other.

The outing that the tiring Gibson would endure on opening day (April 6) would portend evils imminent for the Cards, as he and Diego Segui blew a five-run lead to the Pirates for a 7–5 defeat. Gibson's next start on the twelfth—which would become the Cards' fifth straight loss to start the season—involved a matchup with Seaver, in which both pitchers sailed high, hard ones in the direction of each other's head and led to heated verbal exchanges between the two rivals. Seaver claimed he was retaliating for a pitch that came close to his head the previous August and for a similar pitch that Gibson delivered to Mets teammate John Milner in spring training. Seaver, with a two-inning save from journeyman Phil Hennigan, would outlast Gibson for a 2–1 score as frustration quickly began to mount in the city, with many calling for the immediate removal of both Schoendienst and Devine. The Cardinals would win only twice in their first seventeen games, as the team would bat .216 in April, entering May with only three victories. And truly at the eye of the fans' storm was Busse, who had shown so much promise in the early spring. He began the year hitless in his first seventeen at-bats and made eleven errors in twenty-four games, which in part prompted Dick Kaegel to wonder if the old Browns had returned to town disguised as the Cardinals. A sympathetic Schoendienst tried to be understanding of Busse's attempt to fit in. "I never got on players for making errors, and there is a difference between an error and a mistake. Throwing to the wrong base is a mistake. Booting a ground ball is an error." But in the midst of such a losing streak it was too much to take, and a switch was needed.

The lone bright spot in those sullen early days of 1973 was Sizemore, restaking a claim to his second base position with a .333 average and great fielding. When called upon to bunt, Sizemore continued to use his special twenty-four-ounce bat, especially at home—a suggestion that came from Kissell, who felt that using a lighter stick in bunting on the artificial surface would "deaden" the ball a lot easier, as opposed to pushing the ball too far forward toward the fielders. But on April 25, the only hot hitter in the Cards lineup would tear a hamstring, and Sizemore was thus lost for a month. Taking his place was Kelleher, recalled from the minors in the presumption to take over for Busse at short while Tyson would man second, along with other untested candidates. "In fifteen years," Gibson asserted, "I'd never been on a Cardinal ballclub that played quite so badly." The grumbling continued in the media with claims that the team, even with all the young prospects supposedly prepared to make a contribution, came out of spring training not ready to play, a thought that was incomprehensible to the writers in view of the poor performance in 1972. Schoendienst and the players refuted the notion, saying that the camp had been one of the most physically demanding ever.

But in what would become one of the most up-and-down seasons in club history, the first turning point came in a mid-May showdown with their counterparts to the north.

On May 16—a day before television coverage of the Watergate hearings would begin—the Cards arrived at Wrigley Field in Chicago with baseball's worst record (9-23), while the Cubs were again in an early first-place standing to start the year with a 21-13 mark. Lockman was now getting a full chance on the North Side, with the near misses of the Durocher era in the rearview mirror as Chicago fans hoped that the talented team had finally turned the corner. (By December, nearly all vestiges of the Durocher era would be put to rest, with Santo being dealt across town to the White Sox for pitcher Steve Stone and three other players, while Fergie Jenkins was sent to the Texas Rangers in October. The Santo trade was particularly unthinkable to Chicago fans, and one to which Santo would later regret agreeing.) Two weeks earlier, the Sears Tower had officially opened in downtown Chicago as the world's tallest building and had been filled with corporations desiring the new location; in a like manner, business was promising once again for Phil Wrigley. A fortuitous beginning to the season had seen Tony LaRussa—just acquired by the Cubs—appear as a pinch runner in the ninth inning against Montreal on opening day and score the winning run; it would be his last appearance in the big leagues as a player.

(LaRussa would return to the Minor Leagues and stay there for four more seasons with the Pirates, White Sox, and the Cardinals before being released for the final time at the end of the 1977 season. In 1979 he would take over at midseason as manager of the White Sox for Don Kessinger, the regular Cubs shortstop on this day in 1973 and since the mid-1960s.) As the Cardinals took the field in Chicago, a noticeable difference was present: Busse had been finally yanked from the starting lineup the night before in St. Louis by Schoendienst, an 8–4 win over the Phillies as Tyson, Kelleher, and Sizemore (the latter returning from his injury) began rotating at the shortstop and second base positions. The Cardinals would take both games in the Windy City, the second contest being whittled through record-low thirty-seven-degree temperatures as Chicago's Beckert extended his hitting streak to twenty-six games, but Simmons trumped him for St. Louis with a four-for-five effort. Over the past three years, Ted was developing his reputation as a Cub killer, as he was now batting .377 against them. Joe Torre even thought, at this point, that Simmons had become the best hitter in all of baseball. "I never saw any man hit a ball consistently hard more often than Simmons did," said Torre of the catcher's performance during the 1973 season.

After a disastrous beginning, the team could feel the tide about to turn. "The Cardinals have shown they could play under the gun after all," wrote Jack Herman of the *St. Louis Globe-Democrat* when the two-game sweep was completed. In less than three weeks, Busse would be sent back to Houston, as the experiment had failed. The shake-up, however, was not exclusive to the position players. In the midst of Gibson's weaving his only shutout of the year on May 26, yet another amendment to the pitching staff was made, as Al Hrabosky was summoned from the farm system for the final time on June 8, shortly after the promising Bibby had been dealt to the Texas Rangers. There were rumors that Hrabosky—who had spent most of the past two seasons in the minors—might immediately step into the starting rotation, as Reggie Cleveland continued to disappoint through the first half of the season.

Whether it was the elevation of Hrabosky, the change in the infield, or some other catalyst, the Redbirds rose from their doldrums and became almost unbeatable overnight. After leaving Chicago and losing the first game of a double-header in Montreal on May 20, they ripped off eight in a row, as well as another five straight after that streak ended. Suddenly, the only thing faster than the Cardinals was Secretariat, the thoroughbred horse that captured racing's Triple Crown in dominant fashion with its victory at the Belmont Stakes on June 9 (the team was even hotter than the July 12 fire that destroyed the entire sixth floor of the National Personnel Records Center in St. Louis, a branch of the National Archives). On June 13 Wise would shut down the Big Red Machine in Cincinnati in taking a no-hitter into the ninth inning, having to settle for a one-hit, 8–0 shutout after Morgan spoiled things with a meager single (Wise had also no-hit the Reds as a member of the Phillies in 1971). After accounting for all three team wins in April and the gem against the Reds in June, Wise would go on to be named the National League's starter in the All-Star Game. And by the time Leonid Brezhnev had spoken to the American people on television on June 24—the first Soviet premier to do so—the Cardinals had clawed back from their awful April to near the .500 mark at 33-34, within six games of the Cubs. Highlighting the offensive side in addition to Simmons was Torre, who batted for the cycle at Pittsburgh on June 27 in leading a twenty-two-hit onslaught in a 15–4 win. In accomplishing the feat, Torre had doubled in the first inning, homered in the third, and tripled in the fourth. After hitting into a double play and later walking in the eighth, Torre motioned to the dugout to be replaced for a pinch runner, but Schoendienst declined, leaving him in the contest for one last shot at the rarity. Torre would proceed to single in the ninth inning to attain the cycle, in the process raising his season average to .338.

By the third week of July, the steamrolling Cards would overtake the Cubs for first place, as Gibson moved into second place behind Walter Johnson on the all-time strikeout list (a few weeks later, Brock would pass Babe Ruth on the all-time strikeout list for *batters,* with number 1,331 for his career, climbing his way up toward Mantle's all-time record of 1,710). The Cardinals had won a total of fifty-three games over May, June, and July, and by early August, they vaulted into first place by five games, and were eleven contests over the .500 mark.

Stunningly, it was at this point that the leader was struck down once again. From this latest injury, however, the aging Bob Gibson would never regain the form he once had.

On August 4 in New York, he batted in the Cards' third trip to the plate. Gibson dropped down a perfect bunt single that appeared to start a big inning. Sizemore, following a Brock sacrifice fly, drove a screamer to the left side. Thinking that the ball would surely reach the outfield, Gibson broke for second but had to stop abruptly as the Mets' third baseman, Ken Boswell, snared the liner. In jerking his body to make the reversal back toward the bag, Gibson felt something give way in his right knee. It was torn ligaments, which he later said was the cumulative result, he believed, from the many years of driving hard off the pitching mound. Hrabosky started jogging in from the bull pen in the bottom half of the inning to take his place, but Gibson waved him off, determined to continue. When Bob tried one pitch, however, he could not put any pressure on the leg and had to be replaced. Dr. London, who was watching the game from behind the Cardinals dugout, later announced that Gibson would have surgery in four days, and "we hope to have him back pitching in four to six weeks." In the meantime, Wise, Cleveland, Foster, and journeymen Mike Nagy and Tom Murphy would attempt to piece together a four-man rotation and keep the Redbirds on top.

Just as in past years, the main man once again had to be replaced. And in a valiant effort, the staff came together to nearly pull it off—but the great surge did not happen until the final week of the season.

On September 25, the Cards took a 3–1 lead into the ninth inning in a crucial contest against the Cubs at Busch Stadium. Alan Foster threw valiantly into the final round, but permitted pinch-hitter Adrian Garrett to single with one out. Hrabosky then came to the rescue for Foster and induced Kessinger to pop out for the second out, but walked Billy Williams before Diego Segui entered and allowed three Chicago runs to cross the plate, making it a 4–2 Cub advantage. On the mound for Chicago was Jenkins, who had nearly equaled Foster before being removed at the plate by Lockman in favor of Beckert in the ninth. Bob Locker came in to try to save the game for Jenkins in the bottom half and allowed the Cardinals to score a run and then load the bases with one out. Carbo, however, grounded into a double play, and in an instant, their pennant hopes seemed to vanish once again. By the impending off-season for the victorious Jenkins, he gleefully thought it was one final dagger to impale in his chief adversary, the Cardinals, as his days in the blue pinstripes were coming to an end with a trade to the American League after the season before returning to the Cubs in early 1980s.

St. Louis was now four games back—and behind three other teams—with five games to play. Shaking his head in the visitors' locker room at Wrigley Field, a dejected Carbo muttered, "This is the end."

"I haven't given up," said Simmons as he tried to uplift him. "I'm still breathing." And with the catcher leading the charge, the pitching staff would launch a nearly unprecedented assault on enemy bats starting the following day.

With Gibson still down but looking to return within a few days, Wise and Cleveland were the first to respond to the challenge as the troops reformed, throwing back-to-back shutouts at the Cubs over the next two days. In the case of Cleveland, his contribution was a one-hitter on the twenty-seven, facing only the minimum number of batters as Brock won the game with a two-run homer. "I felt sluggish before the game," Cleveland said. Unlike the previous season in which he started quickly and then faded, the pitcher this time had rebounded from his horrible start to the 1973 campaign to post fourteen wins and an ERA near three. "And during the warm-up, my fastball looked like a watermelon. I told our pitching coach, Barney Schultz, that I wasn't well and he said, 'Great, you'll probably go out there and pitch a no-hitter.'" Brock had been the lone offensive force in Wise's 1–0 blanking as well, singling in the first inning, stealing second, and being driven home on a Simmons hit for the game's only run. Wise did not waste any pitches—with the exception of hitting Jose Cardenal, who was now the Cubs' new right fielder, in the third inning.

A third straight shutout seemed unlikely, even though the struggling Phillies were coming to town. Taking the hill for the Redbirds was Mike Thompson, making only his second start in a Cardinal uniform; he had come to the organization in a March trade but had also spent most of the year in the minors. Thompson, however, was as dazzling as his predecessors had been the past two days, going four no-hit innings before the rains started to fall in downtown St. Louis. With the Cardinals holding a 1–0 lead, Reitz started to bat when the home plate umpire, Vargo, lifted his mask and called for a rain delay, which lasted only five minutes. When play was resumed the downpour then increased in ferocity, as Reitz was sent back to the dugout and the teams were then seated for an hour and a half. Unable to get loose after the hiatus, Thompson handed the ball over to Segui, who atoned for his blown performance from a few days earlier and posted five scoreless innings himself, giving up two hits as the staff had now authored three shutouts in a row by downing the Phils 3–0. The feat would not be approached by a Cardinals pitching staff until late May 2009, when the team would outscore opponents 18-2 over a five-game span.

The team was still stuck in third place, however, a half game behind the Pirates and a full two in back of New York—the latter with the only winning record in the division at 80-78.

Next, the ball was Gibson's. Even though the knee had not fully healed, he knew that his club needed him. He responded with furor, going six strong innings on the twenty-ninth and gaining relief help from Orlando Pena in a 7–1 dismantling of Carlton and the Phillies as he pulled St. Louis to within a game and a half of the lead. It was Carlton's twentieth loss in a severe downfall from his outstanding 1972 campaign, a season that saw his ERA climb from a league-best 1.97 in '72 to 3.90—the heights of which would not be seen by Carlton until he was essentially done as a regular starter in the close of his career in the late 1980s. In the Cardinals' final game, on the thirtieth, Wise would battle the Phillies and Jim Lonborg—their archenemy pitcher from the 1967 World Series with Boston—but would still need help from other teams to overtake the Mets.

Helping in the torrid stretch drive was Bake McBride, who had been up with the Cards from the minors since July 26 and batted over .300 but, surprisingly with his famous speed, did not steal a base in that time. In addition, Alou had been reacquired by the team on September 6 and appeared in eleven games, almost exclusively in a pinch-hitting role (Alou would be sold to San Diego in a month's time; the same day Kelleher would be sold to Houston, as the team looked to Tyson and Sizemore as the future of the middle infield). Another veteran outfielder, Tommie Agee, had also been picked up in August, but Agee, a hero of the Miracle Mets from 1969, would struggle in his final Major League days, batting .177 in limited duty. A personal highlight for him would include homering in the season's final week at Shea Stadium in New York, the site of his greatest glories.

Agee's drive with the Mets to the '69 title had been very similar to New York's end to the 1973 schedule, as on September 30, the mathematics showed that the season could finish the following day with a possible five-way tie atop the National League Eastern Division among the Cards, Mets, Pirates, Cubs, and Expos. On the thirtieth, Jenkins—in his last effort for the Cubs before returning nine years later—would lose the second game of a doubleheader to Jerry Koosman and the Mets to eliminate Chicago (and the Cardinals as well) from the race, while Pittsburgh knocked out Montreal with a 10–2 drubbing of the upstart Canadian team. Thus, in what would become known in baseball history as an exciting but erratic 1973 divisional chase in the East, the Mets finally took the crown with a paltry 82-79 record with a slim margin over the 81-81 Cards, as no other team in the division could capitalize on the Cards' second poor stretch of the season (for after the horrendous April and May, Schoendienst's club went 18-29 after Gibson's injury in early August). The aging Broeg, hungry for another championship, would lament often about the Cards' missed chance in 1973, but naturally, it hurt the men on the field the most—particularly in how the team, once again composed of many newcomers, had molded together. "Our near miss was especially agonizing for me and Brock," Gibson would reflect, "who, having been through the cycle with the ballclub, would have savored the accomplishment of climbing back to the top with a whole new cast. I had to face the fact that I wasn't the same pitcher anymore. My ninety-five-mile-an-hour fastball made only rare cameo appearances."

And 1973 was indeed the first of three straight heartbreaking ends to seasons to close the career of Bob Gibson.

The 1974 off-season was not unlike the others the Cardinals had seen since their glory years of the 1960s, with numerous roster shake-ups taking place, a front office seemingly scrambling to find the right parts. The latest of these moves came shortly after the 1973 campaign had been completed in October, with Wise traded with Carbo to Boston for outfielder Reggie Smith. Smith was a rare talent, one who like Cedeno in Houston could do all facets of the game well. "Smith is the best all-around player in the game today," Chicago White Sox manager Chuck Tanner went so far to proclaim in early 1974 as his club faced the Cardinals in spring training in Florida. "He can do everything that a scout looks for: run, hit for average, hit with power, and throw strong and accurately, plus switch-hit. [He's] a definite blue-chipper." Smith's background was nearly as diverse as his baseball skills; having been born in Shreveport, Louisiana, he later grew up in the rough Watts neighborhood of Los Angeles and became an accomplished musician, a master of the trombone, saxophone, cello, and the drums. He even liked to raise thoroughbred horses like Dick Allen.

Shortly thereafter, Segui and Cleveland would be shipped to the Red Sox as well in December, as in exchange the Cards received promising young hurlers in Lynn McGlothen, Mike Garman, and John Curtis. Even Scipio Spinks—shortly removed from his impressive beginnings before being injured in the collision with Johnny Bench—was traded, sent to the Cubs for outfielder Jim Hickman in March. Spinks would again never show the same flash as in his first few months with the Cardinals, as he failed to ever appear in a game in a Chicago uniform.

Schoendienst was itching to get back to the top—literally. "My World Series ring is getting small," he said of the 1967 version rubbing into his right hand. "My fingers are getting bigger. I need a new ring. With a little luck, we have a good chance of overtaking the Mets in our division." He was also confident that the debacle that occurred at shortstop stop in early 1973 would not repeat itself. "Mike Tyson is a winner," he promised of the new holder of the spot. "And Reitz is a winner." Reitz was progressing so quickly on defense, in fact, that Vern Benson predicted he would go down as one of the best third basemen ever. Reitz began taking an incredible amount of pride in his defensive work. Once when he made three errors in one game, he proceeded to douse his glove in gasoline and set it ablaze.

For 1974 Schoendienst was also happy with the overall look of the pitching staff. "Everyone's been mentioning the other pitchers, but what about a kid like Bob Forsch?" he proposed. When Forsch signed with the Cardinals as an infielder out of a Sacramento high school in 1968 (having foregone a scholarship offer to Oregon State, where his brother Ken had gone to play), he flew to Florida the same night, was picked up in a van at the Tampa airport early in the morning, and was driven to Sarasota, where he was told he needed to report to practice right away. As a kid Forsch saw his only big league game in 1963, Musial's final season, when the Cards played in San Francisco. After batting .224 in the Gulf Coast League, he hit .303 in twenty-six games in the Northwest League and then .235 in the California League. Later, when he was batting .088 in the Midwest League, he was brought in to fire three innings of emergency relief in a blowout game, and the organization thenceforth decided to make him a pitcher after the scoreless showing. By 1971 he was a Midwest League all-star *off the mound* with an 11-7 record and a 3.13 ERA for Cedar Rapids. Gaining a reputation for always tugging at the seams of the ball on the mound in an attempt to raise them for a better grip, Forsch would proceed to pitch two no-hitters in the Minor Leagues—a feat he would ultimately duplicate in the majors.

Forsch was making a strong case to be the newest addition to the rotation. But by the break of camp, he would be sent back to Tulsa for further seasoning to start the year. Yet with all the changes to the pitching staff that had occurred via trades, the most significant move would take place in center field, perhaps the most unsettled position on the team since the departure of Flood. With Vada Pinson, Jose Cardenal, and most recently Jose Cruz as well as others not filling the bill, the job was given to young Bake McBride.

McBride was a natural athlete, having competed in basketball and track at Westminster College in Fulton in addition to baseball (and where he still holds the school's record in the 200-meter dash of 20.90 seconds, set in 1969). Even with baseball running deep in his blood (as Bake's father had played for the Kansas City Monarchs in the Negro Leagues), McBride did not play the sport in high school—nor was he able to tell anyone from whence his nickname came. Being signed after two years at Westminster, Bake planned to return to finish off his physical education degree but had found time to do so difficult with the launch of his professional career.

As was seen in the Cardinals' spring training camp the year before, McBride's running speed soon became the stuff of legend. He was sometimes even too fast for *himself*—as he put on display in his first at-bat at Triple-A ball, where he belted a pitch to the outfield wall and showed off his amazing gait around the bases for an apparent triple. However, in his excitement, McBride failed to touch second base and was called out.

As the clubs were getting ready for the season, the United States was facing an energy crisis in the spring of 1974, as long lines began to form at gasoline pumps (in part due to market unrest from the outbreak of the Arab-Israeli War) while the government ordered daylight savings time to being four months earlier than normal. The shortage on gas was predicted to hit the big league team as spring training began. "Many gas stations are closed," Francis Stann of the *Sporting News* reported from Florida as exhibition games were about to begin. "I spent two days visiting 11 stations and hit the jackpot on the last one—a $2 limit at 56 cents a gallon. Unless something dramatic happens soon, there will be more Opels than Cadillacs parked at the players' entrances."

Atmospheric conditions were proving to be just as unstable that spring. On April 3 what would become known as the "Super Outbreak" of tornadoes hit North America, with a twenty-four-hour-record total of 148 identified twisters hitting thirteen states and part of Canada in claiming more than three hundred lives. The massive storm stretched from northern Illinois to the Gulf coast of Mississippi, and from Virginia to the heartland in a path length estimated to be twenty-seven hundred miles. With the traditional Major League opener scheduled to take place in Cincinnati the following day, it was wondered if ballparks and cities around the Midwest would be in shape to play.

Not a game on the slate, however, would be threatened. The Atlanta Braves took the field against the Reds as planned, as all eyes were on Hank Aaron. The slugger entered the season with 713 home runs, one behind Babe Ruth for the all-time record. After looking at four pitches from Cincinnati's Jack Billingham in the first inning, Aaron jumped on a 3-1 offering that caught a large part of the plate and drove the ball over Pete Rose's head in left. Rose would later claim to know, from the moment of contact, that the ball would leave the yard; thus, he admitted to retreating away from the wall as it sailed over, hoping to catch the historic sphere on the rebound off the secondary wall beyond the playing surface. Rose would later win the game in extra innings on a wild pitch from Atlanta's Buzz Capra, but only one man would be remembered on this day. After the historic blast, Aaron was greeted near the Braves' dugout by Vice President Gerald Ford and Kuhn. Before the season started, the commissioner directed the Braves to play Aaron in at least two of the three games in Cincinnati—approximately the ratio of total games he had played over the 1973 season, so as to ensure the Atlanta fans a fair shot of Aaron's returning home to tie or break the record early the next week. Aaron would sit the second game of the Cincy series, go homerless in the final contest, and knock his epic shot off Al Downing of the Dodgers in the Braves' home opener on April 8 as he received an eleven-minute standing ovation from the fans.

Out in San Diego, things were not so happy. In the fourth game of the season (and his fourth as owner of the struggling Padres), an enraged Ray Kroc stormed up to the press box and grabbed the public address microphone at the team's home opener on April 9. In an unprecedented scene, he began to berate his team over the loudspeaker. "Ladies and gentlemen, I am suffering with you. . . . [T]his is the most stupid baseball playing I've ever seen," was one of his opening comments. Taking away from his moment, however, was a male streaker who bolted onto the field just after Kroc began his remarks.

The Cardinals, on the contrary, had begun the year in fine fashion as opposed to the nightmarish April of 1973, winning seven of their first nine and dispelling any chance of the early hole in which they had buried themselves the previous year. Throughout the first part of the 1974 season, the young team was getting into the habit of winning, and finding new ways to do so. Such was the case on May 24, as they headed into the ninth inning in a scoreless tie with the Cubs at Wrigley Field. Wrigley had been the scene of countless inexplicable displays of poor baseball over the years, but was still a beloved destination. "Wrigley Field is old," Ed Wilks admitted as he visited the park once again for another Cubs-Cardinals series. "Quaint may be the word for it in these days of large, rounded ballyards with their wall-to-wall carpets. But to the Cubs, Wrigley Field is home." Ted Simmons, for one, always found a way to frustrate the Cubs at their home park. "I've always hit the Cubs," he confirmed. "I don't know what it is. It's like the way Billy Williams has hit against us." He would wind up the 1974 season with softball-like numbers against Chicago, getting thirty-four hits in seventy-three at-bats for a stunning .466 mark. And on this date, he beat them with an unexpected body part—his legs, as the traditionally poor exhibition of Cubs baseball would reappear with Durocher's talented teams having gone by the wayside.

With Simmons on third and one out in the ninth inning of a 0–0 game, McCarver hit a ball down to first to Billy Williams, who was playing the position in his last season in Chicago (Williams could no longer run down balls in the outfield, and like the Cubs stars of the 1960s that went before him, Williams would be sent out of town shortly as well). When he fielded the grounder off McCarver's bat, he threw home to catcher Tom Lundstedt, who in turn threw to Matt Alexander at third as they had Simmons held up in a rundown. Like Williams, Alexander was playing a position foreign to him as well, filling in at third for the injured Bill Madlock. He was thought to be the fastest player on the Cubs' roster, however, and when he started chasing Simmons toward home plate, everyone figured the Cardinal runner was a sure out and thus would keep the game scoreless. Simmons glanced toward the plate vacated by Lundstedt passing him by, and without Williams or pitcher Rick Reuschel covering, he sprinted toward home with his long hair sailing through the breeze, a mane that would give him the nickname "Simba" among his teammates. Incredibly, he got to the plate without Alexander touching him, and his run held up in a 1–0 win for Sonny Siebert, who had been added to the starting rotation in coming over from the American League.

Victories like these—unlikely ones, coming in crucial situations—seemed to miss the Cardinals in past seasons, but were part of a charmed existence they were enjoying as their usual tormentors, the Pirates, would incredibly sink to last place by early June. The Cardinals were willing themselves to win, and the personification of this new attitude first appeared on June 11.

Until that date the struggling Al Hrabosky had saved only one game on the year and possessed an ERA over 4.00. It seemed that the club had been ready to give up on him, but Schoendienst saw an opportunity in one of those crucial moments. With two out in the ninth, the left-hander came in to relieve starter Lynn McGlothen and his 1–0 lead with runners on first and second. When Hrabosky entered, Dodgers manager Walter Alston countered by inserting the right-handed-hitting Tom Paciorek as a pinch hitter for Bill Buckner. With time to contemplate the moment as Paciorek was readying to hit, Hrabosky decided to take a short stroll behind the pitcher's mound and turn his back to the plate. Appearing to be speaking to himself, the little southpaw mumbled a few more words, took the ball out of his mitt, and slammed it back in again to the delight of the crowd. He proceeded to strike Paciorek out looking on three straight pitches as the roar grew louder each time. A phenomenon had started, as Hrabosky then decided to initiate every one of his appearances in this same manner. Later in the year, he was asked by a reporter what, exactly, he says to himself when going through his idiosyncrasies. "It's unprintable," Hrabosky responded. "I really don't often say much out loud, but I can always hear myself."

Yet it is rarely remembered that the glove pumping was not the only change to the Hrabosky routine in mid-1974. He believed that shaving off his mustache in spring training had something to do with his poor start to the season as well. "There were rumors that I might be sent back down, and I was out of contract options," Hrabosky said of the time. "During the All-Star break, I started growing facial hair. I knew I wasn't pitching well clean-shaven so I decided to grow it back."

On the day that Hrabosky began his tradition, the Cardinals were simultaneously making Santa Ana, California, high school shortstop Garry Templeton its number-one choice in the amateur draft (in the second round the Cards selected future Hall-of-Famer Paul Molitor, but he did not sign).

The win put McGlothen's record at 8-3; he would then proceed to take four more straight decisions by July 3. Twenty-four hours later, the Cardinals were in first place on Independence Day for only the third time since 1950—with their pennant years of 1967 and 1968 being the others.

While the team soared, the master mostly sat and watched. With yet another poor individual start to the season, Gibson had a 3-8 record by mid-June as the pain in his arm and leg became almost unbearable. After four starts in April his ERA was over seven, with a particularly ugly outing against the Expos in which he walked five in three innings before being pulled by Schoendienst. Aaron, just after hitting his record-breaking homer, was saddened to see one of his chief competitors headed for the end, as was he himself. "One of the young guys on our club—I won't mention his name—hit a fly ball to left field off Gibson in 1974 and came back to the bench throwing his helmet and cussing, saying things to the effect of how Gibson wasn't so tough and he should have taken the old man out of the park," Aaron remembered. "I didn't say anything, but it was all I could do to hold my tongue. Inside I was thinking, 'Son, a couple of years ago hitters like you were lucky to get a loud foul off Mr. Gibson." As in 1973, Gibson would be able to shut out only one team throughout all of 1974. Time was fading on him, as Jim Hickman—obtained from the Cubs only a few months earlier for Scipio Spinks—was let go on July 16 to make room for yet another young pitcher, yet another one to be the heir apparent to the number-one slot on the staff.

Even so, Gibby was still a man of great pride; the day after the Hickman trade on July 17, he tallied another notch onto his belt of achievements. "The nostalgia was mixed with some rapidly-changing current events," Russo later recalled about the evening in which the Cardinals also lost a beloved member of the family. As the Cardinals got ready to play the Reds at Busch Stadium that night, word had filtered down to the locker room that Dizzy Dean had just died. The man to whom Gibson had always been compared as the team's greatest pitcher had been struck by a heart attack while golfing in Reno, Nevada, and passed on a few hours later. Dean—whose lankiness became famous as a player, with his uniform jersey flapping in the breeze as he whipped his legendary right arm through the air—had put on significant weight over the years, approaching three hundred pounds at the time of his death. After being pushed out of the broadcasting business, he retired to his wife's home area of Bond, Mississippi, and spent his days telling stories to the folks on the park benches on the downtown square of nearby Wiggins. "Quail hunts with Charlie Mathis," wrote Robert Gregory about the final days of the Great Dean in the Magnolia State. "Sunday drives with Jim Rabby. Naps beneath Warren Watts's pecan tree. Miss Glo's Blueberry cobbler. Gin rummy with Boyce Holleman. And putts longer than a Faulkner sentence that always went straight in at Bond's Pine Burr country club." People inside of baseball remembered him fondly as well. "Going anywhere with him was like going with a brass band," said Phil Wrigley, who bought Dean for the Cubs from the Cardinals in 1938 even though the pitcher had a damaged arm. "He had a great sense of humor, nothing harmful. He was just a very interesting character." Dean was buried in Bond Cemetery, a nondescript resting place at the end of a peaceful dirt street in town. It is near the final house in which he and Pat had lived until her death in 1981, which today serves as an orphanage for as many as twenty needy youngsters at any given time. Joe Medwick, Dean's teammate and batting star for the Gas House Gang, would follow his in death the following March, as Medwick was continuing his work at the Cardinals' spring training camp with the hitters at the time of his passing.

Fittingly, on the date of his death, it was as if Diz was finally ready to pass the torch to Gibby, for a new level in the career of the Omaha right-hander was about to be achieved. With one more strikeout, he would join Walter Johnson as the only hurlers to pass the three-thousand mark. Many had expected Gibson to accomplish the milestone five days earlier against Atlanta, but he was able to whiff only a pair of batters.

In the second inning, he got ahead two strikes on the Cesar Geronimo, after which the Reds' center fielder was able to foul off a pitch. Gibson then came back with a high, sailing fastball that jumped like a jackrabbit when it approached the plate, one more similar to Gibson's prowess from a decade earlier. Geronimo feebly swung under it, and it was done. The strikeout had ended the top of the second inning as appreciative, tear-filled fans in the lower boxes at Busch could not be held in their seats as number 45 limped off the field.

Six years later Geronimo would become the three-thousandth strikeout victim of Nolan Ryan as well. But for now, in joining Johnson as the only two men to surpass the mark, Gibson had crossed the threshold in just 492 games pitched, while Johnson—playing in a different era, with fewer free swingers—needed 802.

And more interestingly, not only did Gibson's latest feat coincide with Dean's death, but it was also the fiftieth anniversary of Haines's crafting the last National League no-hitter in the city, perhaps worthy as the third member of the St. Louis Pitching Triumvirate.

After the game the worsening pain in Gibson's knee was once again treated by Dr. London, as the physician drained fluid from the joint as usual.

Gibson's three-thousandth strikeout was an event that provided a tonic for the team, as it was in the midst of a rough 1-13 stretch from July 7 to 19 that saw them going from having a three-game lead to a three-game deficit in the division. The first loss on the seventh was the Major League debut of Forsch, who left Tulsa and joined the team in St. Louis, from which they were flying to Cincinnati where Forsch would start in a series opener against the Reds (having just left Cincinnati were the Dodgers, whose relief pitcher Mike Marshall on the Fourth of July set a record with his fourteenth straight appearance in gaining the 3–2 win). They got to the airport and went to the hotel, but the baggage truck was late. Forsch sat patiently in the lobby to wait for his bag, retrieved it, and walked up to his room. He passed an open door to another room where McCarver and Torre were playing cards, and Forsch recalled their "welcoming" message to the rookie.

"What are you doing?" they asked sharply.

"Carrying my suitcase," Forsch answered.

"The bellman's supposed to bring it up, and you're supposed to tip him. They've got kids in college. Do you want their kids to have to drop out of college?"

It was one of those playful but standard lessons that first-year players received, such as at the next stop on the trip at Houston where Forsch was fined twenty-five dollars by Gibson for talking to a player on the other team—even though it was his brother Ken Forsch, who pitched for the Astros. As opposed to the careless attitude of modern players of being friendly with the opponent, Gibson hated any form of fraternization with the enemy, his reasoning for not even wishing to participate in All-Star Games.

When Forsch took the mound that first night in Riverfront Stadium, he made himself finally raise his head and look up at the crowd in the second inning; he would later write in his autobiography that the fifty thousand in attendance scared him to death.

The events Forsch experienced in his rookie year continued to make an impression on him. He was also startled that season in noticing that all the players seemed to be using hair dryers, something usually absent from the Minor League locker rooms. On a cold day in September at Wrigley Field, Schoendienst after the game had gotten out of the shower in the visitors' clubhouse, which had no separate area for coaches. While using the same shower area as the players, someone with a hair dryer was waving it about frantically in front of the mirror and accidentally bumped Schoendienst into the hot, old-fashioned radiator in the corner of the locker room. Red's response was to throw some ice onto his burned arm, and a chair in the direction of the culprit.

Forsch certainly arrived to the team during a low point in 1974. But with the Cardinals struggling, it once again would be a "Simmons incident in Chicago" that sparked them back to life.

The Cardinals' catcher had been in a two-for-thirty-two slump as the team came to Chicago in late July, mirroring the overall troubles of the team in the past month (although they had rebounded recently in taking five of their past six before invading Wrigley). In the fifth inning of the game on the twenty-eighth, Simmons barreled into Billy Grabarkewitz to try to break up a double play. As Simmons came off the field, a fan in the fourth row, a man whom the Cardinal player claimed had been riding him ever since Ted entered the majors, started heckling him. In the sixth Simmons gave the Cards the lead with a three-run homer in his next trip to the plate, which quieted the man down briefly. The next inning Simmons got between Siebert and Billy Williams after a pitch came close and Williams approached the mound; Simmons tried to get Williams to go after him instead, saying that he called for the pitch, but Williams would not bite. Finally, in the eighth inning, Simmons threw out Matt Alexander—the man he had outrun to home plate earlier in the season—trying to steal, and Ted wound up having four hits on the day at the plate, raising his average back up to .266 (as well as .500 against the Cubs so far on the year, in another tremendous personal performance against Chicago). Rygelski and Castle point out that the series' three-game attendance of seventy-eight thousand was almost 8 percent of the Wrigley total for the year. The attendees were among the final few to enjoy the voice of Pat Pieper, who was retiring at the end of the year after having been the Cubs' public address announcer since 1916—an unfathomable run that had even seen Pieper use a megaphone for the first fifteen years on the job before Wrigley Field installed an electronic public address system in 1932.

While evidence was piling up against President Nixon and certain advisers in the Watergate scandal—culminating with Nixon's resignation on August 8, to be effective the following day, with Ford (who would pardon Nixon one month later) taking over as the chief executive—Brock was continuing to pile up stolen bases at an unprecedented rate, even for him. When Brock had failed to steal a base in the first six games of the season, assumptions were being made that the thirty-five-year-old was, like Gibson, winding down and no longer expected to be productive. But by the end of August his total had soared to 94, as his capture of Maury Wills's record of 104, set in 1962, appeared almost a certainty (in August alone Brock had swiped 29 bases in thirty games played that month). He started September by stealing numbers 95, 96, 97, and 98 in one game at San Francisco, the same afternoon that McCarver left the team once again in being sold to the Red Sox. Thus, despite the success of one of his longtime teammates in Brock, Gibson thus could not fully share in the joy of the moment with the departure of his trusted, longtime "personal" catcher. The pitcher only wished he could sprint out on the last edge of his career in the spectacular manner in which Brock had been doing.

Also drawing attention away from Gibson's preeminent sports status in St. Louis was the newfound success of the football Cardinals under coach Don Coryell, who brought a losing franchise up to playoff form in the fall of 1974 with a 10-4 record (the "Big Red" would put up 11-3 and 10-4 records over the next two years as well, but would never get to host an NFL playoff game in Busch Stadium).

Also bearing witness to Brock's heroics in San Francisco was young local native Keith Hernandez, who was called up to make his Major League debut on August 30 after batting a league-leading .351 at Tulsa and would start in all three games of the series with the Giants. The smooth-fielding, smooth-swinging first baseman had grown up in Pacifica, California, like Reitz reared only a few miles from the Giants' home park. Hernandez had been a forty-second-round draft choice after a brief stay at a local junior college. His low draft status was due in part to his not playing his senior year of high school after getting into an intense argument with the coach. His father had been a top first base prospect in the 1940s for the Cards but did not make it in the big leagues and had now been intent on seeing his son make it in his stead. "John Hernandez, Juan to his son, is an obsessive and overbearing man who taught Keith Hernandez how to hit and field," wrote William Nack in *Sports Illustrated* in 1986 during the World Series in which the Mets, Hernandez's team at the time, was playing. "John's understanding of Keith's stroke has been the tether that has kept these two men together. At the same time, he has felt the compelling need to break away from his father and make it on his own, to be his own man."

With Brock's exploits making daily news that was comparable to people following Joe DiMaggio's hitting streak in 1941, excitement and speed were suddenly consuming the sports world. On September 8 Evel Knievel tried in desperation to rocket-propel himself across the Snake River Canyon in Idaho, only to fail; two nights later in St. Louis, Lou Brock was successful in his own venture into uncharted waters. Playing with an injured hand that was heavily bandaged, Brock would steal bases 104 and 105 at home against the Phillies to break the record. Over the course of the season it had again been Sizemore, batting in the number-two slot, who provided Lou with many chances to run. "He hit 0-2 [count] more than any hitter I ever saw," Folkers would notice, "because with Brock getting on base, he took and took and took, waiting for Lou to steal bases. And without a good number-two hitter, you're not going to steal a lot of bases. . . . Sizemore would still hit .270 and do that almost always with two strikes on him, which I thought was incredible. . . . Ted never got the credit."

An eleven-minute ovation interrupted play when Brock set the mark in the seventh inning, with "the Cardinals pouring out of the dugout as if for a fistfight rather than a celebration," according to Broeg. The base was yanked from the ground and presented to new standard-bearer by St. Louis's own James "Cool Papa" Bell, the legendary base runner from the Negro Leagues. Number 105 on the season also brought Brock's career total to 740, which was two more than the previous career record holder in the National League, Max Carey, had stolen.

Taking away from the moment was the fact that, over the past several weeks, Brock had decided to keep a bodyguard with him. He—as with Aaron in the home run chase—was reported to be receiving death threats about the stolen base record. One specific letter included McBride in the threat as well, in which the writer claimed he would be missing out on fifty thousand dollars in lost bets on Pittsburgh to win the division if Brock and the Cardinals did not lessen their quality of play. The letter, which Brock chose to reveal when he openly read it at a press conference when the team got to Chicago later in the month, on the twenty-sixth, included a passage that read: "I'm going to follow you to St. Louis, Chicago, Montreal, and L.A. and Cincy. . . . [M]eanwhile you two bastards [Brock and McBride] can sweat it out. . . . [E]very time you go out to the outfield, you can look anxiously towards the stands, and be sure to say goodbye to your family each morning, for between now and the next two weeks or so, you will have said goodbye for the last time." Brock had released the contents of the letter to the media against the advisement of the St. Louis Police Department, but he felt it was best to "bring details of the letter into the open."

Alongside the individual feats, the wins kept coming for the Cardinals—and kept coming in unconventional fashion. On September 11 and 12, the Cardinals won the longest game ever, a twenty-five-inning journey that left them victorious when, at 3:13 in the morning, McBride beat out an infield single and then circled the bases when a pickoff attempt on him by Hank Webb of the Mets went down into the right-field corner with Reitz at bat. The teams had sent more than two hundred batters to the plate during the struggle, as numerous other Major League records for duration were set. When Jack Buck did his usual "Star of the Game" interview for KMOX afterward, he knew everyone wanted to keep it short and go home. It went like this: "And now, the star of the game—Ken Reitz. Congratulations, Ken! And good night!" (earlier, Reitz had hit a ninth-inning home run to tie the contest).

The Redbirds went on to win five more in a row, allowing them to build a three-game lead on the Pirates by beating Reuss (who had been picked up by Pittsburgh after the 1973 season) in the final game of the streak, as the former Cardinal threw all thirteen innings of a 2–1 St. Louis victory. As part of the team's newfound identity, not all were happy with Hrabosky's routine after entering a game, and understandably many of them were players on opposing teams. By September 17 in Pittsburgh, his act had become so well known that he was booed by the opposing fans for the first time when performing it (according to Russo) as he ran his record to 7-1 in getting the win. "We're just an after-hours team," Reggie Smith warned the rest of the league about the Cards' ability to win in overtime. "Any team that gets us beyond the ninth or tenth inning is in trouble." As for Hrabosky, he paid no mind to the crowd, as he had now allowed only one earned run in his last forty-two innings of work. And between his finishing job of more than four innings along with the last five that the starter Gibson hurled that night, the two men had thrown nine combined innings of no-hit ball. "Let them boo," the defiant lefty, who was now being called the "Mad Hungarian" in the press, said afterward. "I hate people anyway. I think all relief pitchers should hate people."

Resentment from other players against Hrabosky was only beginning. Five days later in a game against the Cubs at Busch Stadium (before which Dizzy Dean's jersey number 17 was retired), Madlock—along with McBride, a serious Rookie of the Year candidate—waited outside the batter's box for two minutes after Hrabosky got on the rubber, in an effort to give the pitcher some of his own medicine. After Madlock even tried to wander back over to the Cubs' on-deck circle, umpire Shag Crawford ordered him back to get the game going— but the batter did not budge. "He didn't hear me," Crawford assumed, "so I told him again." Crawford then called a strike on him for delaying the game (as he is directed to do under the baseball rules, section 6.02c), as Madlock was again invited to return before another strike would be called on him. With Jim Marshall (who by now had replaced Lockman as the Chicago manager) standing on home plate arguing, Hrabosky sent a pitch somewhat close to Madlock's head. As the Cub third baseman stormed toward the mound, Simmons sprung forward and intervened by hitting Madlock in the jaw, and a bench-clearing brawl was sparked. Cubs first baseman Andre Thornton came from behind and punched Simmons, and Chicago's Jim Tyrone similarly knocked McGlothen down. But in the end, neither Madlock nor Simmons was thrown out of the game. "It was a close situation," Simmons tried to explain after the game. "I was getting bumped around, and Madlock looked at me and I said to him, 'What are you looking at?'" Thornton's defense was that "I had to get at Simmons because he took a free shot at Billy." As for Marshall, his argument to Crawford—the latter of whom was on a U.S. Navy ship in World War II that was hit by a Japanese kamikaze plane—was that the umpire should have directed Hrabosky to get on the mound in the first place instead of focusing his attention on Madlock. Crawford's decision to permit both men to remain in the game was an important one, as Simmons would slay the Cubs once again by singling home the winning run in the bottom of the ninth for a 6–5 final. "They must have done this for Diz," Mrs. Pat Dean said as she watched the brawling victory on the day her husband's jersey number was laid to rest. "It looked like the old Gas House Gang."

Sizemore was impressed with Kessinger and Cub Rick Monday, who were actually trying to keep the fight from escalating further. As for Schoendienst, he was simply happy that no one was seriously injured in the melee. Hrabosky, the origin of trouble in the minds of the Cubs, had turned into one of the game's dominant relievers and proved he had the confidence to match. "Barring a home-run pitch, I simply feel that I can't be scored upon. I don't feel there's any way I can give up two or three hits in one inning."

The thrilling win kept them a game and a half ahead of the Pirates, as one writer in another National League city called the Cards "the team too tough to die." Tickets for would-be playoff games went on sale at the Busch Stadium box office the following morning, on Monday the twenty-third, as pennant fever was finally returning to St. Louis. In the coming final days of the season, the drum-tight National League Eastern Division race would rival the excitement seen twelve months earlier.

By the end of the day on September 29 (four days after Dr. Frank Jobe wrapped up what was believed to be the first successful elbow ligament transplant for a pitcher, conducted on Dodgers hurler Tommy John), Brock had stolen his 118th base of the year, helping John Curtis—one of the pitchers swapped from Boston in the off-season—get his tenth win of the year in downing the Cubs 7–3 at Wrigley Field. The win put the Cards in a dead heat in first place with the Pirates at 85-74. The teams had exchanged the top spot three times in the past week, including Pittsburgh jumping ahead with a 13–12 eleven-inning triumph at Busch Stadium on the twenty-fifth. A three-game "season" was now on tap to decide the title, with the Cardinals traveling to Montreal while the Pirates would host the Cubs in Three Rivers Stadium. The Expos, while standing in third place and seven games behind Pittsburgh and St. Louis, had nonetheless gone on an incredible run themselves in September, sporting a 17-4 mark coming into the series with the Cardinals; thus, if the Redbirds were to take the top spot, they would have to go through the league's hottest team to do so.

It was the rookie Forsch's turn in the opener at Montreal's Jarry Park, as temperatures dipped into the forties. Gibson, whom Forsch claimed had said nothing to him all year, came up beside him at the urinals in the locker room. "You nervous?" Gibby asked him in a teasing nature about the big game. The grave implications of the contest could not be interpreted from looking at the grandstand; just over fifty-three hundred people decided to attend, as the focus in Quebec was instead turning to preseason hockey. In a battle between two men who would become first-rate starting pitchers in the years to come, Forsch rose to the occasion and spun a complete game three-hitter in winning 5–1. In doing so, he had pinned the twenty-second loss of the season on young Steve Rogers, the talented second-year pitcher from Springfield, Missouri, who had been named the *Sporting News's* Rookie Pitcher of the Year in 1973 but, like Forsch, was still learning the trade at the big league level. Simmons pounced on Rogers early, striking a three-run homer in the first to settle Forsch down—his twentieth of the season (again breaking his own club homer record for a catcher), and his 103rd RBI. Fellow switch-hitter Reggie Smith would join him in the 100-RBI club the following night.

"Some people say his defense wasn't good," Forsch said years later of the man who would catch him for several more seasons, "but I thought he had a bad rap. He didn't have a strong arm, but he got rid of the ball quick. He pitched out a lot, but that didn't bother me because I had pretty good control . . . and Teddy called a good game." It was also the first time the native Californian could recall pitching with snowflakes wafting around him. The Pirates, meanwhile, would match the Cards' win in Pittsburgh, nipping the Cubs 2–1 on a seventh-inning triple by Richie Zisk that scored Sanguillen, giving Chicago's Bill Bonham twenty-two losses as well.

His arm and reinjured leg both throbbing, Gibson was in no mood for jokes the following night, as the pressure was turned up in his starting assignment against former teammate Mike Torrez. He saw it as a chance for redemption in his own subpar season (11-12), and also a chance to stave off remaining naysayers about his current ability to be a competitive pitcher.

His teammates attacked first, giving him a one-run lead in the fourth courtesy of a leadoff homer from Smith, a man who like Dick Allen had risen to quick popularity in St. Louis with his productive bat during his first season. The Expos equaled things in the sixth, but the Cards rebounded in the seventh behind McBride, who stole second and third before Tyson singled him home.

With the Cards retaking the lead, Gibson was energized heading into the Montreal half of the eighth inning. He pounded his old 1960s-style fastball in onto the hands of Bob Bailey and Ron Fairly, who tapped easy plays to Tyson and Smith, respectively. With two out, veteran outfielder Willie Davis—in his first season in Montreal after being a star with the Dodgers for the past fourteen years—rocketed a single to center as the surprised Gibson looked behind him. Davis then quickly stole second as Gibby lost his concentration for a moment, not thinking that the veteran had any of his old speed left (Davis would come to St. Louis to play for the Cardinals in mid-1975, but outrageous salary demands by the player caused his stay to be only a half season long).

With the tying run now in scoring position, Expos first baseman Mike Jorgensen was the batter, a left-handed hitter who despite his reputation had been nearly as adept at handling southpaws (.306) as he had been right-handed pitchers (.311) during the 1974 season. Even though both knew he was tiring, Schoendienst allowed the ailing Gibson to stay in the game despite the fact that the lefty Hrabosky was ready in the bullpen. Jorgensen, who had gotten the Expos' first hit off Forsch the night before with two outs in the seventh inning, had homered off Gibson in his first at-bat as an Expo back in 1972. He was normally a low-ball hitter, but he slapped at a pitch Gibson had permitted to rise in the strike zone and sent a liner through the cold Canadian wind, a gale that had held up other normal fly balls on the evening, and the result was a homer that gave the Expos the lead.

The Cardinals tried to rally in the ninth, as Cruz singled with one out. Reserve outfielder Jim Dwyer was sent in to pinch-hit for Gibson and grounded into a double play to end the game. The defeat ensured Gibson's first losing season as a full-time starter in the big leagues, as he started to see his waning professional moments go into overdrive. "I would have given anything to be twenty-eight that summer instead of thirty-eight," Gibson would lament about the summer of 1974 twenty years afterward. "We would have blown away the division that year if I had been twenty-eight."

In Pittsburgh pinch hitter Bob Robertson nailed a two-run homer in the eighth inning against Cubs pitcher Dave LaRoche that would give the Pirates a come-from-behind 6–5 win, as the Bucs now held a one-game lead on St. Louis with just one to play.

The media unloaded on Schoendienst the next day, scolding him for leaving the fatigued Gibson in the game and not opting for the reliever to face Jorgensen. But for those who appreciated the manager's allegiance to his main horse, they recalled a similar circumstance back in the 1968 World Series with Northrup's big hit over Flood's head. "I remain grateful to Schoendienst for sticking with me," Gibson wrote in his autobiography about the World Series game. "The obvious thing would have been to pinch-hit for me in the eighth inning, and Red's decision to leave me in the game had more to do with consideration than strategy." So once again, although it cost the Cardinals the game (and perhaps more), Gibby would never forget Red's loyalty to him.

As for Schoendienst, it was his *instinct* to leave Gibson in, just as much as it was his faithfulness to his old trusted pitcher. "When I managed," he would say years later, "we didn't have all the computer printouts and charts and data that are available to managers today. I think some of the guys rely too much on all that stuff, going strictly by the numbers and 'by the book' and never taking a chance or a gamble on a gut feeling. . . . [B]aseball is still a people game, and managers have to remember that." Over his many years in baseball—with the genuine respect, honesty, and integrity he displayed—Red cemented a trust with his charges, and it was never more clearly demonstrated than in his confidence in Bob Gibson. "If you can't play for Red Schoendienst," Orlando Cepeda had once said, "you can't play for anybody."

As Schoendienst, Gibson, and the rest of the Cardinals lay in their hotel rooms that night, pondering their final fate in the standings the next day, the snow started to fall on Montreal.

8　Finished

Bob Gibson is the luckiest pitcher in baseball. He is always pitching when the other team doesn't score any runs.

—Tim McCarver, *St. Louis Post-Dispatch*, August 16, 1972

The winterlike conditions would make Jarry Park unplayable on Wednesday, October 2, 1974, the final day of the regular season. With club executives not wishing to pay for an extra night in the Queen Elizabeth Hotel in Montreal if unnecessary, the team was forced to sit around to wait for word about the last Cubs-Pirates game before their next move was made. It was a night game in Pittsburgh, so in addition to there being no radio or television coverage of the game, the Cardinals had to entertain themselves all day beforehand. Forsch and Dwyer were roommates (and had been in the minors as well) and quickly became bored, so they went out and bought a dartboard, cleared the pictures off their hotel room wall, and played darts for six hours until the Cubs-Pirates game began. As members of the team gathered in a corner of the lobby, one of the St. Louis television commentators, Jay Randolph, gave them play-by-play that was sent to him via telephone in St. Louis from KSD-TV reporter Ron Jacober, who was able to pick up the game on Chicago's WGN station. Faces brightened as Randolph told them Chicago had built a 4–0 first-inning lead in Three Rivers Stadium. If the Cubs could hold on and the Cards won their makeup game with the Expos the next day, a playoff game would ensue between Pittsburgh and St. Louis for the division title; if the Cubs blew their lead and lost, the final Expos-Cardinals game would not have to be played, as the Pirates would have a game-and-a-half advantage over the Cards. It was the exact same situation as 1973, with the Cubs being able to give the Cards a tie for the lead if they won in the season's final hours. It seemed as if now was the time.

Gradually, the Pirates got back in the game. They plated a run in the third, a run in the fifth, and yet another as their starter, Jim Rooker, found a groove in quieting the Chicago bats. With two out in the ninth and the Cubs still holding the 4–3 lead, Rick Reuschel apparently had struck out the previous night's hero for Pittsburgh, Robertson, to end the game—but the pitch squirted away from rookie catcher Steve Swisher for a passed ball, allowing Sanguillen to score the tying run as joyous Pittsburgh fans for four minutes littered the field with bottles (the fans, in protest of an umpire's call, had conversely thrown bottles in *anger* the previous inning as well). Swisher, not paying attention in his self-disgust, allowed Robertson to get all the way to second, although he would be stranded (a week earlier in St. Louis, Swisher had a grand slam that was part of a Chicago onslaught that beat the Cards 19–4, as the St. Louis team at that time appeared measured for the grave, and Swisher, in his giddy excitement for a rare big hit, wanted to retrieve the ball from the stands).

The final Pirates assault would resume in the tenth. Sanguillen lined a single off Oscar Zamora into the outfield to score Al Oliver, who had tripled with one out, to win the game and the National League Eastern Division for Pittsburgh. The Pirates had risen to the top once again after having posted baseball's worst record in the first two months of the season. As the Cardinals got the incredible news in the lobby of the Queen Elizabeth back in Montreal, it was the third time in the past four years that they would finish in second place.

It was one too many near misses for their owner to take. According to Broeg, Gussie Busch was watching the Cubs-Pirates game at the Bevo Mill on Gravois Avenue, a St. Louis landmark that would close its doors permanently in 2009. When Sanguillen's game-winning hit occurred, a sad Busch turned at the restaurant table to his friend Ben Kerner, the owner of the old St. Louis Hawks basketball team. He said, "Drive me home, Hawk," as he called his buddy, and he did not utter another word. Many close to Busch marked it as the last time he was actively involved with the team.

Forsch recalled that, on the plane ride home, his elbow was so sore from playing darts with Dwyer that he could not even straighten his arm—and thus if they *had* made the playoffs, he did not think he would have been able to pitch.

Once again, a power vacuum on offense had hurt the club. The Cards finished last in the league in home runs for the third season in a row (a streak started shortly after the departure of Dick Allen) and last in the majors for the second straight year. Having Allen would not necessarily have helped them in 1974, for he once again disappeared from baseball in early September as he had done with the Cardinals in 1970 and the Phillies in prior years, with the current victims being his Chicago White Sox. Allen would hit his last home run for the Sox on August 16, which gave him a total of thirty-two and the lame-duck American League title in the category, as no one could catch him in the season's final six weeks (thus, Schoendienst's comment of Allen's "not seeming to play the last month of the season" wound up being just as prophetic as it was ex post facto; even after signing his record contract with the Sox, Allen's final game in 1973—August 2—had been even earlier). Evidence of the St. Louis power problem was also shown in the fact that despite reaching base 255 times via hits and walks, Lou Brock scored only 105 runs, as the rest of the team could not drive him in—while still an impressive figure, it likely should have been much more. Nonetheless, his season on the base paths caught the imagination of baseball followers nationwide. It was still not enough for the MVP award, as Brock was beaten out by Steve Garvey of the Dodgers. The Cardinals organization had decided that, in the spacious home ballpark in which they were playing, a premium should be placed on speed, and McBride was thought to be the future centerpiece of this strategy. He and Brock set a record for combined stolen bases by teammates in a season (148), as McBride took away the Rookie of the Year award in the National League, outdistancing Greg Gross of Houston and a third-place finish by Madlock—the first Cardinal to claim the honor since Virdon in 1955. "McBride was much faster," Gibson years later opined in comparing the two, "but Brock's knowledge of pitchers was so thorough that he was able to steal 118 bases on cunning."

McBride's emergence also prompted Devine to finally give up on Jose Cruz, who was sold to the Astros for twenty-five thousand dollars. Similarly, the successful audition of Keith Hernandez—who hit .294 in fourteen games—would prompt Devine to release a veteran in his place for 1975 as well. In October Joe Torre would be traded to the Mets for Ray Sadecki, one of the original Cardinal "bonus babies" and a fellow starting pitcher with Gibson on the 1964 championship team. (Hernandez would actually split 1975 with Tulsa and the Cards, as he was sent down to the minors on June 3 with his big league average sinking to .203. He answered the challenge by batting .330 at Tulsa before returning to the Cardinals at the end of the year and finishing with a .250 mark at the Major League level.) Simmons and Hrabosky, meanwhile, had parlayed their success and popularity into having a new radio show over the winter, hosting an hourlong show called *The Hot Stove League* on KMOX once a week during the off-season. Bluntly answering the call-in questions from listeners, the two unabashedly gave their views of the team—including their assertion that the club did not get enough of a return on the Torre trade. "Honesty is one of the things that makes our show," Simmons, a speech major during his time at Michigan, plainly said. "It's foolish for us to hedge and act as if we have no opinion." They were so bold as to even publicly pick their own "All–Hot Dog" and even "All-Ugly" teams from among the Major League rosters.

The overall team defense had vastly improved in 1974, setting a club record with 190 double plays turned. With bona fide young stars emerging in the field with McBride, Hernandez, Reitz (who led National League third basemen in fielding percentage), and pitchers Forsch, Curtis, McGlothen (the latter of whom won sixteen games by September 3), and Hrabosky (whose sixty-five games pitched was a team record for left-handers), it was hoped that the Cards could finally supplant the other teams in the division and make the postseason before Gibson's playing days were over. "I hope the team can stay together," Sizemore said. "I'd like one more shot with this club. It's a closely-knit bunch of guys and we can win with this nucleus."

The surrounding cast would indeed have only one more chance to win for the great one. In January 1975, Bob Gibson announced that he would be embarking on his final baseball season.

Over the decades several notable baseball stars have been asked how each would like to end his career. Former Royals third baseman George Brett, for example, said he wanted to ground out to the second baseman in his final at-bat—so that he could run as hard as possible to first base in order to show his respect for the game. When the question was posed to Gibson several years earlier, he answered by saying that he probably belonged to another era—perhaps on the starting staff of the Gas House Gang in 1934, just as Dizzy Dean had dreamed aloud when he visited the team on March 12, 1971, in spring training. The Gang was certainly one outfit worthy of his competitive fire.

"Maybe my last game," Gibson wondered in talking to Ed Wilks back in 1970,

> I'm going to have to walk a guy intentionally and when he throws those elbows and bat out over the plate—knowing he's being walked—I'm going to plunk him. In the ribs.
>
> And sometime, maybe in that last game, I'm going to find a guy like Cincinnati's Bernie Carbo [at the time with the Reds]—the kind of guy who's next up and won't stay in the on-deck circle, but keeps meandering off behind the plate to see what you're throwing. I'm going to plunk him with a pitch, too, while he's back there giving a look.

This was Gibby's dream; this is how he wanted to walk off the field, and not look back.

In the days of Dean, the acts Gibson described would hardly be given a second thought by the umpire, the commissioner, or perhaps even the opposing team. And as Gibson saw his career go into its final twilight, he continued to witness the further evolution of the game into something he could not recognize. Higher pitches that used to be called strikes were now decided in the batter's favor—which, in Gibson's mind, was due to the owners' desire for more offense and, presumably, an ensuing rise in attendance. "They keep calling your pitch a ball—the one you want to make when you're in trouble—when for ten or eleven years they've been calling it a strike," he said in a miffed tone. "It takes time to overcome it. And you keep telling yourself they can't call it a ball. But what you've got to do is stop complaining and start pitching."

For the opening day of the 1975 National League season, there was no other choice for Red Schoendienst for his starter on the mound. It was April 7 at Busch Stadium, three days after a man named Bill Gates started a company called Microsoft. Old number 45 would once again take the hill, as he had done to kick off Cardinal seasons in so many years past. The first game would be against Montreal, the same team he faced on that cold, cruel night north of the border back in September when a playoff berth for his team slipped through his own fingers. His pitching opponent in this his final inaugural was Dave Mc-Nally, another man in his final season in the big leagues. McNally had escaped to the Senior Circuit after finishing his highly successful career in Baltimore the previous autumn, noted by surrendering Al Kaline's three-thousandth hit in the season's final days. It was truly an ironic setting as the two veterans got set to clash, two titans of the pitching rubber for the past ten years. The matchup went far beyond their mere statistics and achievements. McNally himself represented the "new money" that was part of the changes in the game that found disfavor with Gibson. Bob himself continued to be a dichotomy in this regard, as he was extremely well paid but simultaneously also disdained the fact that the dollar was becoming the center of baseball, yet another morsel pilfered from the traditional ways of the sport, and it sickened him. In 1975 McNally and another fellow pitcher, Andy Messersmith of the Dodgers, had officially become the first individuals in an employment category that Curt Flood had pursued all along—that of a "free agent." Both men had effectively ended the role of the reserve clause by playing out the 1975 season without a signed contract and, in doing so (according to the arbitrator on the case, Peter Seitz), must be granted free agency by their teams at the conclusion of the season. Whereas McNally would retire at the end of the season anyway, Messersmith would break the bank with the Atlanta Braves in 1976 with their new owner, Ted Turner.

That day Gibson threw like an angry man. Issuing the final double-digit strikeout game of his career, he sent no fewer than twelve Expos batters back to the dugout via the right arm of the umpire. But again, Montreal got the best of him in an 8–4 defeat.

He battled, and he lost. But at least he kept Jorgensen at an 0-for-4 day.

With the last of the American troops leaving Vietnam during the fall of Saigon as the big league season got under way, it was hoped that a measure of stability was finally returning to American life. All the same, it was bound to be a strange, surreal summer in St. Louis. For the first time since the passing of his father, Gussie Busch was stepping down as the director of the brewery and turning the reins over to his own son, August III. Gussie, however, wished to retain control of the ball club (he had given up the role of team president after the 1973 season, giving way to Dick Meyer that year, but would take it back in 1974). People indeed grow older and have to give way to the younger generation.

It was not only Gibson who was feeling the physical pain of aging in his profession. As Brock got older, his legs started aching from the artificial turf. According to Forsch, somebody thought, in a moment of pity, that if they watered down left field, it would be cooler for him and more comfortable. One wet patch was seen in the outfield, and after one inning, Brock had had enough. "It's like a sauna out there!" he yelled.

The new players continued to come and go from the Cardinals, paraded in front of Gibson and Brock just as they had done in every year since the pennant seasons of the late 1960s. As had been done with Ernie Banks as a first baseman in Chicago, a new pitcher was seen each year to be the one to replace Gibson as the go-to guy on the mound in St. Louis. For 1975 with the Cardinals pitching staff the hot new thing was John Denny, a talented but hot-tempered youngster. "Everything had to go almost absolutely perfect in order for him not to get upset," said one of his pitching coaches, Claude Osteen. Taken in the twenty-ninth round by the Cards in the 1970 draft, Denny was the son of an Arizona rancher. Just about the time that Denny arrived at the big leagues in late 1974, his older brother Gary—whom John looked to as a father figure after their parents' divorce—was killed in a domestic dispute.

While Forsch would rise to the top of the staff, no one could truly replace the man in charge. On July 31 in Detroit, Teamsters Union president Jimmy Hoffa went missing; earlier that same month, an irreplaceable man went missing from the Cardinals' starting rotation. As it turned out, July 8 would mark the date of the last time that Bob Gibson would start a game for the Cardinals, as he was sent to the bull pen.

Gibson initially felt humiliated in becoming a reliever. Earlier in his career he had set a Major League record with 303 straight starts without making a relief appearance, but on July 28 he got his first victory in relief since 1964, as Simmons homered in the seventh to win it. The victory would be Gibson's last of any kind. "I didn't conceal my anger at being sent to the bullpen," the pitcher admitted, "but I suspect now that some of it actually stemmed from my frustrations at home." A pending divorce had indeed been a severe distraction, as Gussie Busch—caring for his players as he had always tried to do—was calling Gibson often at his house to make certain things were okay. "To see it all fall apart was a crusher for Bob," Reggie Smith said of the situation. "And to make it worse, at that stage of his career he suffering from all sorts of injuries." He would continue to fight through the pain—it being emotional now, as well as physical—as he always had, wishing to give his mates one final season of greatness. Serving as a relief pitcher for most of the summer, he helped the Cards ultimately get within two games of the Pirates in the National League East by August, but no further. "There was one game toward the end," Smith continued, "where he came in against Houston and pitched an inning. He reared back that night and struck out the side on ten pitches, every one of them mammoth heat. I was awed." Smith was speaking of the game on August 13, in which Gibby's display of his old form would be the second of two saves he would get in 1975 in consecutive appearances.

When Labor Day weekend rolled around, Gibby was honored at Busch Stadium, as his mother was flown in from Omaha for the ceremony along with his two daughters, Annette and Renee. At first, Gibson was too moved to speak when he approached the microphone down on the field. Several times he stepped toward it again, but had to pause with every attempt, as each standing ovation was louder than the one a moment earlier. "I'm more nervous than I was before a World Series game," he admitted later. After steadying himself, he spoke in a manner that seemed to instead be addressing a future generation of big league players, especially ones who in later decades would inject shortcuts to success. "One thing that I've always been proud of," he began, "is the fact that I've never intentionally cheated anyone out of what they paid their money to come and see. But most of all I'm proud of the fact that whatever I did, I did it my way." Then he turned and looked at Gussie Busch, and continued, "The last couple of years certainly haven't been easy. I know I was pitching badly at times. But Mr. Busch would call me up at the ballpark, wish me well and tell me to hang in there—when it seemed everyone else was down on me." Gibson's mother also thanked Busch "and all St. Louis for what they have done for my son," as she opened a case of champagne that well-wishers had sent along with her from Omaha.

Then it was Gussie's turn to speak. "It's both a sad day and a proud day," Busch began, also mentioning that Gibson's number, 45, would join Dean's 17 as a retired Cardinal number. "It's sad because it marks the end of one of the greatest baseball careers of all time. But it's a proud day to say, 'Bob Gibson, you have done a great job. You're a symbol of what it means to work hard.'" Busch then gave Gibson the keys to a brand-new thirty-three-thousand-dollar mobile home as a gift—but not before the team owner drove Bob and his daughters around the perimeter of the field in a victory lap as fifth-year stadium organist Ernie Hays cranked out "Auld Lang Syne."

The Cardinals helped him celebrate by beating the Cubs 6–3. Gibson would pitch in one final game, which occurred two days later in the series finale. And it was not how he wanted to go out. Gibson entered in relief in the seventh inning against the Cubs with the game even at six. The Cardinals had been behind 6–1, but a five-run rally in the sixth inning, which included a three-run double by Brock, had gotten them tied. Gibson started swiftly and intently, retiring Madlock—who would win the first of his two consecutive National League batting titles in a few weeks—to fly out to Brock in left. But Gibson then walked Jose Cardenal and permitted a single to Champ Summers, a part-time player with a .231 average, as tension began to fill the stands. After a walk to Thornton loaded the bases, Gibson uncorked a wild pitch past Simmons that gave the Cubs the lead, as Jerry Morales was subsequently walked intentionally to load the bases once again for the pitcher's spot in the batting order. To pinch-hit, Chicago manager Jim Marshall sent a man named Pete LaCock to the plate, like Summers a second stringer on the Cubs' roster. Seeing a curveball that was merely spinning and not breaking, LaCock unloaded on the legend and drove a grand slam far into the right-field bleachers as the embarrassed Gibson watched the Cubs take an 11–6 lead. Legend has it that it was the last pitch Gibson ever threw, but he actually stayed in the game to retire Kessinger on a groundout to Reggie Smith playing first, a ball on which Gibson had to cover the bag and take the throw. "That's it, I'm out of here," he said to himself in going back to the Cardinal dugout. He could not believe, for all the sweat, blood, records, and championships he had given St. Louis over the years, that he was hearing pockets of derision from the stands.

Going 11-21 in the final five weeks of the season, the team fell into lethargy behind injuries to Smith and McBride as Gibson became a largely forgotten man. For Broeg, the end of the 1975 season was just the latest disappointment in the recent round of near misses for the Cardinals. "For the third consecutive year, up to manager Red Schoendienst's freckled forehead in a division championship fight until September, the Cardinals have faltered, this time even more embarrassingly than they did two years ago when the New York Mets didn't win the bauble—St. Louis bobbled it." Once again, consolation had to be found in a few individual achievements. A year removed from their boxing match at home plate in Busch Stadium, Simmons finished second in the National League batting race to Madlock, but was still more than 20 points behind him (.354 to .332). His total of 188 hits while catching was a league record for the position. And Forsch, the man who as a third baseman had a bat that kept him in the minors, won the Silver Slugger Award in his first full season in the big leagues, batting .308 as a pitcher.

As for the negatives, Broeg did not reserve criticism for those players not named Bob. "Gibson, whose knee surgery cost the Cardinals a sure-thing pennant two years ago, went from great to mediocre overnight." Due in part to the fact that he had only fourteen starts in twenty-two appearances, Gibson did not throw a shutout for the first time in fifteen seasons. The pitcher's ERA hovered near five virtually the entire season, and he received no great sympathy in the national media either. "In retrospect, it undoubtedly would have been better all around if Gibson had retired last year," C. C. Johnson Spink of the St. Louis–based *Sporting News* curtly wrote.

Demoralized, Gibson had hinted that he would quit the season early if the Cardinals were out of the pennant race, and on September 18, the announcement was put forth by Schoendienst, even though St. Louis could still mathematically catch Pittsburgh. Before the Cards' game with Montreal that night at Busch Stadium, it was announced by the club that Gibby would no longer be with the team after the contest, with the team moving on to Pittsburgh and Gibson heading back home to Omaha. Schoendienst did not think he would summon the veteran to the mound in this final game, even if the situation warranted his use. "I'd ask him, but I don't think he'd want to. Why?" Added Brock when he heard the news, "He had a tremendous career, and he's walking away proud." Gibson was saddened about missing the team's final road trip of the season but saw no point in going. "It felt like the last day of high school, when I had no idea what I would be doing with the rest of my life. It was scary."

Bing Devine offered Gibson an undisclosed job with the organization, but Gibson turned him down, saying he needed time to think. In terms of offering him a full-time position, the Cardinals never called on him again.

Gibson, as he consistently stated all along, would do it *his* way.

Epilogue

After falling short of the division title once again, Busch felt it was time to make a more drastic move. "There are times, regardless of one's capabilities, when a different perspective is in order," Gussie would say on October 5, 1976, three days after the close of the regular season. "Red Schoendienst's distinguished career as both a player and a manager are in the record books for all to see." Schoendienst's twelve-year run at the helm was over, the longest tenure in Cardinal history before Tony LaRussa would start his own run in 1996. Schoendienst was replaced by St. Louis native Vern Rapp, a former Cardinal farmhand as a player who had just led the Denver Bears to the American Association championship in 1976. Rapp quickly hammered down the discipline on the players, which was not well received—particularly by Hrabosky, who was ordered by the new manager to shave his mustache. "I felt like a soldier going to war without his rifle," the pitcher would say about his Fu Manchu being absent. In early 1978 Ted Simmons would be called into Rapp's office in the locker room after a game, but Ted had forgotten to close the door before Rapp spoke; thus, when the yelling started, everyone heard Rapp call Simmons a "loser," and the manager would soon be fired, as Ken Boyer was given the job after a two-game interim stint by Jack Krol. It was the same year in which Devine's run with the team would end as well.

Schoendienst would return to lead the Cardinals in two brief stretches—once in 1980, in advance of the arrival of Whitey Herzog so that Herzog could temporarily concentrate on personnel moves, and once in 1990 in between Herzog's departure and Torre's taking the job.

Having to remove Schoendienst, the loyal officer who had accomplished so much for the organization, hurt Busch deeply. He viewed Red as one of the few men of honor remaining in the game, a game—as Gibson had felt—that continued to warp in front of his eyes to his disliking. Busch never recovered from the shock of Curt Flood's defiance, and thus his mind-set toward his players would alter the path of St. Louis baseball for decades to come. A permanent bitterness had settled in on the man who had paid Roger Maris more money in 1968 ($75,000) than all of the starters on the 1934 champion Gas House Gang Cardinals put together; as Bob Broeg would note in 1988, "For Busch, the fun had become a funny business." (And when Flood stated in his own words that he would accept not a penny less than $100,000, the damage for the owner had been irrevocable, as he felt betrayed by the man to whom Busch would pay $250 for each family portrait Curt painted.)

In looking further at Flood, his impact on baseball can be viewed in two ways—progressive or detrimental. Since the advent of the free agent in Major League Baseball, Flood has essentially been deified as the martyr who sacrificed himself for the betterment of players to come after him. In the spirit of American capitalism, he believed in his innate right to offer his labor skills to the highest bidder—as he made clear in his letter to Bowie Kuhn on Christmas Eve, 1969. Unquestionably, this romanticized version of Flood, as well as praise for his cause, has received the greater share of his analysis in the past forty years.

On the other hand, those who have been enamored with what they deem as Flood's "noble pursuit" fail to realize that the very thing he was looking to destroy—the reserve clause—was, in one aspect, a powerful positive force in the corner of the small-market teams in baseball, protecting the rosters of clubs like St. Louis from being raided by the New Yorks and Bostons of the baseball world—the very cities that are now, perhaps without coincidence, broadcast on the national networks seemingly every weekend. Bob Howsam, the man who cut his teeth under Branch Rickey in St. Louis, would later have his own dynastic team—the Cincinnati Reds of the mid-1970s—stripped bare as a direct and indirect result of free agency, leaving yet another small midwestern city at a disadvantage in trying to field a competitive team. Howsam never apologized in contending to his dying day that the reserve clause was something good for the game.

Furthermore, the deeper motives of Flood should be examined, if anyone will ever know for sure what exactly they were. If he was so adamantly and categorically against the reserve clause, why did he not fight it at some other point in his previous fourteen years in the Major Leagues? There is little evidence that Flood had any feelings on the issue until it affected him personally. He had good reasons in not wanting to leave St. Louis, as he had set up an art studio and a photography business in addition to being a recognized Cardinal. "That was understandable," affirmed Gibson of his teammate's desire to stay in town. "But what I didn't understand at first were remarks about not accepting the trade. I didn't see that as an option, but Curt did." Since the very formation of the Major Leagues, every single player—Flood included—was aware of the possibility of being traded, and it was understood as part of the game. But while Flood contended that he was making his point on "principle," he was also seeking $1.4 million in "damages." Finally, if Flood thought Philadelphia was so bad and did not wish to report there, why did Bill White—another African American player—never complain about being sent there from the Cardinals? White maintained the same popularity among fans and writers in Philadelphia as he had built in St. Louis, even to the point of being offered a broadcasting job by the team before he was traded back to the Cardinals. Flood, in passing away in 1997 from throat cancer, took these answers with him to the grave. He had given many wonderful years to Busch and the Cardinal fans, and if things could have been different, he had hoped to give many more.

Through 1976 the entire dirt infield at Busch Stadium had remained; after that season, the stadium floor was converted further, as only the sliding-pit areas around the bases and the pitchers' mound were left as the dirt areas, similar to what had been done only at Candlestick Park in San Francisco. But it did little to slow down Lou Brock, as only Father Time would lessen the effectiveness of baseball's greatest base stealer, a title Brock would hold until the retirement of Rickey Henderson and a distinction Brock still holds among National League records. By early 1978 another long-sought goal was in reach for the Cardinal outfielder as well. "I want 3,000 hits," he said to Broeg on the team bus in St. Petersburg in spring training that year. "Not only because so few players have achieved it, but to prove that I've been a hitter as well as a base-stealer." Even though he had called the possibility of the milestone "remote" when he got his 2,000th in late September 1972, Brock finally reached the plateau two months before he retired in 1979, knocking an infield single off the Cubs' Dennis Lamp at Busch Stadium in August (the hit was literally *off* Lamp—as Brock stroked a line drive that nailed Lamp's pitching hand and caromed to the third baseman). On the previous pitch, Lamp had knocked him down with a fastball near his chin, but Brock retaliated in his own way on the next offering.

Simmons left the club the following year in 1980, having caught more games than anyone in team history (1,440) and having broken Pete Rose's National League record for home runs by a switch-hitter with a final total of 248. Simmons, however, would miss out on the postseason bounty that Herzog would bring to St. Louis in the 1980s, with the catcher ironically battling the Cardinals in the 1982 World Series as a member of the Milwaukee Brewers.

At the time of Gussie Busch's death in 1990, he would bequeath the ball club to family members who were largely indifferent to the game. Within a few years the seemingly indivisible marriage between baseball and beer and St. Louis would come to an end with the team being sold. "August III [Gussie's son] didn't really care much about baseball," Buck frankly stated. "[To him] it was just another division of the brewery, and as long as it didn't lose money, it was okay with him." Buck, however, was still there to call it all, and by the late 1970s he was every bit the "official voice of baseball in the Midwest" that Caray had been. Mike Shannon, proving that he could indeed do the job on a long-term basis, teamed with Buck to form the most outstanding of broadcasting duos. They called Cardinals games together until Buck's death in 2002, while Shannon continues on today with his own unique style.

Just as Gussie Busch gradually faded away from the team, Bob Gibson did as well. For fifteen years Gibson had been the mainstay of the team, a leader in every way imaginable (even in batting skills among the pitchers, for his total of 24 home runs remains far-and-away the club record, with Forsch second at 12 and Dean third with 8). With the exception of limited instructional appearances at spring training, many years would pass before the pitcher would make a formal return to the Cardinal family. Both Gibson and Busch shared a common fondness for the old ways of baseball, a belief felt by Gibson's old rival Fergie Jenkins as well. "We had a lot of fun doing it," Jenkins said of the individual battles with Gibson. "It's too bad that some of the guys now don't reach back and think about how the game was really played."

But with bitterness still lingering between the pitcher and his owner, Gibson would not mention Busch in his Hall of Fame induction speech in 1981, despite thanking nearly everyone else on the long path of his career. Beginning with Busch's clubhouse rant in the spring training of 1969, Gibson could feel a widening discord between the two men. And the same businesslike demeanor with which Gibson dominated batters caused a gradual freezing of his relations with many baseball followers in the city as well, noted by *Post-Dispatch* writer John Sonderegger as beginning way back in 1972. "Bob Gibson, by his very nature, does not endear himself to many baseball fans in St. Louis." Sonderegger even went on to suggest that the pitcher's brusque personality caused St. Louisans to predict a quicker end to his career. "His name is probably a bigger drawing card on the road than it is in town. Perhaps Gibson's indifference to baseball fans and their desire for the personal touch—i.e., an autograph—is one of the reasons he's prematurely buried at the beginning of every season or after every loss."

But Gibson, to his credit, still did not care. "Sometimes I signed autographs and sometimes I didn't," the pitcher said during the last weeks of his career in 1975. "Personally, I think anyone wanting an autograph is crazy." Understandably, Gibson found it especially bothersome when someone would interrupt his meal in a restaurant to have him sign something. In the same spirit as his farewell speech at Busch Stadium that September, he once said that "I owe the public just one thing—a good performance."

The competitive fire that drove Gibson to excellence never left him, even as he blended into life as a "regular person." In 2002 at the age of sixty-six, he chased a motorist in his car for ten miles on Interstate 80 west of Omaha, angry that the other driver had cut him off back in town. Confronting the man at a gas station off the highway, Gibson exchanged blows with him, and both were charged with third-degree assault. Naturally, the media wanted a statement from the old pitcher, but he would not give one, considering the standoff to be no big deal—it was just something he had to do. In no uncertain terms, Gibson permitted no one—and that meant *no one*—to gain the upper hand on him, as even his family knows.

"I've played a couple of hundred games of tic-tac-toe with my little daughter and she hasn't beaten me yet," he was once proud to say.

"I've always had to win. I've got to win."

Notes

Preface

"I doubt we'll ever see that happen again"—Castle and Rygelski 1999, 141.

1. Like Family

"Northrup hit a fastball away"—Feldmann 2007, 357–58.

"Things were never the same again"—Gibson and Wheeler 1994, 208.

"When I saw Flood looking for the ball, I knew I was in trouble"—Ibid., 358.

"The hardest ball to judge"—Golenbock 2000, 501–2.

"He has saved many a ballgame for me"—Ibid.

"He has saved many a ballgame for me"—Broeg 1988, 196.

"Do you still speak to Curt Flood?"—Gibson and Wheeler 1994, 206.

"Virtually everybody approved the trade"—Broeg 1988, 196.

"I believe Stan Musial had something when he said"—Ibid.

"We had a lot of formal dinners"—Schoendienst and Rains 1998, 149.

"The Cardinal players were uncommonly proud"—Halberstam 1994, 360.

"I respectfully decline the honor, thank you"—Gibson and Wheeler 1994, 208.

"My slider wasn't bothered much"—Ibid., 209.

"But the umpires seldom called a strike at the letters"—Ibid.

"The commissioner's office was reaching straight into my pocket"—Ibid.

"The rancor between the pitcher and the hitter"—Feldmann 2007, 372.

2. Becoming a Business

"Uh, Mr. Busch"—Feldmann 2007, 8.

"My right knee is what they call '100% disability'"—Associated Press, March 2, 1969.

"They're out of line"—Bob Broeg, *St. Louis Post-Dispatch*, March 2, 1969.

"Aghast to find pay increases"—Broeg, *St. Louis Post-Dispatch*, March 15, 1969.

"It's unfortunate that we don't have the time"—Broeg, *St. Louis Post-Dispatch*, March 2, 1969.

"Maybe someday"—Ibid.

"Did you know that there were more than 20,000 strikeouts"—Neal Russo, *St. Louis Post-Dispatch*, April 2, 1969.

"Ray should come in"—Broeg, *St. Louis Post-Dispatch*, March 3, 1969.

"He's not far away"—Broeg, *St. Louis Post-Dispatch*, March 16, 1969.

"He's old for his years"—Ibid.

"That was quite an inducement"—Broeg, *St. Louis Post-Dispatch*, March 25, 1969.

"I don't think my wife would appreciate this"—Broeg, *St. Louis Post-Dispatch*, March 14, 1969.

"This is the latest I've ever reported to camp"—Broeg, *St. Louis Post-Dispatch*, March 15, 1969.

"Management was messing in a major way"—Gibson and Wheeler 1994, 211.

"Cepeda will hit a lot of home runs"—Broeg, *St. Louis Post-Dispatch*, March 19, 1969.

"I can't compare Torre with Cepeda defensively"—Broeg, *St. Louis Post-Dispatch*, March 18, 1969.

"I have a lot of respect for Mr. Devine"—Ibid.

"Maybe this is one of the pleasant benefits"—Broeg, *St. Louis Post-Dispatch*, March 20, 1969.

"He's got a good hitting park"—Broeg, *St. Louis Post-Dispatch*, April 11, 1969.

"Inequitable in its impact"—Broeg, *St. Louis Post-Dispatch*, March 18, 1969.

"The speech demoralized the 1969 Cardinals"—Golenbock 2000, 504.

"A few days later"—Golenbock 2000, 505.

"The brewer-sportsman has a fine track record"—Broeg, *St. Louis Post-Dispatch*, March 24, 1969.

"It was at that moment that Coach Powles came into my life"—Broeg, *St. Louis Post-Dispatch*, March 12, 1969.

"It is conceded that St. Louis will dominate"—Leonard Koppett, *New York Times*, March 15, 1969.

"The East is the personal property of the St. Louis Cardinals"—Arthur Daley, *New York Times*, March 17, 1969.

"Infielders, outfielders, and catchers"—Russo, *St. Louis Post-Dispatch*, April 5, 1969.

"None of the starting pitchers reported"—Broeg, *St. Louis Post-Dispatch*, April 8, 1969.

"Bill fits the bill"—Russo, *St. Louis Post-Dispatch*, April 3, 1969.

"I had my best years in St. Louis"—Ibid.

"The Mets aren't going to be making as many mistakes"—Russo, *St. Louis Post-Dispatch*, April 4, 1969.

"That kid is capable of hitting 40 home runs a year"—Russo, *St. Louis Post-Dispatch*, April 8, 1969.

"I just can't wait"—Ibid.

"I've played on some bad diamonds"—Feldmann 2007, 78.

"The infield was soft and lumpy"—George Langford, *Chicago Tribune*, April 20, 1969.

"When blame is assessed"—Broeg, *St. Louis Post-Dispatch*, May 5, 1969.

"Since August 2"—Broeg, *St. Louis Post-Dispatch*, May 6, 1969.

"They [the Cardinals] are almost hopelessly behind the Chicago Cubs"—*San Francisco Chronicle*, May 20, 1969.

"This club is going to be a contender"—United Press International, May 22, 1969.

"That's the farthest I've ever seen Brock thrown out"—Russo, *St. Louis Post-Dispatch*, May 31, 1969.

"Bench compares with the best"—Ibid.

"The only team with enough talent"—Robert Markus, *Chicago Tribune*, July 11, 1969.

"Had a World Series atmosphere"—Castle and Rygelski 1999, 79.

"A disconsolate group of Cubs"—Harry Mitauer, *St. Louis Globe-Democrat*, September 15, 1969.

"We'd like to take Simmons"—Russo, *St. Louis Post-Dispatch*, October 2, 1969.

"The 1969 team was clearly a better team"—Halberstam 1994, 363.

"I've never seen a ball club"—*Post-Dispatch* Wire Services, October 1, 1969.

"After the 1968 pennant year"—Buck, Rains, and Broeg 1997, 158.

"They should have been with us in the Depression"—Ibid., 10–11.

"When I told Bobby he was going to be a regular"—Earl Lawson, *Sporting News*, September 4, 1969.

3. "A Well-Paid Slave Is Still a Slave"

"Reformed sportswriter"—Broeg, *St. Louis Post-Dispatch,* July 12, 1970.

"Being transferred"—United Press International, May 19, 1970.

"He told me that was my business, and goodbye"—Ibid.

"Release and transfer from one National League club to another"—Ibid.

"I really hate to leave St. Louis because I enjoyed playing there"—*St. Louis Post-Dispatch,* October 8, 1969.

"After twelve years in the Major Leagues"—Feldmann 2007, 372.

"You'll never get another job in baseball"—Halberstam 1994, 365–66.

"It would have allowed him to negotiate with the clubs"—*Post-Dispatch* Wire Services, March 5, 1970.

"Long philosophical letters"—Gibson and Wheeler 1994, 219.

"A well-paid slave is still a slave"—Golenbock 2000, 515.

"I think McLain has been punished in a substantial way"—United Press International, April 1, 1970.

"He should be barred for life"—*Post-Dispatch* Wire Services, April 20, 1970.

"Did he forget most of us have wives?"—Milton Richman, United Press International, June 2, 1970.

"I advised Mr. Bouton of my displeasure"—Ibid.

"I have no plans to write any more books"—Ibid.

"We felt we needed a power hitter for the ballpark"—Golenbock 2000, 517.

"I have no intention of returning here"—Bob Posen, *St. Louis Post-Dispatch,* October 8, 1969.

"If it had meant my life, I wouldn't have gone back to Philadelphia"—Broeg, *St. Louis Post-Dispatch,* March 13, 1970.

"Get a place somewhere"—*Post-Dispatch* Wire Services, October 9, 1969.

"If you want to make the deal, go ahead"—Golenbock 2000, 518.

"I don't know Allen"—Bob Posen, *St. Louis Post-Dispatch,* October 8, 1969.

"I bet a few dollars here and there"—Broeg, *St. Louis Post-Dispatch,* March 13, 1970.

"I'm no angel"—Ibid.

"I was enthusiastic about the idea of acquiring Allen"—Gibson and Wheeler 1994, 217.

"We played in a time when black people were supposed to stick together"—Ibid., 165.

"Good and happy years for me"—Curt Flood, *Sport* 49 (1970).

"We will not negotiate further"—Broeg, *St. Louis Post-Dispatch,* March 11, 1970.

"I don't care if he ever pitches a ball for us again"—Broeg, *St. Louis Post-Dispatch,* March 12, 1970.

"I'm not mad; I'm disappointed"—Broeg, *St. Louis Post-Dispatch,* March 11, 1970.

"Been on time for spring training in six years"—Broeg, *St. Louis Post-Dispatch,* March 13, 1970.

"He swung that big ol' forty-two-ounce bat like nobody"—Gibson and Wheeler 1994, 224.

"Allen has got as much power as anybody who ever played this game"—Broeg, *St. Louis Post-Dispatch,* March 4, 1970.

"The commissioner has had his little experiment"—*Post-Dispatch* Wire Services, March 25, 1970.

"Flood just may have played his last big league ball game"—Broeg, *St. Louis Post-Dispatch,* March 6, 1970.

"He's a real good center fielder"—Broeg, *St. Louis Post-Dispatch,* March 17, 1970.

"I wasn't enjoying it anymore"—Broeg, *St. Louis Post-Dispatch,* March 17, 1970.

"When I came over, they asked me if I wanted 15"—Broeg, *St. Louis Post-Dispatch,* March 17, 1970.

"The condition, a defect of the filtering function of the kidneys"—Ibid.

"There is an extreme possibility I might die of it"—Broeg, *St. Louis Post-Dispatch,* March 19, 1970.

"Richie gave 150 percent when he was on the field"—Russo, *St. Louis Post-Dispatch,* May 26, 1970.

"Allen's been throwing a lot better from third base"—Russo, *St. Louis Post-Dispatch,* March 30, 1970.

"Sure, it hurts"—Broeg, *St. Louis Post-Dispatch,* March 20, 1970.

"We're together because of it"—Ed Wilks, *St. Louis Post-Dispatch,* April 5, 1970.

"Those are white-collar fans"—Ray Sons, *Chicago Daily News,* April 1, 1970.

"I wish I could get Santo to be like Billy"—Ibid.

"The Clinton County League, a collection of small town Illinois teams"—Dick Kaegel, *St. Louis Post-Dispatch,* July 21, 1972.

"Blew his job"—Buck, Rains, and Broeg 1997, 125.

"Sittin' in the catbird seat"—Ibid., 157.

"Another reason Jack stood apart from the rest of the broadcasters"—Schoendienst and Rains 1998, 141.

"He didn't want me to get the job in the first place"—Buck, Rains, and Broeg 1997, 83.

"What nice things can I say about Harry"—Wilks, *St. Louis Post-Dispatch,* April 8, 1969.

"I wonder if Harry would be able to get a job in today's marketplace"—Buck, Rains, and Broeg 1997, 113.

"The 1960s was a golden era for broadcasting"—Ibid., 124.

"Wherever there is artificial turf"—Broeg, *St. Louis Post-Dispatch,* May 21, 1969.

"The installation is just over eleven and a half inches"—Bill Beck, *St. Louis Post-Dispatch,* March 22, 1970.

"Astroturf now looks like grass"—Broeg, *St. Louis Post-Dispatch,* May 21, 1969.

"The possibilities are limitless"—Beck, *St. Louis Post-Dispatch,* March 22, 1970.

"Anybody who hits the ball on the ground"—Broeg, *St. Louis Post-Dispatch,* July 20, 1970.

"This is strictly speculative"—*Post-Dispatch* Wire Services, May 2, 1969.

"You're going to have to have fast outfielders for Astroturf"—Russo, *St. Louis Post-Dispatch,* April 6, 1970.

"The defenses will have to be better than ever"—Ibid.

"I don't have to be as good a fielder as I used to be"—Russo, *St. Louis Post-Dispatch,* October 2, 1970.

"I'm going to make a prediction"—Russo, *St. Louis Post-Dispatch,* April 14, 1970.

"Allen is a great athlete"—Russo, *St. Louis Post-Dispatch,* April 9, 1970.

"Why should I worry about Seaver?"—Wilks, *St. Louis Post-Dispatch,* May 9, 1971.

"Beating Gibson doesn't mean I replace him"—Ibid.

"I got chills when Allen got that ovation"—Russo, *St. Louis Post-Dispatch,* April 11, 1970.

"I feel that I'm right there"—Russo, *St. Louis Post-Dispatch,* April 12, 1970.

"I didn't see that many in the park"—Ibid.

"I've got to think the Cardinals are a stronger"—Russo, *St. Louis Post-Dispatch,* April 21, 1970.

"The Cardinals weren't hungry last year"—Russo, *St. Louis Post-Dispatch,* April 23, 1970.

"My number one nemesis"—Gibson and Wheeler 1994, 229.

"Nobody better ever say that Gibson is over the hill"—Broeg, *St. Louis Post-Dispatch,* April 27, 1970.

"What's wrong with Bob Gibson?"—Wilks, *St. Louis Post-Dispatch,* September 8, 1970.

"Hurry back—they're eating me up at third"—Eisenbath 1999, 275.

"When I came to this country from Cuba to play baseball"—Russo, *St. Louis Post-Dispatch,* April 20, 1970.

"If I had gone on and played"—Wilks, *St. Louis Post-Dispatch,* May 4, 1970.

"Why, he might even assault the unbelievable"—Broeg, *St. Louis Post-Dispatch,* May 18, 1970.

"I'd sure like to get it"—Associated Press, August 30, 1971.

"I think the leadership in the American League"—Associated Press, April 3, 1970.

4. Nephritis
"If I were going to criticize Schoendienst"—Broeg, *St. Louis Post-Dispatch,* July 30, 1970.

"Managers don't make rules"—Eisenbath 1999, 387.

"Schoendienst [is] dealing with a different breed"—Ibid.

"Behaved or misbehaved"—Broeg, *St. Louis Post-Dispatch,* May 8, 1970.

"There were times when I didn't enjoy being around"—Buck, Rains, and Broeg 1997, 158.

"When you asked a player to do something"—Schoendienst and Rains 1998, 154.

"I don't give a ____—I've got a ballgame to pitch"—Feldmann 2007, 330.

"Anything that is one-sided in our society is wrong"—Koppett, *Sporting News,* June 6, 1970.

"Whatever [Judge Cooper] decides, the losing side will appeal"—Ibid.

"LaRussa has done the job for"—United Press International, May 29, 1970.

"It was like the first day of school all over again"—Gibson and Wheeler 1994, 225.

"I had to shake him off the first five or six pitches"—Ibid.

"I just hope I'm around longer than the man who used to wear it"—*St. Louis Post-Dispatch,* June 16, 1970.

"Hrabosky has a good fastball"—*St. Louis Post-Dispatch,* June 15, 1970.

"I'm not sorry to see the park go"—Russo, *St. Louis Post-Dispatch,* June 26, 1970.

"Forbes Field was my worst park"—Ibid.

"It looks like I've found a park I can hit in"—*St. Louis Post-Dispatch,* July 1, 1970.

"Ty Cobb holds the record"—Broeg, *St. Louis Post-Dispatch,* March 30, 1971.

"The next time we have a day game"—Kaegel, *St. Louis Post-Dispatch,* July 3, 1970.

"The players should be happy to play this game"—Russo, *St. Louis Post-Dispatch,* July 28, 1970.

"We should not lose sight of the fact"—Eisenbath 1999, 387.

"The infield is probably the poorest"—Broeg, *St. Louis Post-Dispatch,* July 13, 1970.

"Jose ought to lead the league in steals"—Russo, *St. Louis Post-Dispatch,* June 19, 1970.

"How's this grab you"—Wilks, *St. Louis Post-Dispatch,* July 29, 1970.

"We were so bad"—Gibson and Wheeler 1994, 222.

"Clearly, the preponderance of credible proof"—Associated Press, August 13, 1970.

"$100,000 a Year—What a Way to Be Mistreated"—Broeg, *St. Louis Post-Dispatch,* August 14, 1970.

"I think the pennant means more to Billy and the club"—Associated Press, September 4, 1970.

"Sometimes a player can get so wrapped up"—Ibid.

"A strange phenomenon is the typewriter schizophrenia"—Broeg, *St. Louis Post-Dispatch,* August 25, 1971.

"Vic's a thinking-type hitter"—Russo, *St. Louis Post-Dispatch,* May 15, 1970.

"What's that pirate's name"—*St. Louis Post-Dispatch,* August 28, 1970.

"Steve Carlton spent his holdout trimming trees"—Wilks, *St. Louis Post-Dispatch,* October 1, 1970.

"For a change, our offense was actually better than our defense in 1970"—Gibson and Wheeler 1994, 223.

"We had Ken in mind for the organization"—Russo, *St. Louis Post-Dispatch,* October 1, 1970.

"The young players at Arkansas liked Boyer"—Ibid.

"Devine, whose adroit deals built the Cardinals"—Broeg, *St. Louis Post-Dispatch,* October 3, 1970.

5. "I'll Never Throw a No-Hitter"
"If the strong man from Wampum, Pennsylvania"—Broeg, *St. Louis Post-Dispatch,* October 3, 1970.

"Uncle Sam says Julian owes $84,320 in back taxes"—Zanger and Kaplan 1971, 114.

"He had a reputation of being a difficult player"—Schoendienst and Rains 1998, 153.

"We did produce power"—Russo, *St. Louis Post-Dispatch,* October 5, 1970.

"I wanted one season that I could play in peace"—Broeg, *St. Louis Post-Dispatch,* October 6, 1970.

"I even kept away from the race tracks all season on the road"—Ibid.

"I ought to hit a lot more doubles in St. Louis"—Zanger and Kaplan 1971, 112.

"He's got everything"—Broeg, *St. Louis Post-Dispatch,* March 7, 1971.

"I couldn't believe it"—Broeg, *St. Louis Post-Dispatch,* March 2, 1971.

"I mentioned a figure and Bob mentioned a figure"—Russo, *St. Louis Post-Dispatch,* October 2, 1970.

"We're with you forever, Bob—win or tie"—Ibid.

"I sometimes think Red believes anybody can play third"—Eisenbath 1999, 295.

"The 20,455 fans at the Garden"—*St. Louis Post-Dispatch,* March 8, 1971.

"Was precipitated by a protest meeting"—*St. Louis Post-Dispatch,* March 28, 1971.

"Me and Gibby"—Broeg, *St. Louis Post-Dispatch,* March 12, 1971.

"In general, we've got the kind of depth we had"—Broeg, *St. Louis Post-Dispatch,* March 10, 1971.

"I think all three of them could play regularly in the major leagues"—Ibid.

"I like Cruz the best of the lot"—Russo, *St. Louis Post-Dispatch,* April 17, 1971.

"Felipe got $200, and I got $200"—Broeg, *St. Louis Post-Dispatch,* March 26, 1971.

"Matty is as good with his glove now as Curt Flood was"—Ibid.

"The Cardinals have their demi-dynasty behind them"—Wilks, *St. Louis Post-Dispatch,* March 3, 1971.

"This is no means a reflection on George"—Broeg, *St. Louis Post-Dispatch,* March 6, 1971.

"Batting second is a great challenge"—Eisenbath 1999, 279.

"He's got a 25-year-old body"—Wilks, *St. Louis Post-Dispatch,* March 24, 1971.

"To be sure, black experience teaches"—Flood 1972, 26.

"Flood penned what has to be a most discouraging sentence to all"—Broeg, *St. Louis Post-Dispatch,* March 4, 1971.

"Blue is baseball's new boy wonder"—*St. Louis Post-Dispatch,* April 14, 1971.

"There's no telling how good he can become"—Ibid.

"I knew it would be hard to come back after the layoff"—Associated Press, April 6, 1971.

"If he had claimed bankruptcy"—*St. Louis Post-Dispatch,* May 5, 1971.

"Willie Montanez is the best thing to happen to baseball in Philadelphia"—Associated Press, July 6, 1971.

"Even now, as the Redbirds open tomorrow"—Broeg, *St. Louis Post-Dispatch,* April 5, 1971.

"I don't want to embarrass the team"—Associated Press, April 2, 1971.

"If I'm not happy, I can't play"—Wilks, *St. Louis Post-Dispatch,* June 27, 1971.

"From 30 feet"—Russo, *St. Louis Post-Dispatch,* April 7, 1971.

"I normally don't see him make a pitch like that to me"—Ibid.

"It was not down the middle"—Ibid.

"The ball Williams hit was on the outside corner"—Ibid.

"The kind with no buttons, no zippers, no flies"—Paul Stillwell, *Columbia Missourian,* January 27, 1971.

"They're lighter and more comfortable than the old models"—Broeg, *St. Louis Post-Dispatch,* April 12, 1971.

"With Richie Allen gone"—Broeg, *St. Louis Post-Dispatch,* March 16, 1971.

"I've never enjoyed a spring more"—*St. Louis Post-Dispatch,* April 2, 1971.

"Javier's been swinging the bat better"—Wilks, *St. Louis Post-Dispatch,* May 16, 1971.

"I feel that I finally know how to pitch"—Russo, *St. Louis Post-Dispatch,* May 28, 1971.

"That whole group of Cardinals"—Golenbock 2000, 522.

"I felt as if I were a rookie"—Wilks, *St. Louis Post-Dispatch,* September 2, 1971.

"I can really push down the food"—*St. Louis Post-Dispatch,* May 6, 1971.

"Schofield was one of the great 'red-asses' of all time"—Gibson and Wheeler 1994, 230.

"I knew that [team physician] Stan [London] would need ten days"—Broeg, *St. Louis Post-Dispatch,* June 3, 1971.

"One thing about the rainout"—Wilks, *St. Louis Post-Dispatch,* May 13, 1971.

"It wasn't difficult for me to accept the job"—Associated Press, June 10, 1971.

"That Beauchamp wore me out in the Winter League"—Russo, *St. Louis Post-Dispatch,* June 22, 1971.

"It's hard to believe that Hague"—Broeg, *St. Louis Post-Dispatch,* July 1, 1971.

"The National League rules say it's $100"—Wilks, *St. Louis Post-Dispatch,* July 10, 1971.

"The longest I ever hit"—Wilks, *St. Louis Post-Dispatch,* July 14, 1971.

"He's the one I have to fear the most"—Associated Press, July 29, 1971.

"I'm not mad about not being picked this year"—Russo, *St. Louis Post-Dispatch,* July 12, 1971.

"If there were any doubts that [Reggie] Cleveland"—Russo, *St. Louis Post-Dispatch,* July 17, 1971.

"With all my chatter"—Ibid.

"Italian smorgasbord"—Wilks, *St. Louis Post-Dispatch,* July 29, 1971.

"Jose has nothing against Milwaukee"—*St. Louis Post-Dispatch,* August 1, 1971.

"Armed with transistor radios"—Broeg, *St. Louis Post-Dispatch,* August 16, 1971.

"I was throwing hard"—Russo, *St. Louis Post-Dispatch,* August 15, 1971.

"The greatest thrill of my life"—Ibid.

"Not the hardest I'd ever thrown, but close"—Gibson and Wheeler 1994, 232.

"All those people who said Gibson was washed up"—Russo, *St. Louis Post-Dispatch,* August 15, 1971.

"Physically, I'm all right"—Associated Press, August 16, 1971.

"It was a sucker punch"—Russo, *St. Louis Post-Dispatch,* September 7, 1971.

"Tim lost his cool, all right"—Ibid.

"I was agitated and apparently misunderstood something"—Broeg, *St. Louis Post-Dispatch,* September 14, 1971.

"It tore my heart out"—Buck, Rains, and Broeg 1997, 161.

"The Cardinals ought to have a good club"—Russo, *St. Louis Post-Dispatch,* September 17, 1971.

"Last spring, everybody said we didn't have enough pitching"—Wilks, *St. Louis Post-Dispatch,* September 24, 1971.

"[Who] will follow the Cincinnati Reds"—Wilks, *St. Louis Post-Dispatch,* October 6, 1971.

"Postal regulations"—Red Smith, *New York Times,* October 12, 1971.

"I thought Red [Schoendienst] did his best job this time"—Broeg, *St. Louis Post-Dispatch,* October 1, 1971.

"Torre was anything but a speed merchant"—Gibson and Wheeler 1994, 229.

"For the first two months of the season"—Eisenbath 1999, 275.

"After July [1971], I began to hold onto the wall after leaving the shower"—Ibid., 296.

"You might take a look at what *you're* doing"—Golenbock 2000, 518.

6. Loss of the Lefties

"He [Carlton] was being very difficult to sign"—Golenbock 2000, 519.

"Wise was a reliable pitcher"—Gibson and Wheeler 1994, 234.

"Mr. Busch sometimes would take a very strong stance"—Eisenbath 1999, 306.

"To win on this club"—Associated Press, June 24, 1971.

"Darn it, I don't feel like I'm a .500 pitcher"—Eisenbath 1999, 310.

"If we had kept Carlton"—Schoendienst and Rains 1998, 157.

"Maybe the day has come to alter the reserve clause"—Broeg, *St. Louis Post-Dispatch,* March

10, 1972.

"I want to finish my career here, but not this year"—Broeg, *St. Louis Post-Dispatch*, March 3, 1972.

"Obviously, Bing has reached the limit"—Broeg, *St. Louis Post-Dispatch*, March 6, 1972.

"I realized the difference"—Broeg, *St. Louis Post-Dispatch*, March 10, 1972.

"He raised himself from a journeyman's salary to a superstar's salary"—Eisenbath 1999, 295.

"Bouton has made enough money"—Broeg, *St. Louis Post-Dispatch*, March 16, 1972.

"I never saw a catcher throw harder"—Ibid.

"I can't speak for other clubs"—Ibid.

"We've agreed to make certain"—Broeg, *St. Louis Post-Dispatch*, March 24, 1972.

"Pay me, or I quit"—Feldmann 2007, 211.

"Javier wasn't in shape"—Broeg, *St. Louis Post-Dispatch*, March 25, 1972.

"All they [the players] would be entitled to"—*St. Louis Post-Dispatch*, March 31, 1972.

"I think the players are damn greedy"—Associated Press, April 1, 1972.

"I was lucky over there"—Broeg, *St. Louis Post-Dispatch*, March 7, 1972.

"Fans shake their heads and cluck over the greediness"—Richman, United Press International, March 17, 1972.

"There are actually people still alive today who remember"—Jeff Meyers, *St. Louis Post-Dispatch*, March 22, 1972.

"The fastest way to clear this up"—*Chicago Sun-Times*, April 4, 1972.

"The majority of the players are ready to go out and play ball"—Associated Press, April 7, 1972.

"Have a home in Chicago for many years"—United Press International, April 2, 1972.

"Standing firm"—United Press International, April 11, 1972.

"If we play 162 games"—Kaegel, *St. Louis Post-Dispatch*, April 11, 1972.

"Lucky as hell"—*St. Louis Post-Dispatch*, April 7, 1972.

"Represent the fans and express their views"—*St. Louis Post-Dispatch*, April 9, 1972.

"This [the strike] would never have happened if"—David Condon, *Chicago Tribune*, April 14, 1972.

"The room looks like Los Angeles in the smog"—Russo, *St. Louis Post-Dispatch*, April 18, 1972.

"The job was more or less misrepresented to me"—*St. Louis Post-Dispatch*, October 1, 1971.

"I have a poor radio voice"—Meyers, *St. Louis Post-Dispatch*, May 26, 1972.

"The Cardinals gave me a $6,000 raise"—interview, March 14, 2012.

"This was a deal I had to make"—Golenbock 2000, 520.

"Spinks was named"—Eisenbath 1999, 287.

"He talks to Brock sometimes, talks to Torre"—Ibid.

"The obvious question must be"—Broeg, *St. Louis Post-Dispatch*, April 17, 1972.

"I would hope not"—Kaegel, *St. Louis Post-Dispatch*, April 17, 1972.

"June swoon just came a month early this year"—Russo, *St. Louis Post-Dispatch*, May 18, 1972.

"That's the only time in my career"—*St. Louis Post-Dispatch*, June 7, 1972.

"The players are giving one hundred percent and getting booed"—Gary Mueller, *St. Louis Post-Dispatch*, May 19, 1972.

"I learned as a player that the most important thing"—Schoendienst and Rains 1998, 136.

"Beaten by a better pitcher"—Castle and Rygelski 1999, 150.

"Two-hour games, or less, were the norm"—Ibid., 139.

"It's amazing to see him"—Kaegel, *St. Louis Post-Dispatch*, June 22, 1972.

"It's incredible that a man so sharp"—Broeg, *St. Louis Post-Dispatch*, June 21, 1972.

"How many men can field like he does"—Kaegel, *St. Louis Post-Dispatch*, July 19, 1972.

"You're 15 minutes too late"—Ibid.

"Distinguished and still graceful at 57"—Broeg, *St. Louis Post-Dispatch*, July 10, 1972.

"Chick Hafey, Joe Medwick, Johnny Mize, and Terry Moore"—Ibid.

"Safe for the day, out for the year"—*St. Louis Globe-Democrat,* July 5, 1972.

"All Jenkins has done is gripe"—Broeg, *St. Louis Post-Dispatch,* October 6, 1972.

"The problem was, everyone thought I loved to pitch against Fergie"—Castle and Rygelski 1999, 140.

"If I gave up two or three runs"—Ibid.

"If I didn't want to pitch"—Kaegel, *St. Louis Post-Dispatch,* July 25, 1972.

"His loyalty, it has been said"—Phil Pepe, *New York Daily News,* July 26, 1972.

"I've never experienced anything like that"—*St. Louis Post-Dispatch,* July 5, 1972.

"The toughest point in adjusting so far"—Kaegel, *St. Louis Post-Dispatch,* September 19, 1972.

"The defense down the middle"—Bob Hartsell, *Tulsa Tribune,* August 29, 1972.

"A 20-year-old throwback to an era"—Broeg, *St. Louis Post-Dispatch,* March 14, 1972.

"I strum the guitar, agitate the piano, and cry the blues"—Ibid.

"The way he gloves a ball at third base"—Ibid.

"He's too fat to pitch"—Russo, *St. Louis Post-Dispatch,* September 24, 1972.

"He's got a body to hit and run until he's 40"—Broeg, *St. Louis Post-Dispatch,* September 26, 1972.

"Remote"—Broeg, *St. Louis Post-Dispatch,* March 6, 1973.

"It seemed that Roberto Clemente"—Charles Feeney, *Sporting News,* January 20, 1973.

"Big changes"—Associated Press, August 3, 1972.

"Don't room higher than the second floor on the road"—Broeg, *St. Louis Post-Dispatch,* March 13, 1973.

"Mom, did they take any of his clothes?"—Schoendienst and Rains 1998, 157.

"I can't picture myself going to spring training with the club we have"—Kaegel, *St. Louis Post-Dispatch,* September 28, 1972.

7. Close to the Top Once Again

"Are the fabled Yankees"—Jack Lang, *Sporting News,* January 20, 1973.

"Always been an Indians fan"—Ibid.

"There is nothing in life quite so limited"—Doug Mittler, *ESPN Magazine,* January 27, 2010.

"It does baseball no good"—Associated Press, March 19, 1973.

"Knowing damn well"—Gibson and Wheeler 1994, 239.

"It was good just to get back some of the Cardinal spirit"—Ibid.

"You wouldn't take a talent like Hector"—Eisenbath 1999, 162.

"Morale is good, and that gives us a chance"—Broeg, *St. Louis Post-Dispatch,* March 5, 1973.

"During the three years I was with the Cardinals"—Golenbock 2000, 524.

"Carbo's got the best right field arm"—Russo, *St. Louis Post-Dispatch,* September 30, 1972.

"I never got on players for making errors"—Schoendienst and Rains 1998, 137.

"In fifteen years"—Gibson and Wheeler 1994, 240.

"I never saw any man hit a ball consistently hard more often"—Eisenbath 1999, 278.

"The Cardinals have shown they could play under the gun after all"—Jack Herman, *St. Louis Globe-Democrat,* May 27, 1973.

"We hope to have him back pitching in four to six weeks"—Russo, *Sporting News,* August 18, 1973.

"I haven't given up"—Eisenbath 1999, 94.

"I felt sluggish before the game"—Ibid., 153.

"Our near miss was especially agonizing for me and Brock"—Gibson and Wheeler 1994, 242–43.

"Smith is the best all-around player in the game today"—Eisenbath 1999, 281.

"My World Series ring is getting small"—Russo, *Sporting News,* March 2, 1974.

"Everyone's been mentioning the other pitchers"—Ibid.

"Many gas stations are closed"—Francis Stann, *Sporting News,* March 2, 1974.

"Ladies and gentlemen, I am suffering with you"—*Sporting News* 1992, 549.

"Wrigley Field is old"—Wilks, *St. Louis Post-Dispatch*, September 18, 1970.

"I've always hit the Cubs"—Kaegel, *St. Louis Post-Dispatch*, September 21, 1974.

"It's unprintable"—Russo, *St. Louis Post-Dispatch*, September 18, 1974.

"There were rumors that I might be sent back down"—Craft and Owens 1990, 103.

"One of the young guys on our club"—Gibson and Wheeler 1994, 243.

"The nostalgia was mixed with some rapidly-changing current events"—Russo, *Sporting News*, August 3, 1974.

"Quail hunts with Charlie Mathis"—Gregory 1992, 389.

"Going anywhere with him was like going with a brass band"—C. C. Johnson Spink, *Sporting News*, August 3, 1974.

"What are you doing?"—Forsch and Wheatley 2003, 21.

"John Hernandez, Juan to his son"—William Nack, *Sports Illustrated*, October 13, 1986.

"He hit 0-2 [count] more than any hitter I ever saw"—Golenbock 2000, 522.

"The Cardinals pouring out of the dugout"—Broeg 1988, 205.

"I'm going to follow you to St. Louis"—Russo, *St. Louis Post-Dispatch*, September 30, 1974.

"And now, the star of the game"—Broeg 1988, 204.

"We're just an after-hours team"—Russo, *St. Louis Post-Dispatch*, September 18, 1974.

"Let them boo"—Ibid.

"He didn't hear me"—Castle and Rygelski 1999, 221.

"It was a close situation"—Ibid.

"They must have done this for Diz"—Kaegel, *St. Louis Post-Dispatch*, September 23, 1974.

"Barring a home-run pitch"—Meyers, *St. Louis Post-Dispatch*, September 25, 1974.

"The team too tough to die"—Eisenbath 1999, 95.

"Some people say his defense wasn't good"—Forsch and Wheatley 2003, 74.

"I would have given anything to be twenty-eight that summer"—Gibson and Wheeler 1994, 243–44.

"I remain grateful to Schoendienst for sticking with me"—Ibid., 206.

"When I managed"—Schoendienst and Rains 1998, 139.

"If you can't play for Red Schoendienst"—Eisenbath 1999, 387.

8. Finished

"Drive me home, Hawk"—Broeg 1988, 205.

"McBride was much faster"—Gibson and Wheeler 1994, 245.

"Honesty is one of the things that makes our show"—Russo, *Sporting News*, February 1, 1975.

"I hope the team can stay together"—Russo, *St. Louis Post-Dispatch*, October 3, 1974.

"Maybe my last game"—Wilks, *St. Louis Post-Dispatch*, October 1, 1970.

"They keep calling your pitch a ball"—Wilks, *St. Louis Post-Dispatch*, September 17, 1970.

"It's like a sauna out there!"—Forsch and Wheatley 2003, 13.

"Everything had to go almost absolutely perfect"—Eisenbath 1999, 171.

"I didn't conceal my anger at being sent to the bullpen"—Gibson and Wheeler 1994, 246.

"To see it all fall apart was a crusher for Bob"—Ibid., 247.

"I'm more nervous than I was before a World Series game"—Russo, *Sporting News*, September 20, 1975.

"It's both a sad day and a proud day"—Ibid.

"That's it, I'm out of here"—Gibson and Wheeler 1994, 249.

"For the third consecutive year"—Broeg, *St. Louis Post-Dispatch*, September 28, 1970.

"Gibson, whose knee surgery cost the Cardinals"—Ibid.

"In retrospect, it undoubtedly would have been better"—Spink, *Sporting News*, October 11, 1975.

"I'd ask him, but I don't think he'd want to"—Russo, *St. Louis Post-Dispatch*, September 18, 1975.

"He had a tremendous career, and he's walking away proud"—Ibid.
"It felt like the last day of high school"—Gibson and Wheeler 1994, 247.

Epilogue
"There are times, regardless of one's capabilities"—Eisenbath 1999, 387.
"I felt like a soldier going to war without his rifle"—*St. Louis Post-Dispatch,* April 23, 2009.
"For Busch, the fun had become a funny business"—Broeg 1988, 197.
"That was understandable"—Gibson and Wheeler 1994, 218.
"I want 3,000 hits"—Broeg 1988, 206.
"August III [Gussie's son] didn't really care much about baseball"—Buck, Rains, and Broeg 1997, 133.
"We had a lot of fun doing it"—Castle and Rygelski 1999, 142.
"Bob Gibson, by his very nature"—John Sonderegger, *St. Louis Post-Dispatch,* July 16, 1972.
"Sometimes I signed autographs and sometimes I didn't"—Russo, *Sporting News,* September 20, 1975.
"I've played a couple of hundred games of tic-tac-toe"—Angell 2004, 189.

Bibliography

Newspapers

Chicago Daily News
Chicago Sun-Times
Chicago Tribune
Columbia Missourian
New York Daily News
New York Times
St. Louis Globe-Democrat
St. Louis Post-Dispatch
San Francisco Chronicle
Sporting News
Tulsa Tribune

Web Sites

Baseball-reference.com
Baseballlibrary.com
Retrosheet.org

Other Sources

Angell, R. 2004. *The summer game.* Lincoln: University of Nebraska Press.

Broeg, B. 1988. *Redbirds: A century of Cardinals' baseball.* St. Louis: River City Publishers.

———. "Ted Simmons: Losing drives me crazy!" *Baseball Digest* (June 1973): 21–24.

Broeg, B., and J. Vickery. 1998. *St. Louis Cardinals encyclopedia.* Lincolnwood, Ill.: Masters Press.

Buck, J., R. Rains, and B. Broeg. 1997. *That's a winner!* Champaign, Ill.: Sagamore Press.

Castle, G., and J. Rygelski. 1999. *The I-55 series: Cubs vs. Cardinals.* Champaign, Ill.: Sports Publishing.

Craft, D., and T. Owens. 1990. *Redbirds revisited.* Chicago: Bonus Books.

Eisenbath, M. 1999. *The Cardinals encyclopedia.* Philadelphia: Temple University Press.

Feldmann, D. 2007. *El Birdos: The 1967 and 1968 St. Louis Cardinals.* Jefferson, N.C.: McFarland.

———. 2009a. *Miracle collapse: The 1969 Chicago Cubs.* Lincoln: University of Nebraska Press.

———. 2009b. *The 1976 Cincinnati Reds.* Jefferson, N.C.: McFarland.

Flood, C. 1972. *The way it is.* New York: Pocket Books / Simon and Schuster.

Forsch, B., and T. Wheatley. 2003. *Bob Forsch's tales from the Cardinals' dugout.* Champaign, Ill.: Sports Publishing.

Gibson, B., and L. Wheeler. 1994. *Stranger to the game.* New York: Viking Press.

Golenbock, P. 2000. *The spirit of St. Louis: A history of the St. Louis Cardinals and Browns.* New York: Harper Collins.

Gregory, R. 1992. *Diz.* New York: Penguin Books.

Halberstam, D. 1994. *October 1964.* New York: Villard Books.

Schoendienst, A., and R. Rains. 1998. *Red: A baseball life.* Champaign, Ill.: Sports Publishing.

Sporting News. 1992. *Baseball.* New York: Galahad Books.

Weiss, S. 2007. *The Curt Flood story.* Columbia: University of Missouri Press.

Zanger, B., and D. Kaplan. 1971. *Major League Baseball, 1971.* New York: Pocket Books / Simon and Schuster.

Appendix

National League East Standings, 1969–1975

1969	W	L	Pct.	GB
New York	100	62	.617	----
Chicago	92	70	.568	8
Pittsburgh	88	74	.543	12
St. Louis	**87**	**75**	**.537**	**13**
Philadelphia	63	99	.389	37
Montreal	52	110	.321	48

1970	W	L	Pct.	GB
Pittsburgh	89	73	.549	----
Chicago	84	78	.519	5
New York	83	79	.512	6
St. Louis	**76**	**86**	**.469**	**13**
Philadelphia	73	88	.453	15.5
Montreal	73	89	.451	16

1971	W	L	Pct.	GB
Pittsburgh	97	65	.599	----
St. Louis	**90**	**72**	**.556**	**7**
Chicago	83	79	.512	14
New York	83	79	.512	14
Montreal	71	90	.441	25.5
Philadelphia	67	95	.414	30

1972	W	L	Pct.	GB
Pittsburgh	96	59	.619	----
Chicago	85	70	.548	11

New York	83	73	.532	13.5
St. Louis	**75**	**81**	**.481**	**21.5**
Montreal	70	86	.449	26.5
Philadelphia	59	97	.378	37.5

1973	W	L	Pct.	GB
New York	82	79	.509	----
St. Louis	**81**	**81**	**.500**	**1.5**
Pittsburgh	80	82	.494	2.5
Montreal	79	83	.488	3.5
Chicago	77	84	.478	5
Philadelphia	71	91	.438	11.5

1974	W	L	Pct.	GB
Pittsburgh	88	74	.543	----
St. Louis	**86**	**75**	**.534**	**1.5**
Philadelphia	80	82	.494	8
Montreal	79	82	.491	8.5
New York	71	91	.438	17
Chicago	66	96	.407	22

1975	W	L	Pct.	GB
Pittsburgh	92	69	.571	----
Philadelphia	86	76	.531	6.5
New York	82	80	.506	10.5
St. Louis	**82**	**80**	**.506**	**10.5**
Montreal	75	87	.463	17.5
Chicago	75	87	.463	17.5

Index

References to photos appear in italics

About the Author

Doug Feldmann is a professor in the College of Education at Northern Kentucky University and the author of ten books. He is a former scout for the Cincinnati Reds, the Seattle Mariners, and the San Diego Padres. He lives in Cincinnati.